'This short volume provides a unique overview of the Portuguese empire, decolonization, and today's Lusophone (Portuguese-speaking) world hitherto unavailable in a single, comprehensive volume. It sums up admirably how decolonization and the struggle to democratize in Europe's last empire left an important legacy in today's Africa. More importantly, it captures how the struggle to find a basis for cooperation among national societies outside Europe and the Americas – linked together by a distinct cultural *milieu* spanning Africa and Asia and a European language and culture outside Europe – have been transformed into a continuing cultural identity that transcends colonialism and current economic and political realities.'

Professor Lawrence Graham, University of Texas

The Last Empire

Thirty Years of Portuguese Decolonization

Edited by Stewart Lloyd-Jones
and António Costa Pinto

intellect™
Bristol, UK
Portland, OR, USA

Published in Paperback in UK in 2003 by
Intellect Books, PO Box 862, Bristol BS99 1DE, UK

Published in Paperback in USA in 2003 by
Intellect Books, ISBS, 920 NE 58th Ave. Suite 300, Portland, Oregon 97213-3786, USA

Copyright © 2003 Intellect

All rights reserved. No part of this publication may be reproduced, stored in a retrieval system, or transmitted, in any form or by any means, electronic, mechanical, photocopying, recording, or otherwise, without written permission.

Cover Design: Gabriel Solomons
Copy Editor: Holly Spradling

A catalogue record for this book is available from the British Library

Electronic ISBN 1-84150-897-7 / ISBN 1-84150-109-3

Contents

Preface and acknowledgements — vii

PART I: Portugal, the colonies and the 1974 Revolution

The influence of overseas issues in Portugal's transition to democracy — 1
Richard A. H. Robinson

The transition to democracy and Portugal's decolonization — 17
António Costa Pinto

PART II: Case Studies

São Tomé and Príncipe: decolonization and its legacy, 1974-90 — 37
Malyn Newitt

Macao, Timor and Portuguese India in the context of Portugal's recent decolonization — 53
Arnaldo Gonçalves

PART III: Portugal and the PALOPs

Portugal and the CPLP: heightened expectations, unfounded disillusions — 67
Luís António Santos

What good is Portugal to an African? — 83
Michel Cahen

Portugal's lusophone African immigrants: colonial legacy in a contemporary labour market — 99
Martin Eaton

PART IV: Testimonies

Portugal, Africa and the future — 113
Douglas L. Wheeler

The empire is dead, long live the EU — 127
António de Figueiredo

Bibliography — 145

Preface and acknowledgements

This book is the result of a conference on Portuguese decolonization, which took place in Edzell, Dundee on 11-14 September 2000 as an initiative of the Contemporary Portuguese Political History Research Centre (CPHRC) and the University of Dundee's Department of Politics. This event brought together European and North American researchers who have, during the last few years, studied Portuguese decolonization within the context of the country's transition to democracy.

In the first part of the book, Richard Robinson analyses the significant influence of the colonial wars on the nature of Portugal's transition to democracy. Noted for its fierce resistance to decolonization, the dictatorship of António Salazar finally succumbed to a *coup d'état* that placed the country's armed forces at the forefront of Portugal's transition. Robinson examines the initial crisis of the Portuguese Revolution of April 1974, which was dominated by conflicts concerning the nature of Portugal's withdrawal from its empire.

One of the main factors explaining the accentuated crisis of the state that characterized Portugal's democratization, and which differentiated its transition from those of Spain and Greece, was the manner in which the transition to democracy occurred simultaneously with the decolonization process. In the second chapter, António Costa Pinto examines how the prospect of Portugal's integration into the European Economic Community constituted an alternative vision to the 'end of empire', and how it became an important factor in the consolidation of Portugal's democracy by enabling the Portuguese to quickly forget the trauma of decolonization.

The second part of the book includes the examination of two case studies of examples that have largely been neglected in English language scholarship. In the third chapter, Malyn Newitt examines some of the ways in which the actual process of decolonization influenced the direction in which São Tomé and Príncipe developed after independence from Portugal. His contribution looks at three questions: the extent to which the decolonization had its own momentum rather that being simply a by-product of the general decolonization in the other colonies; the extent to which the choices made at the time of decolonization became major determinants of the way the country has developed; and thirdly, whether there were practical alternatives to decolonization and independence that might better have secured the prosperity and development of such a small and fragile state.

In the following chapter, Arnaldo Gonçalves provides another case study, this time examining the various destinies of the remains of Portugal's empire in India and Asia. He divides his analysis between Goa, Damão and Diu, which were invaded by the Indian Union in 1961, at the very outbreak of the colonial war in Africa; East Timor, which was invaded by Indonesia in 1975; and the particular status of Macao—Portugal's final colonial possession, which was transferred to Chinese control in 1999.

The third part of the book analyses the changing relationship between Portugal and its former colonies in Africa. In chapter five, Luís António Santos explains how Portugal, after 20 years establishing itself in Europe, began to look once more at its relations with its former colonies. He analysis the problems and delays involved in creating the *Communidade de Países da Língua Portuguesa* (CPLP—Community of Portuguese Speaking Countries), and Portugal's uncertainty regarding the nature of its relationship with its former possessions in this new organization, and the debates between forces with opposing visions of just what the CPLP is meant to represent to each of its member states.

In a rather provokative chapter, Michel Cahen takes a look at the CPLP from the point of view of the *Países Africanos da Língua Oficial Portuguesa* (PALOP—Portuguese Speaking African Countries), pointing out that there is little interest in these countries for the establishment of privileged relations with Portugal. Finally, Martin Eaton examines one of the greatest impacts of decolonization—the presence in Portugal of large numbers of immigrants from the PALOPs.

In addition to these communications, we are able to publish the testimonies of two of the participants at the conference in part four of the book. The first of these, by the renowned historian of lusophone Africa, Douglas L. Wheeler, is a previously unpublished document that he presented to the United States' Department of State just a few weeks prior to the April revolution. Many of his conclusions were subsequently confirmed by events on the ground. The second testimony is by the well-known journalist and Portuguese activist, António de Figueiredo, who fled the dictatorship to exile in the United Kingdom during the 1950s. Figueiredo's contribution represents an important autobiographical account of a lifetime opponent of the Portuguese dictatorship. Figueiredo was a participant in General Humberto Delgado's democratic opposition campaign for the Portuguese Presidency in 1958—a campaign that led to one of the dictatorship's greatest crises.

Preface and acknowledgements

★ ★ ★

The CPHRC would like to thank the Fundação Calouste Gulbenkian and the British Academy for their generous support of this our first conference. We would also like to thank the Instituto Camões in Lisbon and the International Conference Group on Portugal for the financial support they provided towards the organization of the conference. We are also grateful to the University of Glasgow's Department of Politics for their generous assistance in publicising the event.

A very special debt of gratitude is due to the University of Dundee's Department of Politics both for providing the CPHRC with the facilities necessary for organising and financing this event, and for co-sponsoring the conference. We would especially like to thank Norrie MacQueen, Head of the Department of Politics, for his encouragement and support of the CPHRC. Without this help, the conference would not have taken place.

The editors would also like to thank the other participants of the conference, both panellists and discussants, particularly: Lawrence Graham of the University of Texas at Austin; Patrick Chabal of the Department of Portuguese and Brazilian Studies at King's College London; Norrie MacQueen of the University of Dundee; and Natércia Coimbra of the *Centro de Documentação 25 de Abril* at the University of Coimbra.

The editors would also like to express their gratitude to the Editorial Board of the *Portuguese Journal of Social Science* for agreeing to include this volume in their series and for the revision and translation of some of the chapters, and to Teresa Segurado, Secretary at UNICS-ISCTE, for typing the testimonies.

Stewart would like to thank Mike Harland of the University of Glasgow for his unswerving support for the CPHRC and for his skills as a translator, and Francis Lambert, also of the University of Glasgow, for his inspiring comments. A special word of thanks must go to Linda and Liam Gourlay for their constant support, patience and encouragement, without which the CPHRC would not exist.

PART I

Portugal, the colonies and the 1974 Revolution

1: The influence of overseas issues in Portugal's transition to democracy

Richard A. H. Robinson*

For historians, assessing influence is a perennial and perforce inexact art. Different people weight factors differently. For example, those of the Marxist persuasion are perforce bound by their belief-system to attach particular importance to economic and socio-economic factors with a particular teleology in mind. The revolutionary process of 1974-75 in Portugal, however, was illuminating for non-Marxist observers as they watched Marxist commentators revise their explanatory apparatus from the all-importance of the macro-analysis of socio-economic structures and trends and the unimportance of individuals' activities to include, at least in real day-to-day practice, the supreme importance of individuals' actions and the discernment of regimental political loyalties and potential fire-power. That quondam War Correspondent of the *Manchester Guardian*, Friedrich Engels, would certainly have approved of the latter practice.

Nevertheless, historians of all persuasions continue to demonstrate that they think the comparative weight to be attached to different factors in explaining events of all magnitudes, even if their judgements are disputable. This common historical 'tradition' is continued in this piece, where the judgements are inspired by evidence whose completeness and accuracy is very far from being beyond dispute. As so often in the practice of historians, speculation and guesswork are to the fore: this writer would not wish to disguise these with masking words such as 'insight'.

Background

It could plausibly be argued that overseas events and issues have determined the course of Portugal's history at a number of critical junctures. The very process of 'the Discoveries' brought Portugal a world-historical significance that it would otherwise have lacked and gave it a maritime trading empire in Africa and Asia in the sixteenth century which in turn brought the Portuguese Crown great wealth, enabling monarchs to be free of constitutional constraints which their subjects might otherwise have placed upon them. In 1578 it was in an overseas land close to home – Morocco, 'the Algarve Beyond the Sea – where the 'splendid and most Portuguese Madness' (Ameal 1968: 314) of the crusading King Sebastian led Portugal to disaster at the battle of al-Qasr al-Kabir. Many important elements of the elite were slain or had to be ransomed for enormous sums and the childless monarch was succeeded by his uncle, the properly childless Cardinal-King Henry, after which the line passed to the Spanish Habsburgs. Thus it was an overseas event that led to what Portuguese have customarily called 'the Spanish captivity' of 1580-1640, which nationalist historiography has seen as the veritable loss of national independence.

It would not be plausible to explain the success of the revolt of John of Braganza in 1640 by invocation of overseas (as opposed to international, or foreign) causes. The inability of the Spanish monarchs to defend Portuguese possessions overseas from Dutch and English encroachments could, however, be listed as a contributory background factor. In the late seventeenth and eighteenth centuries it was the wealth of Brazil that made the Portuguese Crown strong, freeing it from constitutional pressures, while the policies of Pombal sought to exploit this wealth more systematically for the good of the homeland. It was foreign, European events in the form of the French invasion of 1807, which put a definitive end to the trans-Atlantic basis for the national recovery of the eighteenth century, but it was the centralising endeavours of the liberal revolutionaries of 1820 in relation to Brazil which led to the 'cry of Ipiranga' (the declaration of independence). The loss of Brazil greatly diminished the Portuguese resource base, making the weakened country more susceptible to outside interference, while the commitment of Pedro IV as Emperor of Brazil brought on the debilitating 'Brothers' War'. Those immersed more deeply than this author in the methodology of the 'ifs of history' could find fruitful material for their counter-factual speculative enquiries in imagining Portuguese development if Pedro IV had been simply King of Portugal after the demise of João VI in 1826, with or without the retention of Brazil as chief colony.

In more recent times, there is evidence that overseas issues have at least played an important part in determining the fate of the homeland. Lord Salisbury's ultimatum of 1890, preventing Portugal giving reality to the pink-coloured map of a Portuguese band of territory in southern Africa stretching from the Atlantic to the Indian Oceans, is said so to have humiliated the liberal regime of King Carlos that it made converts to militant nationalist Republicanism and opened the road that led (for Republicans, inexorably) to the events of 5 October 1910. The opinion is general that it was the retention of African overseas possessions, though some might say the preservation of the Republic of the 'Democrats' whose *raison d'être* was imperial nationalism, that determined Portugal's ruinous intervention in the First World War, which some see as inextricably related not only to Sidónio Pais's seizure of power in December 1917 but also the military movement of 28 May 1926 which put paid to parliamentary liberalism (Teixeira 1996; Meneses 2000).

The policies of Salazar, beginning with the Colonial Act of 1930, tied the politics of the Portuguese homeland even more closely to the overseas by its centralising imperial policies and the eventual full-scale adoption of French-style integration of the overseas possessions which had in 1911 officially become 'colonies', following the French fashion of that time. The formal existence of one indivisible pluri-continental Portugal 'from the Minho to Timor' dated from the constitutional revision of 1951, though the official distinction between 'indigenous' and 'non-indigenous' inhabitants had to wait until the repeal of the Native Statute in 1961.

From *Abrilada* to *Abrilada*

1961-1974 are the dates assigned – without speculation or guesswork – to the last phase of Portuguese colonialism. 1961 marks the start of the African wars in Angola and the loss, after four and a half centuries, of the Portuguese State of India; 25 April 1974 marks the effective end of the forces of the Portuguese Republic's attempts to impose its will by force on its overseas territories in the wake of the military movement of 25 April 1974.

The neatness of the dates is however only superficial as far as the history of the homeland is concerned. From the standpoint of the history of the Salazarist New State, 1958 and the presidential campaign of the volatile ultra-rightist-turned-democrat General Humberto Delgado marks the beginning of the end. Connected with the legal campaign were various attempts to overthrow Salazar's regime by force between 1958 and 1962, inevitably involving military conspiracy. Had any of these plots been successful, or had his legal presidential campaign been allowed to prosper, it would have resulted in the dismissal of Salazar and the presumed inauguration of a policy aimed at replacing Salazarist notions of integration with some sort of 'commonwealth solution' for the relationship of the Portuguese metropole and its various overseas territories.

Potentially more threatening for the regime than Delgado's conspiratorial efforts were the coup plans of Salazar's Defence Minister General Botelho Moniz, known as the *abrilada* of 1961. Had these plans not been thwarted at the last minute by Premier Salazar and President Thomaz, with the help of others including General Kaulza de Arriaga, it seems that Botelho Moniz and his military supporters (who apparently included General Costa Gomes but not General Spínola) would have installed the one-time Colonial Minister Marcello Caetano as the chief civilian in power (Delgado and Figueiredo 1991; Valença 1977; Gomes 1980). It is believed that at that time he was in favour of a federalist solution for the imperial problem which would not in the short term have been incompatible with the ideas then advocated by the United States for immediate liberalisation with a view to self-determination of the colonial territories after a number of years (Rodrigues 2002; Nogueira 1984: 210-417, 458-63, 514-9, 581-7). At this time some have recently alleged that Salazar himself did not rule out self-determination in the long run,[1] but he was implacably opposed to Belgian, British or French policies of 'scuttle' in Africa in the shorter term. He was well aware of the politically immature state in which Belgium left the Congo in 1960 (which was to have a most significant impact on Angola), of the British Colonial Secretary's desire to be the first out of Africa and of the French retreat from the integrationist *Algérie française* position and de Gaulle's offer of independence to the overseas territories of the French Union (an offer immediately accepted only by French Guinea). Salazar's would-be substitutes presumably looked to the Gaullist French Community as an exemplar while Salazar stood firm on his interpretation of the doctrine of unripe time.

In 1961, then, overseas issues failed to change the course of Portuguese political history. In the mythology of the MPLA, 4 February is celebrated as the anniversary of the beginning of the armed liberation struggle on account of the attack on a prison in Luanda, while the massacres occasioned by Holden Roberto's FNLA's insurgency in northern Angola in March 1961 mark the definitive start of Portugal's African wars. At the same time as Salazar's outwitting of the Botelho Moniz conspiracy there appears to have been a certain patriotic closing of ranks in the face of the threat in Angola and it perhaps would be possible to ascribe the longevity of the Salazarist New State to a new lease of life occasioned by the Angolan 'confusion' – and this despite the 'facts' that Botelho Moniz's coup was scheduled for a month after the FNLA's massacres and that the regime's unsuccessful gamble over the State of India led to its loss and Salazar's televised weeping over this humiliation in December 1961. Two years later the commander in Goa, General Vassalo e Silva, was expelled from the Army for his decision to surrender rather than futilely to resist Indian vastly superior numbers and, at least after 25 April 1974, this political scapegoating of the military was conventionally said to have had a profound effect on the officer corps, thus preparing minds for the officers' movement which carried it out (Silva 1975; Morais 1980). This may well be so but there seems to be no hard evidence of discontent in the officer corps until about 1972. Discontent among other ranks could be indicated by a number, but an unknown and not apparently significant number, of desertions from the armed forces in the field and the increasing numbers of conscripts not turning up for service between 1961 and 1974. What is not known is what proportion of these young absentees were put off by colonial warfare and the possibility of extended service in different territories and what proportion was attracted by unprecedented earning opportunities in other booming West-European economies during this period. The matter is further complicated by the truism that in the real world motives are infrequently unmixed.

While it would seem that there is little hard evidence to be had on civilian or military morale and thinking from 1961 to 1968, the situation changes somewhat with the incapacitation of Salazar. The relationship of overseas and metropolitan domestic issues then becomes bound up with assessments of Marcello Caetano's motives and real desires. There are those that contend that, when he became Premier in 1968, he abandoned the ideas of federalist reformism on the overseas question which he had allegedly, and possibly opportunistically, espoused when kept out of power during the preceding decade. Others point to evidence suggesting that Caetano accepted office to reform the regime but had to accept the condition of key conservative members of the military and political elite, including President

Thomaz, that he adhere to the essentials of Salazarist integrationism regarding the Overseas Provinces. In this latter interpretation Caetano failed to make the transition from authoritarianism to democracy because of his inability to resolve the overseas question, which meant increasing military expenditure to a ruinously unacceptable extent, growing war weariness and disappointment of the expectations raised in 1969-70 for genuine political reform. Such interpretations often point to indecisiveness and weakness of character in his failure to force faster evolution on the overseas question than the moves toward constitutional statehood in Angola and Mozambique as well as to the irrevocable alienation of non Communist oppositionists such as Mário Soares with whom he might have been able to do business in a controlled transition to democracy had it not been for the need to prohibit through censorship and other forms of repression public debate on overseas policy objectives on the grounds that such debate would exacerbate divisions on the home front to the advantage of national enemies, internal and external (Caetano 1973; 1974; 1976). Thus unresolved overseas issues are seen as the key determinant in the failure of Caetano to make a transition to a more pluralist and democratic political system in the homeland.

Overseas issues in the form of apparently perpetual and unwinnable colonial conflicts of varying intensities in Africa (and an officially outstanding irreversible military situation on the Indian sub-continent) did indeed bring about and essentially cause the overthrow of the regime on 25 April 1974 by military coup. In published reminiscences it seems that senior military personnel became more agitated about the need for a political way out of the colonial *cul-de-sac* around 1972, when it became clear that political evolution had ground to a halt. Less senior officers involved in the overthrow of Caetano subsequently explained how their consciousness had been changed by reading revolutionary literature for their own psychological warfare purposes and by contact with politically conscious conscripts. Thus large sections of the regular officer corps came to resent the regime's political manipulation, as in the episode of the Congress of Combatants in 1973 and to fear becoming scapegoats for defeat like Vassalo e Silva. The unpopularity of colonial counter-insurgency, despite the modest casualty rate of 4,027 deaths in action (but 8,290 military deaths altogether) in Angola, Mozambique and Guinea from 1961 to 1974 (*Comissão para o Estudo das Campanhas de África* 1988, 264-6), had taken its toll on the attractions of an increasingly poorly paid military career. While the arrival of the SAM-7 missile in Guinea in 1973 and Mozambique in 1974 changed the military balance, the key catalyst for anti-regime organisation among officers was Decree 353/73 in July 1973, which offended regulars by allowing conscript officers to gain rank on an accelerated basis, the government's idea being to try and overcome the growing shortage of junior officers. From these protests came the Armed Forces' Movement (MFA), while the regime was thrown into confusion by allowing publication of Spínola's book, *Portugal e o futuro*, on 22 February 1974, which broke official silence on the overseas question. Military discontent had turned into political discontent. The MFA's 25 April was essentially a consequence of overseas problems and was to change the course of Portuguese politics irrevocably.

From 25 April to 28 September 1974

The course of the revolutionary process is conventionally divided into three phases marked by the episodes of 28 September 1974, 11 March 1975 and 25 November 1975. This general schema will be followed here, with 11 March being seen as an attempt by Spínola to reverse the outcome of the 28 September fiasco that had provoked his resignation as provisional President of the Republic two days later.[2]

At first the world assumed that the coup of 25 April had been made by Spínola and the Captains of the MFA together, and it was not until July that the young officers' group styled the Co-ordinating Committee of the Programme of the Armed Forces' Movement revealed itself as the real power in the land. In publishing the Programme of the MFA, which revolved around the three Ds of decolonisation, democratisation and development, Spínola had been careful to edit out the reference to the self-determination of the Overseas Provinces to allow himself greater flexibility and in the hope of retaining the possibility of resisting the demands of the main Afro-Leninist guerrilla movements. Thus the differences between the new provisional President of the Republic and the Co-ordinating Committee who were for rapid decolonisation were largely hidden from public view. To the outside world Portugal seemed until July to be governed by Spínola as head of the seven-man inter-service Junta of National Salvation presented on television just after the *coup*, to which were shortly added a traditional Council of State and a provisional government led by a liberal lawyer, Palma Carlos, and including the leaders of the three main parties: Sá Carneiro, an independent elected to the National Assembly in 1969 to form a 'liberal wing' of Caetano's system but who had broken with the regime and had just founded the centrist Popular Democratic Party (PPD), as Vice-Premier; the returned Mário Soares (Foreign Minister) for the Socialist Party (PS); and the returned Álvaro Cunhal for the pro-Moscow Portuguese Communist Party (PCP).

In metropolitan Portugal the first two months following 25 April saw the collapse of state authority as workers and employees took over their enterprises and purged those whose past made them politically incorrect in the new situation. In the media committees took over broadcasting stations and newspapers, with the MFA assigning officers to these to prevent abuse and to some extent hold the ideological ring. Against the backcloth of deepening international recession, a more or less gentle anarchy reigned. Overseas the armed forces ceased the fight and expected to return home quickly, while Maoists and Trotskyists in the Metropole further paralysed military efficacy by leading noisy campaigns against any more troops being sent to the colonies. The *coup* had had the effect of depriving metropolitan government of military options in the colonies. Thus in Guinea there was little to do but hand over to the Guinea and Cape Verde African Independence Party (PAIGC), though in the Cape Verdes there was a longer transition to a separate PAIGC regime. In Mozambique, where the MFA were at odds with the white settlers and non-Mozambique Liberation Front (FRELIMO) blacks following clashes before 25

April, there was again little option but to come to meet the terms of FRELIMO after a transitional period.[3] Spínola was frustrated with his inability to hold back the tide of events and began to sense conspiracies and betrayals by prominent MFA officers such as Melo Antunes and Otelo Saraiva de Carvalho. He was therefore ready by the start of July to try and impose some authority at home and in the crumbling empire by trying to assert military hierarchy against the MFA 'Captains' and by going along with a plan for an early presidential election to strengthen his position through democratic legitimation.

The scene was thus set for the crisis of July 1974, which resulted in a defeat for Spínola and a victory for the Co-ordinating Committee. A new coalition provisional government was formed under the pro-Communist MFA Major Vasco Gonçalves while the only functioning military units in the metropole were put under the command of the then politically unaffiliated Brigadier Otelo in COPCON (Operational Command for Continental Portugal). Spínola then had publicly to agree that the populations of Guiné, Mozambique and Angola were ready to determine their own futures and accepted the replacement of the right-wing Silvino Silvério Marques as the metropolitan government's chief representative in Angola by Admiral Rosa Coutinho, who quickly revealed himself as the friend of the pro-Soviet faction of the MPLA Angolan Popular Liberation Movement) and an opponent of the rival FNLA (Angolan National Liberation Front), as of settler interests. It seemed that whereas Spínola hoped to decolonise Angola in such a way as to protect Portuguese interests and stymie the MPLA and the pro-MPLA MFA, the MFA leaders and the PCP, PS and far left *grupúsculos* all favoured handing Angola over to the MPLA as the most-favoured progressive liberation movement, many of whose leaders, unlike those of rival liberation groups, had been educated in Portugal.

Angola was the jewel in the Portuguese colonial crown.[4] Its wealth as a producer of oil, diamonds, coffee and rare metals made it the only Overseas Province to have aided the metropole through its export surplus. Furthermore, given as of 1974 the bitter divisions between the FNLA, MPLA and UNITA (National Union for the Total Independence of Angola) liberation movements, and the internal fragmentation of the MPLA, and the paucity of anti-Portuguese military activity compared with Guiné and Mozambique, the territory seemed to Spínola, who was determined to take control of this part of the decolonising process, a place where there could be consultation of the popular will with the possibility of an outcome favourable to Portugal as opposed to abandonment, however disguised, to the enemy. To bring about the desired outcome in Angola it was essential for him to regain control of the situation in the metropole by outmanoeuvring the Co-ordinating Committee and its left-wing civilian allies. It was necessary to rouse disorientated conservatives, the 'silent majority' who were falling prey to the alleged conspiratorial machinations of cunning and sinister minorities.

In the episode of 28 September it is difficult to separate domestic and overseas issues. Spínola saw Angola as the last hope for a weakened Portugal without a post-colonial mission. Getting the better of the radicals of the MFA and their disruptive political allies would permit the restoration of military hierarchy, the restoration of order and a safer route to an acceptable democracy in Portugal and the saving of Angola from automatic independence under a Afro-Leninist regime. In the event Spínola failed to get his rally, relying on right-wing elements such as the significantly named Popular Party/Portuguese Federalist Movement (PP/MFP) and he failed to overawe key MFA/COPCON units into obeying him and dispersing the leftist vigilantes who had taken it upon themselves to stop any pro-Spínola movement. If the outcome of '28 September' was decided by the balance of forces in and around the capital, the crisis itself was occasioned as much by overseas issues as by domestic developments.

From 28 September 1974 to 11 March 1975

With the victory of the MFA and leftist vigilantes, the pace of the revolutionary process quickened. The Junta of National Salvation was purged of its right-wing members and lost importance to an as yet non-institutionalised MFA revolutionary council of 20 officers. The new provisional President of the Republic was the former Chief of the General Staff of the Armed Forces under Caetano and Spínola, General Costa Gomes, who appointed Vasco Gonçalves head of the third provisional government, still containing representatives of the PCP, PS and PPD as well as the MFA. The Liberal Party and the PP/MFP were banned after 28 September and, although its leader had not supported Spínola over the rally, the conservative Christian Democrat CDS was harried in its attempts to organise. Attempts by leftist political vigilantes to prevent its first congress in Oporto did much to alert foreign opinion to the trend of events in Portugal. The PPD also found its campaigning activities harassed.

While party-political life got off to an uncertain start in late 1974 and early 1975, more radical elements in the MFA camp, most notably the 5th Division of the Armed Forces General Staff which now made psychological warfare on 'unenlightened' sections of the mainland's population (Livro Branco 1984), propagated ideas of a 'People-MFA Alliance' which seemed to marginalise non-leftist parties. Premier Gonçalves and the PCP, which effectively controlled the trade-union movement, Intersindical, also seemed increasingly committed to the creation of some novel political superstructure based on the MFA and its Communist collaborators which would deflect the revolutionary process away from electoral politics, even though the MFA Programme promised elections within twelve months of the overthrow of the old regime.

The months following '28 September' were also marked by divergences of approach within the triumphant MFA. Regarding the overseas territories, the MFA victory safeguarded the agreement with FRELIMO for a transition to independence in June 1975 and variants on this transition model were followed with the PAIGC in the Cape Verdes and the MLSTP in São Tomé and Príncipe for the independence of those islands.

Despite the work of Rosa Coutinho in building up Agostinho Neto's pro-Soviet MPLA, particularly in Luanda and oil-rich Cabinda, the movement was not strong enough in late 1974 to marginalise the Bakongo-based FNLA and its Ovimbundu-based circumstantial ally, Savimbi's UNITA. Much though many MFA officers would have liked to deal with the MPLA in Angola as it had with FRELIMO in Mozambique, the FNLA and UNITA had to be brought into a transition process if secession, civil war or an alliance of these movements with white settler interests were to be avoided. None of these latter scenarios would have fitted with Major Melo Antunes of the MFA's much-vaunted 'exemplary decolonisation'. Thus to further the decolonising process and marginalise settler interests which Spínola would have wanted to take into account in his version of self-determination through popular consultation, a deal was put together and signed in January 1975 at Alvor in the Algarve whereby Portugal would share power with a coalition of the three liberation movements until independence on 11 November 1975.[5] Rosa Coutinho was replaced by less partisan Portuguese representatives but it became quickly apparent that the deal would not stick. The territory began its slide into anarchy as the rival movements and their separate armed forces looked to foreign backers. Were the Gonçalves tendency in the MFA to stay dominant, this would be to the advantage of the MPLA, which had in part been formed by the PCP. Were the MFA to lose control in Lisbon, this would quite change the balance of forces in Angola.

Meanwhile, back in the homeland, the dynamics of the revolutionary process were giving rise to complications. In January 1975 the PCP attempt to railroad through a trade-union law giving *Intersindical*, which it controlled, a monopoly of labour representation, with all that that would mean for future governments, brought popular reaction in the form of unexpectedly strong mobilisation of opposition by the PS of Mário Soares, now freed of its pro-PCP faction since its congress the previous month. The PS would become the natural ally of those MFA elements that believed that genuine political democracy should be inseparable from 'socialism' and Soares became the effective front man for those wary of PCP domination. The new US Ambassador, Frank Carlucci III, and West-European Socialist leaderships rallied to him as the best barrier to further Communist advances.[6]

Spínola hoped to take advantage of these signs that the 'silent majority' was becoming more vocal and of the sentiment in the Armed Forces against MFA radicalism that was growing in the armed forces, where voting for representatives to an MFA Assembly in March went against prominent leftists. Spínola and his coterie seem to have indulged in daydreaming rather than proper planning for a comeback by *coup*. Schemes were mooted for seizing the President and revolutionary councillors when in session in the presidential palace at Belém but other preparations were not very far advanced when MFA disinformation about an 'Easter massacre' of officers potentially hostile to radicalisation of the revolutionary process were fed to Spínola supporters by, among others, the Spanish authorities (Cervelló 1993: 221-7). The consequence was the hasty launch of a largely planless *coup* by Spínola and his military supporters on 11 March which ended in fiasco, thus strengthening the MFA radicals and their civilian leftist allies, many of whom acted as vigilantes on 11 March as they had on 28 September.

The 11 March episode had more to do with domestic than overseas issues. The dynamics of revolution were beginning to raise alarm from the PS rightwards, while the process of decolonisation had been largely accepted. However a successful coup by Spínola would have changed the situation in Angola, where he and his supporters had been circumstantial allies of the FNLA since September and where some of his admirers were to fight for Holden Roberto's forces which, within days of the failure of '11 March', took to the offensive against the MPLA, whose position was secured by the failed *coup* since Portuguese policy (such as it was) did not change. Though the revolutionary dynamics in the homeland were in the foreground on 11 March, in the near background were overseas issues since it would be logical to suppose that a victory for Spínola would have led to an agonising reappraisal of the decolonising process, not only in Angola, but also in Mozambique and the other territories then still in transition to independence.

From 11 March to 25 November 1975

The period from 11 March to 25 November saw the increasing radicalisation of the 'revolutionary process under way' (PREC – *processo revolucionário em curso*) as well as an increasing wave of popular opposition to it. The immediate aftermath of '11 March' saw an (unsuccessful) attempt by MFA radicals to marginalise more moderate MFA luminaries by what was nicknamed a 'wild assembly' of the MFA. It also saw decrees negating the fairly carefully drawn-up economic plans of the MFA in favour of the arbitrary 'socialisation' of all but foreign-owned banking and insurance firms and the tolerated occupation of land, mostly in the southern part of the country: in the end the lands occupied and turned into 'collective units of production' did not perfectly match the lands scheduled for expropriation by the relevant revolutionary legislation (Barreto 1986; Drain and Domenech 1982).

Despite the doubts of the more exuberantly revolutionary elements in the MFA, elections for a constituent assembly were held on 25 April 1975, which usefully reflected opinion in the country as a whole. 91.66 per cent of the registered electorate voted and of these 37.87 per cent voted for the PS, 26.39 per cent for the PPD and 7.61 per cent for the Christian-Democrat CDS (Party of the Democratic Social Centre), whose campaign had been disrupted by the banning of its coalition partner. Parties had had to sign a pact with the MFA to be allowed to take part. The PCP and fellow travellers (MDP – Portuguese Democratic Movement, FSP – Popular Socialist Front) together got 17.76 per cent, while five other leftist groups (MES – Movement of the Socialist Left, UDP – People's Democratic Union, FEC – Communist Left Front, PUP – Popular Unity Party, LCI – Internationalist Communist League) together accounted for another 2.81 per cent (António 1981). Some MFA leftists called on voters to cast blank ballot-papers, but the total of blank and spoiled papers was only 6.94 per cent. Gonçalves's coalition government, containing PS, PCP and PPD representatives, continued unchanged while the MFA's essentially self-appointed Council of the Revolution was institutionalised.

As the PCP leader Cunhal famously observed to the Italian journalist Oriana

Fallaci, revolutionary dynamics, not elections, were the key to the evolving situation (Robinson 1979: 236; Cunha 1992: 191-271). During the 'hot summer' of 1975 the MFA began to fall apart as the Gonçalves faction became ever more closely identified with the PCP, whose burgeoning membership now considered Portugal as beyond the bourgeois-democratic stage on the road to socialism, while COPCON and its unpredictable commander Otelo Saraiva de Carvalho veered to the left of the PCP. In July the PS left Gonçalves's government over its and the MFA's inability to ensure freedom of press opinion, as instanced by a leftist committee of workers preventing the daily *República* being the organ of the PS. The PPD followed suit after a Catholic rally in Aveiro on 13 July was used as a signal for a campaign to destroy PCP organisation in the north and centre of the country, still regions with high levels of religious practice like the Azores and Madeira, where a separatist spectre hovered temporarily over movements rejecting Lisbon's revolutionary course.[7] In the northern and central mainland the anti-revolutionary camp stretched from the PS, through the PPD and CDS, to militants of the exiled Spínola's MDLP (Democratic Liberation Movement of Portugal) and the neo-Salazarist ELP (Portuguese Liberation Army), both the latter Spanish-based. Organisation was in part provided by members of the clergy, most notably Canon Melo of Braga (Abreu 1983; Trinidade 1993: 352-7).

This division of the country between the revolutionaries dominating the capital and the Alentejo and the rest was the background against which the less radical members of the MFA came into the open in early August with publication of the Document of the Nine, in which it was made plain that MFA socialism would have to be inseparable from pluralist democracy. Otelo's COPCON and the Nine, though poles apart in their ideological rhetoric, had a common foe in Vasco Gonçalves and the pro-PCP elements supporting him. By September they had turned the tables on the Gonçalvists in the armed forces and replaced the leftist military commander in Oporto with a more conservative figure. In government Gonçalves was replaced by Admiral Pinheiro de Azevedo as Premier in the sixth provisional government, a coalition including PCP, PS and PPD representatives. Faced with defeat the PCP and its allies continued to woo COPCON while participating in broad revolutionary fronts and giving support to movements aiming to undermine discipline in the armed forces, notably the SUV (Soldiers United Will Win) movement.

With the PCP losing influence in the armed forces, the Nine turned their attentions to neutralising COPCON by creating their own Military Intervention Group (AMI) centred on 9 October based on the Paratroops, the Commandos (whose commanding officer Colonel Jaime Neves the PCP had been unsuccessful in removing) and other special forces. They then successfully pressed for one of their number, Vasco Lourenço, to be appointed commander of the Lisbon Military Region to nullify Otelo's COPCON, where revolutionary officers were seeking to make a last stand in mid-November. As opinion hardened against the revolutionary left in most of the country, in Lisbon revolutionary workers besieged the Assembly of the Republic and made it impossible for government to function.

The situation came to a head on 25 November (Antunes, 1981), when confused and officerless paratroopers tried to take over airbases and were abetted by civilian revolutionaries. The movement was overcome by President Costa Gomes declaring a state of emergency, with troops loyal to Vasco Lourenço and the operational commander, Colonel Ramalho Eanes, restoring order. Key factors leading to this outcome were Otelo's refusal to rally COPCON against Lourenço and the PCP's caution in abandoning the revolutionaries and permitting the Commandos to operate unhindered, for which the party was rewarded by being kept in the government coalition. The leftist threat to a pluralist democratic outcome to the revolutionary process had been surmounted and the aspirations of three out of four electors, as expressed on 25 April 1975, prevailed over the minority.

As this brief account suggests, the climax of the revolutionary process can adequately be explained without reference to overseas issues. The decolonising process resulted in the unhindered independence of Mozambique, the Cape Verdes and São Tomé and Príncipe in the summer of 1975. China was not persuaded to take back Macao then and in East Timor the MFA failed to get agreement between the main political movements and civil war resulted in August 1975 with the Portuguese as powerless bystanders.[8] None of these developments influenced the situation in Portugal.

In Angola Portuguese commanders found themselves unable to prevent the slide into civil war but assisted the MPLA by threatening to block the FNLA's advance on Luanda and allowing the MPLA to receive outside assistance, most notably from Cuba, which was to result in its victory. While Angola was much in Portuguese minds from March to independence in November on account of the arrival of hundreds of thousands of refugees, the unfolding situation seems to have had no noticeable influence on the course of the Portuguese revolution. No returning troops took part in '25 November'. It is sometimes alleged that Soviet policy, desirous of an MPLA victory in Angola, used the PCP to achieve this end and then lost interest in the party after 11 November because it no longer had a part to play in materially helping the MPLA (Gallagher 1983: 227). While it was obviously to the MPLA's advantage to have a friendly government in power in the metropole, since an unfriendly one could have scuppered its chances, there appears scant evidence for the proposition that the Portuguese revolutionary process was directly and seriously influenced by the evolution of Angolan events. Revolutionary dynamics in Portugal interacted with the economic and international circumstances prevailing but not in the last phase of the revolutionary process with the disappearing Portuguese overseas possessions.

Aftermath and conclusion

In my judgement in this paper, overseas issues may have played a role in helping the survival of the Salazar regime after 1961 by encouraging feelings of patriotic solidarity. They certainly played a direct and all-important role in ensuring the failure of Caetanist reformism and the overthrow of the authoritarian regime in 1974. Colonial issues, and particularly the fate of Angola, were intertwined in the making of

'28 September' and the subsequent resignation of Spínola but seem to have been less to the fore in the making of '11 March'. '25 November' is quite explicable without reference to the tragic backcloth of Angola and East Timor. Thus overseas issues brought authoritarianism to an end but were of declining significance for the revolutionary process that ended in the consolidation of pluralist democracy.

After 25 November 1975 overseas issues seem not to have influenced the course of Portuguese political history. Strife and instability in former colonies was regretted and belied claims of an exemplary decolonisation but never again would former colonial possessions influence events in Portugal. Neither did the number of refugees from former overseas territories, estimated at about 700,000, though inevitably presenting social problems with which politicians had to be seen to grapple in 1975-76, prove to be politically influential (Pires et al. 1984).

It could plausibly be contended that, when registered as Portuguese electors, they would be more likely to vote for the CDS and the PPD, parties seen as less associated with responsibility for the sufferings of the victims of decolonisation, than for the PS and PCP. A comparison of the election results of 25 April 1976 with those of the previous year shows that the vote of the CDS, the major party least associated with the revolutionary process, did indeed rise from 7.61 to 16 per cent of the total, but the PPD's share fell from 26.39 to 24.38 per cent. The more rightist PDC (Party of Christian Democracy) could gather only 0.54 per cent. The performance of the CDS could easily be explained by the changed environment in which it was able to campaign in 1976 and to some popular disillusionment with the economic situation and falling living standards, generally perceived by electors more as a consequence of the revolutionary process than of the global recession. That the returnees from former colonies could have exerted only a negligible influence electorally is evidenced by the numerical facts that the CDS in 1976 got 442,615 more votes than in 1975, but the total number of registered voters only increased by 170,663 (António 1981). Perhaps most returnees were so alienated from the whole idea of '25 April' that they did not bother to register; but this is to provide an explanation for which there is no very hard evidence.

References:

*Honorary Reader in contemporary Iberian history, the University of Birmingham, UK.

[1] See the interviews with Silva Cunha (Undersecretary of State for Overseas Administration, 1962-65; Overseas Minister 1965-73; Minister of Defence 1973-74), 'Independências? E porque não?'; Baltasar Rebelo de Sousa (Overseas Minister 1973-74), 'Avançar depressa com autonomias'; and Rui Patrício (Caetano's last Foreign Minister), 'Guiné poderia ser estado federado' in *Diário de Notícias*, 24, 25, 26 July 1999, http://www.dn.pt/dn2/pna/24p6a.htm; http://www.dn.pt/dn1/pna/25p5a.htm; http://www.dn.pt/pna/26p6a.htm.

[2] Accounts of these 19 eventful months are legion; in the English language these include Porch, D. (1977), *The Portuguese armed forces and the revolution*, London: Croom Helm; Harvey, R. (1978), *Portugal: birth of a democracy*, London: Macmillan; Robinson, R. A. H. (1979), *Contemporary Portugal: a history*, London: Allen and Unwin, pp. 191-253; Kayman, M. (1987), *Revolution and counter-revolution in Portugal*, London: Merlin, pp. 69-183; Manuel, P. C. (1995), *Uncertain outcome: the politics of the Portuguese transition to democracy*, Lanham, MA: University Press of America; and Maxwell, K. (1995), *The making of Portuguese democracy*, Cambridge: Cambridge University Press, pp. 56-177.

[3] A good survey is by MacQueen, N. (1997), *The decolonization of Portuguese Africa: metropolitan revolution and the dissolution of empire*, London: Longman, whose balanced treatment contrasts with the polemical nature of earlier works such as Aguiar, L. (1977), *Livro negro da descolonização*, Braga: Intervenção. See also Guerra, J. P. (1996), *Descolonização portuguesa: o regresso das caravelas*, Lisbon: Dom Quixote. In addition, on Guiné there is Silva, A. E. D. (1997), *A independência da Guiné-Bissau e a descolonização portuguesa*, Oporto: Afrontamento, and on Mozambique Newitt, M. (1995), *A history of Mozambique*, London: Hurst & Co., pp. 520-46.

[4] On the decolonization of Angola, apart from MacQueen (1997), see Fola Soremekun, F. (1983), *Angola: the road to Independence*, Ile-ife: University of Ife Press; Heimer, F. W. (1979), *The decolonization conflict in Angola 1974-76: an essay in political sociology*, Geneva: Institut Universitaire de Hautes Études Internationales; and Guimarães, F. A. (1998), *The origins of the Angolan civil war: foreign intervention and domestic political conflict*, Basingstoke: Macmillan, pp. 31-236. Correia, P. P. (1991), *Descolonização de Angola: a jóia da coroa do império português*, Lisbon: Inquérito, is an account by a leading MFA officer.

[5] *Angola: the independence agreement*, Lisbon: Ministry of Mass Communication (1975) is an English translation.

[6] For Mário Soares's views see Soares, M. (1976), *Portugal: que revolução? Diálogo com Dominique Puchin*, Lisbon: Perspectivas e Realidades; and Avillez, M. J. (1996), *Soares: ditadura e revolução*, Lisbon: Público. The PCP's view of Carlucci's activities is in Carvalho, R. de (ed.) (1978), *'Dossier' Carlucci/CIA*, Lisbon: Avante!

[7] On the Azores see various articles commemorating the anti-Lisbon protest demonstration of 6 June 1975 in *Diário de Notícias*, 6 June 1999, http://www.dn.pt/dn3/pna/6p, and the interview with the Azorean Liberation Front leader José Almeida in *Açoriano Oriental*, 6 June 1999, http://www.acorianooriental.pt/cgi-bin/show.pl?id=104&command=art&artdir=reg&artid=8&back=pp.

[8] See (*inter alia*) Pires, M.L. (1991), *Descolonização de Timor: missão impossível?*, Lisbon: Dom Quixote; Sá Pereira (ed.) (1976), *Jornal 'O Retornado' denuncia ao mundo o pavoroso caso de Timor*, Lisbon: Literal-Selecta; Nicol, B. (1978), *Timor: the stillborn nation*, Melbourne: Visa; Jolliffe, J. (n.d.), *East Timor: nationalism and colonialism*, St. Lucia: University of Queensland Press; and Carey, P. and Bentley, G. C. (eds.), *East Timor at the crossroads: the forging of a nation*, London: Cassell, pp. 1-72.

2: The transition to democracy and Portugal's decolonization

António Costa Pinto

The withdrawal of the United Kingdom and France from Africa was not only caused by the emergence of African nationalism: it was a sign that direct political control of these colonies had become a burden to the national interests of the European colonial powers (Hargreaves 1988). Nevertheless, the force of this indigenous nationalism, the United States' anti-colonial strategy, and the projects for European unification were also powerful agents that served to hasten the transfer of power. In the Portuguese case, the most important explanation for the outbreak of a prolonged series of colonial wars and an obstinate resistance to decolonization was the nature of Portugal's dictatorial regime at that time. The wars were more than the empirical expression of economic interests that were involved in maintaining the colonial system in a condition in which the superimposition of the New State's nationalist ideology was unquestioned. Above all, they were caused and propagated by the dictatorial nature of the New State political system. Resistance to decolonization was a choice made by both the dominant political elite and the dictator; it was also one that led to the most significant crisis within the regime since 1945.

It seems reasonable to state that, given the presence of some democratizing pressures, these would have certainly resulted in a more rapid negotiated solution to the colonial problem. The regime's nature was also an instrumental factor in one of the most significant military mobilizations in Portuguese history, illustrating the thesis according to which dictatorial regimes manage, at least during their first phase, to eliminate 'the social sanctions' against imperialist adventures (Snyder 1991: 540). The future of the regime, therefore, was inseparably linked to the outcome of the wars.

Less paradoxically than it may seem, the war effort coincided with a period of real economic and social development in the colonies during the 1960s, particularly in Angola and Mozambique. The increase in the white population in the two largest colonies was significant, while the 'Europeanization' of Portugal's economy and the wave of emigration to Europe was also to make a difference during this decade.

The effects of the Cold War and of the United States' foreign policy did not favour regime change in Portugal; however, this did not prevent the regime from coming under strong international pressure to decolonize. Portugal was the least significant member of the western bloc, yet the importance of the US base on the Azores, and its membership of NATO were enough for the New State to persuade the Kennedy administration to ease its pressure on Portugal to decolonize (Rodrigues 2001). Curiously, with Marcello Caetano's arrival in power, when Portugal's domestic political system was at its most fragile and when the outlines of liberalizing reforms were making an appearance, the US administration adopted a new African strategy that supported the continuation of white rule in South Africa. Consequently, under the Nixon administration, pressure to decolonise was almost absent.

As one study of the colonial wars has noted, the liberation movements were principally nationalist and the outbreak of armed resistance was a 'decision that was more practical than ideological' (Chabal 1994: 273). The first movements were politically and ideologically diverse in nature, and were further divided in their dependence upon support from neighbouring states. From the perspective of a rapid decolonization, several sections of the elite and the political authorities in contiguous states that had only recently been decolonized themselves supported political movements. While some were prepared for a long drawn out conflict, others hoped for quick negotiated settlements. Nevertheless, as the wars dragged on the idea of an armed revolutionary legitimacy was suggested and increasingly consolidated.

From a purely military point of view, the Portuguese government's global strategy, which was closely linked to economic development, had some success in limiting guerrilla activities and in preventing them from affecting the more developed urban areas. Not one of the movements managed to establish its leadership within the territory, and nor did any movement succeed in appealing to more than a relatively restricted ethnic base. Despite this, however, the liberation movements obliged the dictatorship to engage in a heavy economic, social, and military effort on three fronts, with no prospect of easing and with no room for negotiations.

By the beginning of the 1970s, and after almost 14 years of war, the guerrillas in the Portuguese territories finally became the stereotypical 'communists' and 'revolutionaries' that Portuguese propaganda had applied indiscriminately and almost synonymously to 'terrorists' since 1961. Salazar's successor, Caetano, continued in his predecessor's footsteps by persisting with the war, although he did introduce some decentralizing administrative reforms. The wars, their revolutionary legitimacy, and international and diplomatic pressure made it possible for the international community to recognise the main guerrilla movements.

The democratization of Portugal and decolonization

By mobilizing political actors that were absent in the transitions to democracy in the other southern European countries, the colonial war was a specific and determining factor in the overthrow of the Portuguese dictatorship (Schmitter 1999; Pinto 2002). It was in the emergence of the Armed Forces Movement, a movement of middle-ranking officers who were increasingly attracted to left-wing politics, more than the nature of the dictatorship's fall – a military *coup d'état* – that the uniqueness of the Portuguese transition resides.

Formed initially as a reaction to corporate problems provoked by the emergence of a corps of conscript officers, the MFA's impact on the Portuguese transition was profound. The serious crises of state and the elevated degree of social mobilization that immediately followed the overthrow of the regime introduced a dynamic of rupture that was not limited to the political sphere, and which included strong anti-capitalist pressures. Any brief analysis of the swift demise of the Portuguese Empire must acknowledge that it was during this initial phase of Portugal's transition to democracy that decolonization took place. The colonial question was at the root of the first conflict between Spínola and the MFA, which occurred during the *coup*. The MFA's programme stated that it 'fully recognised the right of self-determination', yet Spínola managed to eliminate this phrase, transforming it into the more vague promise to 'pursue a colonial policy that will lead to peace' (Ferreira 1994: 55).

Between April and July 1974, when the Portuguese government's position was formally clarified with the publication of Law 7/74, the tensions between Spínola and the MFA, in respect of decolonization policy, was great. This conflict continued throughout the summer until Spínola's fall from power in September 1974 and, according to Ferreira, this was the lit fuse that led to 'the emergence of the MFA as a political agent during the pre-constitutional period' (Ferreira 1994: 54).

The first weeks after the fall of the dictatorship saw a series of significant social movements that included strike waves, the purging of public companies, government ministries, and schools. At the local and trade union level, left-wing parties – and particularly the MDP/CDE, the PCP, and parties of the extreme left – began to occupy local authority chambers and trade union offices, while at the same time decolonization emerged as an important demand during their public demonstrations.

Although they had been slowly emerging during the 1950s: growth that accelerated during the 1960s, the political culture of all sections of the left – from moderate socialists and progressive Catholics to the extreme left – was in favour of decolonization on the eve of the regime's overthrow. Decolonization was a part of their political programmes and dominated the ideals of the leaders of the PS, the MDP and the PCP, all of whom participated in the first provisional governments.

Under strong pressure caused by a dynamic of political change that was brought about new social movements, the dictatorship, its elite, and its symbols, even the parties that came to occupy the centre-right and right of the political spectrum either made declarations supporting decolonization – as in the case of the Popular Democratic Party (PPD), which emerged from the liberal wing of the dictatorship; or retreated into the shadows of Spínola's federalist/referendum option that was ended with the general's defeat in the wake of the events of 28 September 1974 (GPDP 1979: 392–420).

Taken by surprise by the coup, the international community was quick to recognise the new regime in Lisbon, although it had little respect for the overall decolonization process. The participation of communists in government, and the successive leftwards turns of the new government, attracted US attention both in Portugal and in Angola.

Even before the nomination of the first provisional government, the Socialist Party leader, Mário Soares, began a series of informal conversations with the leaders of the liberation movements. Almeida Santos and delegates sent by Spínola soon joined him in this endeavour. At the same time as they sought the immediate recognition of their right to independence as a condition for a cease-fire, Spínola began to oppose the MFA, both on African territory and in continental Portugal, thus signalling his arrival as a political actor.

Supported by the parties of the left whilst acting on its own initiative, the MFA moved away from Spínola, opposing his attempts to become the effective leader of the institutionalization of democracy and, particularly, of the decolonization process. With the nomination of the second provisional government, led by Vasco Gonçalves, the MFA launched itself as an autonomous organization. It was by their initiative that Spínola signed Law 7/74 that proclaimed the colonies' right to independence and which outlined the legal framework that would both enable decolonization to take place and define the organs that would be involved in the process. The negotiations accelerated from that moment on, and counted on active participation from the MFA as well as Mário Soares and Almeida Santos, the two government ministers who presided over the discussions.

Spínola continued to defend his referendum option throughout the summer of 1974, seeking third party alternatives to the liberation movements that placed all of his hopes on the white communities within the colonies—particularly in Angola and Mozambique. His position was contrary to that which dominated both the emerging party system and the MFA, which dominated the military institution, and whose members were pressing for a rapid withdrawal from Africa. Spínola's option could only have been possible had there been a strong metropolitan authority with a negotiating strategy that was backed up by the military forces in the colonies; however, none of these conditions were present.

With Spínola's fall, Portugal's decolonization acquired a global character, with a metropolitan society that was in crisis, and which was progressively divided during the turbulent institutionalization of democracy. In a few months, Portugal had moved from being NATO's smallest anti-Communist partner to becoming a 'semi-Communist infiltrator' with Third Worldist foreign policy sympathies that was gaining an international significance that was in direct proportion to the increasing foreign intervention in Portuguese politics.

It was in this context that there was 'a dramatic compression in the timing of the end of the empire' (MacQueen 1998: 212). As we shall see below, as well as the pressure being exerted by the international community and the liberation movements, there was also a general desire to achieve a rapid decolonization that would secure Spínola's defeat. This idea characterised an important segment of the political leaders, from the MFA to the centre-left, at the time. In the words of one Portuguese scholar: 'Opposing the myth of "Portugal: one and indivisible from the Minho to Timor" was the methodology of uniform decolonization. This was the method by which continental Portugal would free itself – for once and for all – from the imperial logic. It was the centre that dispensed with the periphery' (Ferreira 1994: 63).

Decolonization case by case[1]

Guinea-Bissau
The transition to independence in Guinea-Bissau was the most rapid of all; although it was not without its problems. The Portuguese authorities had to deal with the fact that the PAIGC had made a unilateral declaration of independence in 1973. Nevertheless, for some Portuguese scholars, this represented 'the model for Portuguese decolonization' (Silva 1997).

One important aspect of Guinea-Bissau's transition was the independent presence of the MFA that had executed a form of '*coup d'état* that followed that of Lisbon' (Silva 1997). This coup led to the immediate removal of the colony's governor, General Bettencourt Rodrigues, who had replaced Spínola in 1973. General Rodrigues handed in his resignation on his return to Lisbon. The MFA in Guinea also began arresting members of the regime's secret police, the PIDE, who were rapidly evacuated to Lisbon as the military called for a cease-fire with the PAIGC, the organization they believed to be the only representative of the Guinean people.

Portugal's foreign minister, Mário Soares, accompanied by Spínola's representative, held their first meeting with PAIGC delegates in Senegal. At this meeting the Portuguese delegation stated their position that it was too soon to recognise the colony's independence, although they did agree an immediate end to hostilities on the ground. Despite the advice offered him by Senegal's leader, Senghor, who had attempted to explain that the 1971 model was dead, Spínola remained convinced of the desireability of a phased independence process that would be controlled by Lisbon (Spínola 1976).

In the meantime, Spínola sent Lt. Colonel Carlos Fabião to Guinea as a delegate of the National Salvation Junta. Fabião gave an initially cautious speech at a meeting of 1500 troops at which the existence of a local MFA structure was apparent (Silva 1997). Negotiations continued until the end of May in London, without any conclusive outcome. One problem raised by the PAIGC delegation was concerned with Cape Verde, which was considered to be an integral part of the territory that made the unilateral declaration of independence in 1973. The only result to emerge from these discussions was the nomination of a PAIGC delegation in

Bissau. The delegates met again in Algeria some weeks later, but again without any real result.

The PAIGC obtained some diplomatic victories during this period, particularly Brazil's recognition of Guinea-Bissau's independence and the country's admission as a member of the United Nations. At this point rival organizations to the PAIGC emerged in Bissau. These competitors had a very small support base and, with the PAIGC enjoying a good relationship with Senghor, they could not attract international support. The greatest threat to the Guinean liberation movement came from the African commandos who had fought on the Portuguese side during the war.

The divisions between the MFA and Spínola in Portugal and the pressures on the ground continued to increase. On 1 July, the local MFA approved a motion on the decolonization of Guinea, which called for the immediate and unequivocal recognition of the unilateral declaration of independence, repudiating any and all 'reactionary and neo-colonial' pretensions while demanding the immediate restart of negotiations with the PAIGC (Silva 1997). The idea of accepting a former armed enemy as the only legitimate representative of local interests was now gaining strength.

Despite the difficulties in the official negotiations, a Portuguese initiative led to the arrival in Bissau of a PAIGC delegation that entered into discussions with Carlos Fabião. A short time later, following an incident between Portuguese troops and guerrilla's, the Portuguese Military High Command met a PAIGC delegation and, against Spínola's wishes, agreed on a programme for the repositioning of Portuguese troops and the allocation of some Portuguese military bases to the PAIGC.

The passing of Law 7/74 clarified the situation and swept away all legal obstacles to the negotiations. After an initial round of meetings, Portugal and the PAIGC finally signed an accord in Algiers on 26 August 1974. The Portuguese State agreed to withdraw all its troops by the end of October, to officially recognise the Republic of Guinea-Bissau on 10 September, and to confirm Cape Verde's right to independence following a series of separate negotiations.

Demobilised by the Portuguese and abandoned to their fate, some of the African commandos who had fought for the Portuguese military were summarily executed following independence.

Cape Verde
Cape Verde was the first colony to be decolonized by the initiative of Lisbon in a territory in which there was neither armed conflict nor strong international pressure to do so. The Algiers Accords with the PAIGC included some guidance on the decolonization of Cape Verde and, as has been noted, the PAIGC was recognised as the islands' *de facto* legitimate representative in the independence negotiations (Silva 1997). Believed by many historians to be 'one of the most controversial decisions of the decolonization process', the union between the problem of Cape Verde with that of Guinea was legitimated only by the PAIGC's Cape Verdian leaders

under the cover of a 1972 UN resolution (Ferreira 1994: 62).

Cape Verde occupied an important geographic position that the dictatorship had on several occasions attempted to incorporate within NATO (Coker 1986). An important airport, which was used by South Africa, was constructed on Sal. The strategic dimension caused Portugal to fear the intervention of the western powers, particularly the United States, during any transfer of power to the PAIGC. Spínola was to use this possibility as the main justification for his position during his brief mandate.

Despite the fact that a large number of the PAIGC's elite were Cape Verdians, and that the independence of Cape Verde was an integral part of the movement's programme, this party had been unsuccessful in establishing cells there (Lopes 1996). Contrary to some of the optimistic interpretations, however, the PAIGC always experienced a certain degree of internal ethnic tensions – not all of which were provoked by the Guineans. Since the 1960s, several Cape Verdian nationalists had rejected union with Guinea-Bissau, causing serious conflicts within the PAIGC that was accused of ignoring the Cape Verdian front in the movement's political activities.

With the overthrow of the dictatorship, the PAIGC faced the new situation in Cape Verde with some nervousness and radicalism. At this time political groups appeared on the islands that supported various policies; some called for the establishment of more or less autonomous or federal links with Portugal, while others called for the islands' independence from both Portugal and Guinea-Bissau. There was also visible evidence that some sectors of Cape Verdian society, both resident and abroad, feared the PAIGC.

Of the PAIGC's rival parties, the Union of Cape Verde People (UPICV – União do Povo das Ilhas de Cabo Verde), which was led by Leitão da Graça, an anti-PAIGC exile, was the most ideologically radical. The more moderate Cape Verde Democratic Union (UDC – União Democrática de Cabo Verde) was founded in May 1974 by João Baptista Monteiro (Lopes 1996: 331-42). Some emigrant communities were also deeply divided – particularly the Cape Verdian community in the United States (Barrows 1990: 199-217; Nunes 1982). Initially disguised as a unified anti-colonial front organisation, the PAIGC now began to call for the political conquest of Cape Verde. The first steps, according to many observers, frightened a part of Cape Verdian society, particularly the more conservative sectors and the Church.

In Cape Verde, the MFA was quick to establish itself and to form a pressure group with parallel contacts to those of the delegate from Lisbon, Major Loureiro dos Santos. José Judas, one of this group's members who was later to become a member of the Council of the Revolution, was an important proponent of the rapid transfer of power to the PAIGC (Lopes 1996: 370-71). At the height of these tensions, the local MFA approved a document that demarcated it from the remaining political parties, arguing that there was no solution 'other than the recognition of the PAIGC as the legitimate representative of the people of Cape Verde (Lopes

1996: 373).

Following the recognition of Guinea's independence and the removal of Spínola from power, several of the PAIGC's leaders returned to Cape Verde. The nature of the conflicts between the PAIGC and the UPICV were such that in order to maintain public order, the Portuguese military, with the PAIGC, intervened to prevent UPICV demonstrations from taking place. Steps were also taken to arrest members of both the UPIVC and the UDC, who were then imprisoned at Tarrafal (Lopes 1996: 385-400).

Cape Verde's independence was secured in July 1975, seven months after the Lisbon negotiations between the Portuguese government and the PAIGC. The independence agreement established a transitional government composed of three PAIGC and two Portuguese ministers led by a Portuguese high commissioner who would oversee the organization of elections to a constituent assembly that would formally declare the islands' independence. The PAIGC was the only party to contest the elections, obtaining 92 percent of the vote (Davinson 1989). On the day of the elections, all of the prisoners in Tarrafal were granted an amnesty and left for Lisbon with the last Portuguese troops.

Mozambique

25 April 1974 was met with apprehension in Mozambique where the Military Governor and some senior officers remained faithful to the ousted regime. Their attempts to resist were quickly defeated by troops loyal to the new government in Lisbon; however, the MFA remained weak in Mozambique, enabling FRELIMO to exacerbate the military situation in May and June by opening a new front in Zambezi (MacQueen 1998: 126).

While not on the same scale as that of Angola, the war in Mozambique did not affect the colony's white population, which had grown rapidly during the 1960s. Nevertheless, within a few months of the Portuguese coup, Mozambique was to change rapidly with the flight of the white community and FRELIMO's control of the independence process.

Contact with FRELIMO was established largely as a result of pressure from local military leaders, thereby ensuring a more active role for the MFA. Following the example set in Guinea, the MFA recommended that Portuguese troops engaged only in defensive actions and suggested that Lisbon immediately recognise FRELIMO as the legitimate representatives of the Mozambican people. Much to Spínola's annoyance, pressure for a cease-fire agreement increased (Ferreira 1994). Costa Gomes visited the colony in May and, recognizing the poor disposition of Portuguese troops, ordered a *de facto* cease-fire in the north of the country (Spínola 1978).

Just as a strike-wave was having a damaging affect on the country's productivity, Costa Gomes sent some former political prisoners to Dar-es-Salaam with proposals for cease-fire negotiations; however, the National Salvation Junta's preference for Spínola's policy caused FRELIMO to mistrust Portuguese overtures, with the result that they rejected this approach. Both sides remained in contact with one another through the Zambian government, and in early July 1974, Mário Soares and Samora Machel met in Lusaka. The talks did not progress well given that Soares's remit was restricted to the negotiation of a cease-fire. Despite this, the Portuguese delegation accepted COREMO's exclusion from the discussions (Bragança 1987: 437). Machel outlined his conditions: recognition of FRELIMO as the sole legitimate representative of Mozambican society; independence; and the swift transfer of power. Lisbon's indecision resulted in the collapse of the talks and to preparations being made for a referendum in the colony.

A brief resumé of the emergence of parties and movements in Mozambique in the wake of the 1974 coup immediately reveals the difficulties involved in encountering any solid alternatives to FRELIMO. Jorge Jardim, a charismatic personality of the colony's white community, was one of the few supporters of the Rhodesian model. Jardim was one of the few Mozambican entrepreneurs who had the ability to cause concern for both the Portuguese government and FRELIMO; however, his role in the process was turbulent and inconsistent. Following Spínola's overthrow, the MFA stopped all contact with Jardim and prohibited him from leaving Mozambique (Jardim 1976).

Whether they were created to pursue Spínolist projects, or simply organised to defend the interests of the white community, movements such as the Federalists, Democratic Convergence, or the Independent Front for Western Convergence (FICO - Frente Independente de Convergência Ocidental), were swiftly dismissed as reactionary representatives of 'white power'. Only a small minority of whites, represented by the 'Mozambique Democrats', supported FRELIMO – and even then only after they had abandoned many of their founders.

Some of the groups that had been authorised by the colonial authorities as a consequence of Caetano's 'limited pluralism' survived to garner the support of Africans who opposed FRELIMO. One such group was the United Group of Mozambique (GUMO – Grupo Unido de Moçambique), a multi-ethnic group that included Joana Simeão as one of its leaders. During its earlier public demonstrations, when the referendum remained a serious option, GUMO found itself under attack from both FRELIMO and the white right-wing (MacQueen 1998: 139). After a short while, GUMO expelled Simeão and disbanded.

FRELIMO's sole rival during the 1960s was the Zambian based COREMO. This organization began preparations to take its place in the new Mozambique and created several front organizations such as the Mozambican Common Front (FCM - Frente Comum de Moçambique) that included Joana Simeão and two FRELIMO dissidents, Urias Simango and Lázaro Kavandame. On the eve of the signing of the Lusaka Accords, Simango and another COREMO veteran, Paulo Cumane, founded the National Coalition Party (PCN – Partido de Coligação Nacional) in Beira, with the intention of securing a seat at the post-independence negotiations with FRELIMO (Herikson 1978: 222-3).

After several secret informal meetings, however, Melo Antunes and a representative of the MFA in Mozambique met with FRELIMO representatives in Dar-es-Salaam – opening the way to a swift decolonization without the need for any referendum being held. The agreement called for the nomination of a majority FRELIMO transitional government to be in place by 25 June 1975, the date set for independence. Fearing the reaction of Mozambique's white community, and recognizing the continued existence of serious economic problems, the Portuguese were somewhat concerned about the rapidity of the process. Nevertheless, Mário Soares and Almeida Santos accepted the agreement, and it was signed in Lusaka on 7 September 1974.

The Lusaka Agreement provoked a serious revolt by the white community, who were supported by anti-FRELIMO African parties. White rebels associated with FICO, and their anti-FRELIMO allies, which included Cumane, Simeão, and Simango, occupied the airport and the *Rádio Clube de Moçambique* (Mozambique Radio), both of which were controlled by FRELIMO supporters. The rebels freed some PIDE prisoners. Many of the Portuguese military units in the Mozambican capital failed to intervene, apparently because they had received no orders from Spínola. The military situation was clarified, however, when Costa Gomes ordered Portuguese troops from the north of the country into the capital (Spínola 1978).

During the days following the rebellion, rumours of conspiracies were rife. The atmosphere was further coloured by the appearance of terrorist brigades. Two of the rebel leaders, Simango and Joana Simeão, were arrested by FRELIMO forces. While in custody, they declared that Spínola, who officially ratified the Lusaka Agreement on 9 September, had supported the revolt.

While during October, racially motivated attacks resulted in the deaths of several Africans and whites, the exodus of the white population can be dated from the ratification of the Lusaka Agreement. Both the transitional government and the Portuguese High Commission made several appeals for them to return, but to little avail. By the end of October, there were 15,000 mainly white and Indian Mozambican refugees in South Africa. Between 1974 and 1977 almost 160,000 Mozambican returnees (*retornados*) had gone to Portugal (Ferreira 1994: 85).

The new Portuguese High Commissioner, Vítor Crespo, arrived in Mozambique at the height of the revolt, while FRELIMO's Joaquim Chissano – who had been nominated to lead the transitional government – arrived a few days later. In accordance with the Agreement, Portuguese forces began to concentrate in Beira and in the nation's capital, ready to leave for Portugal; however, with the disturbances continuing, some mixed military units were retained for security reasons, while the Portuguese police remained in Mozambique for several months after independence.

The social and economic affairs that had not been part of the Lusaka Agreements remained to be resolved by the transitional government. The main problems concerned the central bank and the Cabora Bassa dam, which the Portuguese were unable to abandon completely as a consequence of the creditors' refusal to accept the transfer of this structure to Mozambican control. Several observers were later to accuse both parties to the Agreement of 'irresponsibility' for not having protected property rights (Newitt 1995: 540).

South Africa and Rhodesia were unsettled by the sudden appearance of independent states on their borders and were quick to respond to the perceived threat that this posed to their existence, and both countries sponsored anti-FRELIMO guerrilla movements. Nevertheless, given the United States' relative lack of interest in Mozambique—especially when compared to Angola – meant that international factors were less important constraints in Mozambique's decolonization than they may have been elsewhere. The US Deputy Secretary for African Affairs, Donald Easum, met Samora Machel in Dar-es-Salaam during October 1974, in what was the United States' first meeting with FRELIMO since the death of Eduardo Mondlane. Machel wanted to establish good relations with the US and sought its economic support for Mozambican independence. All was to come to naught, however, as Kissinger dismissed Easum shortly afterwards. Several years were to pass before the US and FRELIMO were able to normalise their relationship (Schneidman 1987: 439).

Internationalization in Angola

Angola's decolonization was by far the most complex of all. While it would be an exaggeration to say that the drive for decolonization in Angola emerged 'almost by accident' (Brimingham 1995: 68), it is nonetheless true to say that it was not caused by any increased military or political pressure by the weak and divided liberation movements. Angola was the richest and most successful of all Portugal's colonies during the 1960s, and it had the greatest number of white colonists, yet its decolonization was the most difficult and violent of all.

The coup in Lisbon on 25 April 1974 caught the MPLA by surprise while it was in the throes of a serious internal crisis that had divided the movement into three factions – one of which, led by Daniel Chipenda in the east of the colony, was very well armed. On his liberation, the MPLA's honorary president, Father Joaquim Pinto de Andrade, his brother, Mário Andrade – who was the leader of 'Active Revolt' – called for the realization of a congress. The congress took place in the outskirts of Lusaka, and was attended by Agostinho Neto and Chipenda, who each had 165 delegates, and by Andrade's 'Active Revolt', which had 70 delegates. Following several days of debate, Neto and his supporters walked out, thereby consolidating the schism within the movement. In Brazzaville a few days later, and under strong pressure from the leaders of four African states, the three factions agreed to the appointment of a 'provisional leader until independence'; however, it was not long before this agreement fell by the wayside (Marcum 1978: 248-51). In September, Chipenda succeeded in regaining control over his group, and together they abandoned the MPLA to initiate contact with its rival, the FNLA (Jaime and Barber 1999: 145-50).

Despite having become little more than an 'extension' of Mobuto's armed forces in Zaire, the disintegration of the MPLA enabled the FNLA to obtain a leading role in the military field. At the same time it made strenuous efforts to regain United States' support by presenting itself as the West's future champion in Angola (Maxwell 1982: 374).

When the new Governor, Admiral Rosa Coutinho, left for Angola at the end of July 1974, the situation on the ground was much clearer. Portugal had already reached an agreement ending hostilities with UNITA, but had delayed doing the same with the other movements. The FNLA had seen its penetration into Angolan territory halted by the Portuguese armed forces, while the MPLA continued to fight for its place at the negotiating table.

Spínola attempted to lead the decolonization of Angola personally, and outlined several manoeuvres he hoped would mobilise the white community's activists into taking an active role in the process while entering into discussions with Zaire over the Angolan problem (GPDP 1979: 419-20). In Angola too, however, the MFA had emerged as an autonomous force with its own political preferences. At an assembly in Luanda attended by 500 Portuguese officers, the MFA opposed Spínola's policies and approved the proposal for the rapid decolonization of Angola by an overwhelming majority (Ferreira 1994: 71).

During the early months, the white community waited for decisions from Portugal, while the number of white colonist parties proliferated. The fall of Spínola, and with it the dream of a negotiated settlement with important intervention from the white community, saw the recommencement of negotiations with the MPLA and the FNLA as the only interlocutors with the Portuguese government on the Angolan decolonization process. In October 1974 a cease-fire was agreed with the FNLA and Agostinho Neto's faction, despite Chipenda's protests, and these groups began to open delegations in Luanda.

In January 1975, the FNLA, MPLA and UNITA met in Mombassa in order to approve a set of general principles for their negotiations with Portugal. One week after this meeting, they signed the Alvor Accords that regularised and set a timetable for the Angolan decolonization process. In this way the white colonist parties and the smaller African splinter groups were excluded from the process, with only the three historical movements obtaining recognition. Chipenda remained on the outside and solidified his alliance with the FNLA. UNITA had to be quickly recognised by the OAU, which happened only a few days before the negotiations had begun (Wheeler 1980: 6). In their preparations for eventual elections, both the FNLA and UNITA initiated alliances with the white community. Initially enjoying support from both the United States and Zaire, the FNLA, for example, purchased the *Jornal de Angola* in preparation for the campaign.

Following the model that had already been utilised in other cases, they nominated a High Commissioner and a transitional government and scheduled elections to take place the following October, with independence to follow on 11 November 1975. Only the three main movements party to the negotiations were permitted to compete in the elections. Rosa Coutinho, who had been attacked by the white colonists, the FNLA and UNITA and who was accused of favouring the MPLA, was replaced as High Commissioner a few weeks later by another military figure, Silva Cardoso.

Conflicts between the MPLA and its splinter group, led by Chipenda, began in Luanda in February 1975, beginning a cycle of civil war that involved the two super-powers and the direct intervention of Zaire, Cuba and South Africa. In the words of one historian 'the conflict [in 1975] was not about liberation itself, but who should inherit the spoils in a colony that had become rich and successful' (Birmingham 1995: 67). With the beginning of armed confrontation, Portugal's role as mediator was superseded as the extent of international military support increased and the latent civil war heated up (Gleijeses 2002).

The United States immediately 'reinitiated' its contacts with the FNLA; however the internal crisis prevented the provision of any significant support in the immediate wake of the 1974 coup. At the same time, the Soviet Union recommenced its support for the MPLA; support that had, according to some sources, been suspended since 1972 (Schneidman 1987: 441-2).

Mobuto had been seeking to pressurise the United States into supporting Holden and no others. The US, however, also extended their hand to Jonas Savimbi's UNITA. US support to UNITA was initially minimal and determined by political considerations given that the United States' anticipated that the FNLA would win the forthcoming elections given the MPLA's internal difficulties and their belief that all parties would adhere to the Alvor Accords (Spikes 1993: 131-2).

The military escalation on the ground was already obvious by March 1975. The FNLA had attacked the MPLA in Luanda and the Soviet Union, for motives that divide Cold War historians even today, increased its military support to Agostinho Neto. In response, the CIA recommended a substantial increase in arms supplies to both Roberto and Savimbi, even while UNITA was receiving support from South Africa (Marcum 1978: 263).

Several sources indicate that the escalation, like so many others during the Cold War, was not provoked so much by the prospect of the emergence of an African Marxist regime as it was by the United States' strategy of responding to Soviet intervention (Schneidman 1987: 449). Gerald Ford authorised an increase in arms supplies and units of the regular Zairian army entered Angola, while UNITA and Daniel Chipenda obtained their support from South Africa.

In July 1975, the MPLA drove its opponents out of Luanda and the first Cuban troops made a brief appearance at the MPLA's side (Gleijeses 2002). The transitional government began to collapse and with it all that remained of the Alvor Accords. Jomo Kenyatta made an unsuccessful attempt to save the Accords during a series of discussions that took place in Kenya. Significantly, and by the agreement of the participants, there were no Portuguese representatives at the conciliation talks that took place in June 1975.

The mass exodus of Portuguese civilians accelerated. In January 1975 around 50,000 Portuguese fled Angola, and by the summer of the same year an air bridge was established to evacuate the remaining colonists. In an operation that involved the participation of civil and military aircraft, and which also utilised commercial aircraft from the US, France, Switzerland, the United Kingdom, West Germany and even the Soviet Union, more than 200,000 colonists were evacuated from Angola (GPDP 1982).

Several Portuguese delegations were sent to Luanda, reaffirming their neutrality and appealing for all sides to respect the Accords. Given the social and political instability back in Portugal, and by the demobilization of Portuguese troops in Angola, there was very little prospect of Lisbon being able to intervene militarily or for its diplomatic intervention to have any effect (Oliveira 1996: 105). Concentrating on the withdrawal of Portuguese troops and on aiding the refugees, the Portuguese administration threatened to repel any attack on Luanda. Expressing the Portuguese left's sympathies towards the MPLA, Melo Antunes attempted to persuade Kissinger that this was the only movement that could ensure Angola remained unaligned, and that US support for the MPLA would diminish the Soviet-Cuban influence (Schneidman 1987: 426).

By the end of the summer of 1975, UNITA and South Africa dominated the southern part of the country, with Chipenda in the service of the so-called Operation Zulu. The FNLA controlled a front that included Zairians, former Portuguese troops, and several mercenary groups that had in the meantime fought alongside them. It seemed that the MPLA was about to be defeated. An increase in Soviet and Cuban military support, however, with the Cubans sending more troops to Luanda, saved the day for the MPLA at the same time as offers of mediation by the OAU were being rejected by the Soviet Union. In the meantime, increased US support to the FNLA and UNITA was being criticised in Congress, which was getting over the trauma of Vietnam. Congress blocked any US participation in Angola, a decision that favoured the consolidation of the MPLA.

On 11 November, the date established in the Alvor Accords for Angola's independence, the High Commissioner lowered the Portuguese flag, oversaw the departure of the last Portuguese troops and offered independence to 'the Angolan people'. The war did not end on this day, however, and while the MPLA proclaimed the establishment of the People's Republic of Angola in Luanda, the FNLA and UNITA proclaimed the formation of the People's Democratic Republic of Angola.

Timor: from neglect to the diplomatic battle
Timor represents the most extreme of all of Portugal's decolonization processes. A small territory with purely symbolic importance for Portugal, this island was shared with the Netherlands and had not seen the presence of any significant nationalist movements during the 1950s and 1960s, although the Indonesia's independence had had led to some revolts (and corresponding repression) in the colony.

During the first months following the overthrow of the dictatorship, nothing of note happened in Timor apart from the appointment of a new Governor, Lemos Pires, following Almeida Santos's official visit to the territory in November 1974. At this time, three new local parties were being formed: Timor People's Democratic Association (APODETI), which favoured Timor's integration into neighbouring Indonesia; Timor Democratic Union (UDT), which initially advocated association with Portugal; and the Independent East Timor Revolutionary Front (FRETILIN), which consisted of young revolutionaries.

With a difficult transition to democracy, and the decolonization process under way, the Lisbon authorities did not attribute great importance to Timor. Lemos Pires was attempting to manage the conflict between the three parties, which was particularly significant given that the armed forces at his disposal were, in the main, recruited locally (Pires 1991). In June 1975, and at a moment when prospects of the various factions reaching an understanding was unlikely, Vítor Alves visited the colony and decided to hold a summit meeting of all three parties. Both FRETILIN and the UDT refused his invitation. Despite their absence, he resolved to prepare an electoral law and began consultations on the various options available, ranging from complete independence to association with Indonesia while Portugal reaffirmed Timor's right to self-determination.

The first violent clashes took place at the end of July, and by August the first refugees were leaving. Faced with coups by both the UDT and FRETILIN, the Portuguese authorities withdrew to the island of Ataúro just as FRETILIN seemed to win the mini civil war and gain control of the territory. Following several conversations between Portugal and Indonesia, and facing the political preparations for occupation by its powerful neighbour, FRETILIN declared Timor's independence on 28 November. On the same day, the UDT and APODETI formally declared the territory's association with Indonesia, whose troops invaded a few weeks later (Oliveira 1996: 161-5).

Portugal recognised neither the colony's independence nor the Indonesian occupation, and withdrew from Ataúro on the day following the invasion. The Portuguese government severed diplomatic relations with Indonesia and raised the matter at the United Nations, which continued to recognise Portugal as the legitimate administrative authority of a non-autonomous territory.

More than 20 years after Indonesia's annexation of Timor, the end of the Cold War and the beginnings of a complex transition to democracy following the increasing corruption of Suharto's regime, prospects for Timorese independence began to emerge. Indonesian massacres in Timor began to affect international public opinion during the 1990s; however, the decision to hold an internationally observed referendum that gave the Timorese people the option of independence was an unprecedented act in the region. The massacres committed by Indonesian armed forces following the victory of the pro-independence movement resulted in UN military intervention in 1999 that enabled the preparations for independence to be made.

Portugal: from Africa to Europe

The European option that was favoured by the majority of the Portuguese political elite was a product of the transition to democracy that began in 1974. Whilst Portugal was only marginally involved in the reconstruction of Western Europe following the Second World War, the country's decision to opt for the European option was a consequence of decolonization and of the institutionalization of democracy (Pinto and Teixeira 2002).

The European Community, representing developed Europe, was an 'ready symbol' that the democratic elites could utilise to legitimate the new domestic order following the contested transition and the end of the colonial empire that had been so dear to the New State.

Whilst present in the programmes of several of the new political parties from the very earliest days of the revolution, it was primarily in the context of the political cleavages of 1975, when they were faced with socialist and Third-Worldist alternatives, that the parties of the right and the centre-left emphasised 'Europe' and the EEC as a reference for Portugal's future. Within the context of the polarised transition of 1974-5, the European option was an important factor in the break from a dictatorial, isolationist, and colonial past, which simultaneously assumed an anti-Communist and anti-revolutionary dimension.

Portugal did not experience the same levels of international isolation as its Spanish neighbour following the Second World War. Its status as a founding member of NATO and as a participant in other international organizations, such as the Organization for European Economic Co-operation (OEEC) and the European Payments Union (EPU), and its receipt of Marshall Plan funds – albeit on a relatively small scale – are all examples of the Portuguese dictatorship's international acceptance.

Being excluded from, and remaining mistrustful of, the Treaty of Rome that marked the foundation of the European Economic Community, and following positions adopted by its major trading partner, the United Kingdom, membership of the European Free Trade Association (EFTA) was to be an important economic aim for the dictatorship throughout the 1960s. Negotiated on terms that were favourable to Portugal – which saw the majority of its economic activities largely protected – the EFTA agreement was one of the roots of Portuguese economic growth in the 1960s, and for the significant increase in its economic relations with Europe. It was also behind the emergence of interest groups with fewer associations with the colonies.

The Portuguese export sector responded to the EFTA stimulus with dynamism, with the domestic market absorbing an increasing number of Portuguese products – to the detriment of the colonies. The United Kingdom's entry into the EEC in 1973 forced Caetano to conclude a commercial agreement with the EEC. Signed in 1972, this agreement strengthened Portugal's economic links with Europe, and contained a clause that held out the prospect for closer relations at a future date. 'Inevitably, the logic of imperial links and of economic nationalism were progressively being corroded by the changes in economic relations during the 1960s and 1970s' (Corkill 1993: 16). Caetano's indecision helped consolidate the position of a small liberalizing and technocratic pro-European sector within the dictatorship that was to break with the regime on the eve of its overthrow (Castilho 2000). Spokes-people for these groups, some of which had emerged during the limited pluralism permitted during the final phase of the dictatorship, sought to provide a political outline for relationship between Europe, economic modernization and regime liberalization.

Decolonization, Europe and national identity
Both the process of decolonization and the adoption of a pro-European policy led to the production of significant ideological output by some sections of the intellectual elite who began reflecting on their combined impact on national identity – an ever present theme in the Portuguese ideological debate since the end of the nineteenth century (Monteiro and Pinto 1998: 232–45). With decolonization, a central element in the Portuguese nationalist discourse disappeared, as the often heralded 'identity crises' failed to appear in any tangible form.

Following a period of recriminations that emanated mainly from the more conservative groups in their criticism of decolonization during the late-1970s, several small, and largely unsuccessful, extreme right-wing parties were formed that sought to capitalise on the discontent felt among those sectors that had been most affected by the country's new outlook – particularly the *retornados* (Pinto 1998a). Also unsuccessful were those conservative ideological groups whose discourse talked of defending a 'national identity' that was being threatened by the country's integration into the EEC. The ultimate failure of this argument can be seen in the consensus in favour of Europe that united the two main conservative parties (the CDS and the PSD) during the 1970s and 1980s.

The elaboration of nationalist discourses emerged during the 1970s as a reaction against the country's incorporation into Europe, promoted by a conservatism that utilized, instrumentally, the country's exclusively Atlantic vocation. The Communist Party also promoted the economistic defence of the 'interests of the national productive forces' in the face of European capitalism. However, with the myth of the empire ended, the democratic elite managed to engender the belief within Portuguese public opinion that Europe was the only means through which Portugal could recreate important relations with the new Portuguese speaking African states, particularly since almost all economic links had disappeared and political relationships had deteriorated following the granting of independence in 1975 (Pinto and Teixeira 2002).

With Portugal's social and economic development, the former colonies are new viewed as part of the distant past. Even with the known methodological limitations, opinion studies offer us a small window on the evolution of Portuguese public opinion with regards European unification and Portugal's new place in the world since the 1970s and 1980s.

In 1978, three years after decolonization, the majority of Portuguese – almost 70 per cent – believed that 'Portugal was right to grant these countries independence', although they also thought that 'the rights of Portuguese living in them ought to be protected'. Only 2.2 per cent of those questioned were in favour of continuing the fight against the liberation movements (Bacalhau 1994: 257).

Despite this, again in 1978, a substantial minority of 20 per cent thought that Portugal could not survive economically without its former colonies. The gradual diminution of this belief seems to be directly linked to the prospect of EEC accession: 'the accession process and membership itself, besides providing a substitute for the lost colonies, also represented an incentive for change in the nature of the country's economic, social and cultural activities.' (Bacalhau 1994: 257).

Nevertheless, the emergence of the EEC as a positive prospect for Portuguese society was a lengthy process that was initially restricted to the political elite. In 1978, shortly after the formal membership application had been submitted, most Portuguese had little to say on the matter, with over 60 per cent of the population stating that they did not know if EEC membership was essential for the future of the country's economy. It was not until the early-1980s that the population became better informed on the matter. The Portuguese – at least as far as we are able to judge by the opinion polls – do not seem to have experienced any serious identity crisis, either as a result of the loss of the colonial empire in 1975, or as a consequence of the country's new international position within Europe since 1986.

Concluding remarks

The fall of the dictatorship and the nature of Portugal's transition to democracy resulted in the rapid decolonization of Europe's last colonial empire in conditions that were extremely favourable to the guerrilla movements. Being unable to maintain any military pressure in the former colonies, and with a political climate in Portugal that favoured the transfer of power to the liberation movements, the authorities in Lisbon was quick to put an end to Portuguese rule in all of the colonies. Yet, even if Portugal's transition had been less fraught, it remains doubtful whether Lisbon would have had been able to pursue any other course during the 1970s. Spínola's desire for the creation of a 'Lusophone federation' were not practical following the lengthy wars in Angola, Mozambique and Guinea-Bissau.

The limited capacity of the white community to react in Angola and Mozambique is not easy to explain. However, the hypotheses that this was a consequence of the dictatorship, of the lack of decentralization, of the repression of civil society and of any devolutionary pressure may be part of the explanation for their excessive dependence upon Lisbon. The colonial governors, who were mainly military officers, at least until Caetano's government, were usually minor figures within the regime as an expression of Salazar's fear of both heroic candidates for power in Lisbon and of colonial centurions who looked towards Rhodesia or South Africa (Wheeler 1978: 415-426).

Critics of Portuguese colonialism have repeated the conclusions they reached during the 1960s, and have noted that Portugal's obstinacy in maintaining an 'obsolete form of colonialism, they [the dictatorship] provoked, contrary to their intentions', the 'end of both white domination in South Africa and of imperialist control throughout the rest of the continent' (Harris 1972: 223). The Portuguese Empire's abrupt collapse in 1975 did accelerate the end of white domination, and brought a large part of Africa into close proximity with the Soviet Bloc during the Cold War.

One of the legacies of both the colonial war and of the swift decolonization was the consolidation of socialist political regimes in the new Portuguese speaking countries of Africa, including those, such as Cape Verde and São Tomé, in which there had been no armed conflict.

As the final chapter of European decolonization in Africa, the Portuguese example raised increased doubts about African independence, the role of their elites and the advances and setbacks experienced within the post-colonial societies. However, the attempts to demonstrate that 'there is no convincing evidence that the liberation movements carried a majority of their "nations" behind them' (MacQueen 1997: 58), even while it may be true, are retrospective projections of more recent concerns and unknown in the history of the formation of modern states. Ironically, East Timor at the turn of the millennium was the only former Portuguese colony to opt for independence democratically.

As for Portugal, it consolidated its integration into Europe following a serious economic crisis – the blame for which lies more with the 1973 Oil Shock and the transition to democracy than with decolonization – rapidly putting an end to the argument that the end of empire would only have detrimental consequences. The white populations, and especially those who had only emigrated a short time before independence, were the greatest losers; however, their return *en masse* to Portugal was, perversely, beneficial to the Portuguese economy.

References:

[1] This chapter will not discuss São Tomé and Príncipe as that is the subject of Malyn Newitt's chapter (see chapter 3).

Piero Gleijeses, *Conflicting Missions: Havana, Washington, and Africa, 1959-1976*, University of North Carolina Press, 2002.

PART II

Case studies

3: São Tomé and Príncipe: decolonization and its legacy, 1974–90

Malyn Newitt[*]

This chapter examines some of the ways in which the actual process of decolonization influenced the direction in which São Tomé and Príncipe developed after independence. In particular it looks at three questions: the extent to which the decolonization of São Tomé and Príncipe had its own momentum rather than being simply a by-product of the general decolonization process in the other colonies; the extent to which the choices made at the time of decolonization became major determinants of the way the country has developed; and thirdly whether there were practical alternatives to decolonization and independence which might better have secured the prosperity and development of such a small and fragile state.

Introduction

At the time of the Portuguese Revolution in April 1974 São Tomé and Príncipe was the smallest and least significant of Portugal's colonies. The two tiny islands with a land surface of 370 square miles, most of it high mountain, had a combined population of about 90,000. Príncipe with 7,000 people and an area of only 42 square miles is by far the smaller and least important of the two islands. São Tomé's tiny economy rested entirely on the production of cocoa, which was grown on large plantations, called *roças*, which were mostly owned by Portuguese companies or banks. These *roças* had been starved of investment and most of them operated with outdated machinery and agricultural methods.[1] Cocoa exports had been in continuous decline since 1925 and in 1974 only 7,400 tonnes were produced.

The population of the islands was stratified in an unusual and important way. The colonial establishment consisted of Portuguese administrators, police and military, almost all of them metropolitan Portuguese, a class of plantation overseers and managers and a few businessmen. In all the white population amounted to about 2,000. Many of these formed liaisons with local women but their mixed race offspring were not accepted by the São Tomeans and remained an isolated group, socially stranded between the whites and the dominant black group – the *forros*.

The *forros* were the largest and most significant group in the population. The term *forro* literally means a 'freeman' and indicates membership of the old São Tomé families who were the descendants of the original settlers and who, prior to about 1850 had owned or leased all the land in the islands, and had controlled municipal government and the church. The *forros* were a heavily lusitanised creole population. Portuguese was their mother tongue and all of them were catholic. The richer families had traditionally sent their children to Portugal, Angola or even Brazil for education. It was from this class from which São Tomé's small intelligentsia was drawn – they had published newspapers, and produced poets and writers as well as politicians to sit in the Cortes in Lisbon. However, during the twentieth century the *forros* had been typical of a class in decline. They had lost control of 90 per cent of the land in the scramble for plantations in the nineteenth century and had only managed to hang on to the tiny *glebas*, or small holdings, that clustered around the capital in the north of São Tomé and Príncipe. They had also been displaced from important positions within the island government by the metropolitan Portuguese.[2]

A wise Portuguese colonial policy might have fostered relations with this group who were potentially strong allies but instead the Portuguese both despised and feared this class. The commonly held Portuguese view was that the *forros* were lazy, lacked any enterprise and refused to work. They were also considered to be untrustworthy and the Portuguese became increasingly suspicious of the young *forro* men and women from the wealthier families who went abroad for their education and consorted with politically undesirable elements in Lisbon or Paris. The tensions between the *forros* and the Portuguese administration had surfaced during the relative political freedom of the Republic when *forros* elected their own member to sit in the Cortes and the *Liga dos Interesses Indígenas* (LII) acted as a focus for *forro* opinion (Nascimento 1994).[3]

Relations between the Portuguese and the *forros* had taken a disastrous turn in 1953 when the policies pursued by the governor, Carlos Gorgulho, since taking office in 1947 erupted in the events remembered as the Batepá massacre. Gorgulho, who had plans for the economic development of the islands, had commandeered some *forros* for public works and rumours had circulated that *forros* were to be contracted for work on the *roças* who were chronically short of manual labour. In the confused events that followed one member of the security forces was killed and the authorities carried out a repression which led to indiscriminate killings and large numbers being imprisoned, tortured and set to forced labour. Gorgulho was eventually recalled while PIDE investigated his administration and released the prisoners, but the damage had been done and the *forro* families, all of whom had suffered in the Batepá affair, retained a deep hatred of the Portuguese connection and a suspicion that the authorities might at any time plan a repetition of the massacres (Pelissiér 1979; Seibert 1999: Ch.2).

One of the greatest of Gorgulho's crimes in the eyes of the *forros* was that he had attacked their prized status as 'freemen'. This status was principally understood in terms of being exempt from contract labour on the rocas. Not only had Gorgulho threatened to force the *forros* to work on the cocoa plantations, but during the events of 1953 he had enrolled and armed bands of plantation workers to attack *forro* settlements. Imported slaves had originally worked the rocas but when slavery was finally abolished in the Portuguese empire in 1875 contract workers, known as *serviçais*, had replaced them. Until the 1920s contract labour had continued to be a form of slavery. The *serviçais* never returned to their homes in Angola or Mozambique and lived and died in slave barracks on the plantations that they were not allowed to leave. After 1920 some repatriation of workers took place and the *roças* found increasing difficulties in obtaining workers for their outdated and labour intensive processes. Convicts were sent from Angola and Mozambique, often people who had simply failed to pay their taxes, and increasingly Cape Verdians were brought from the drought stricken islands to undertake plantation work. By 1974 the plantation worker class was made up of Cape Verdians, mainland Africans, and children of *serviçais* born in the islands who were called *Tongas*. They all shared in common the lack of education and health facilities, a remoteness from shops, towns or social services of any kind and they faced formidable obstacles if they wished to leave the plantations, farm their own land or own fishing boats or businesses. In 1920 there had been 38,000 *serviçais* and they had constituted 60 per cent of the island population, but by 1974 their numbers had declined to under 20,000 out of a total population of 90,000.

There was one other group, the Angolares. Numerically very small and confined to one small area of São Tomé, the Angolares were traditionally believed to be descendants of survivors from an Angolan slave ship wrecked on the islands. The Angolares were not accepted into the *forro* elite although after independence it briefly suited the government to claim that they were an original, pre-Portuguese population of the islands.

The rise of the *forro* political elite

After the Batepá affair relations between the Portuguese and the *forros* remained very tense and the government did little to repair its relations with this group or provide them with career opportunities in the islands or the empire. Secondary education was only available in the São Tomé and Príncipe after 1952 and young São Tomeans still had to go abroad to complete their education. Small São Tomé communities existed in Portugal and in neighbouring African countries and it was in Lisbon that a new political elite began to form in the years after 1953. Here São Tomé students came under the influence of exiles from the other Portuguese colonies. Among this group were Miguel Trovoada who studied law, Manuel Pinto da Costa who had lived most of his life in Portugal and who went on to take a doctorate in economics in East Germany and Carlos Graça who qualified as a doctor – all of these were eventually to become either prime minister or president of independent São Tomé and Príncipe. The other well-known São Tomean, and the only one who found any position within the Portuguese imperial establishment, was Francisco Tenreiro, a geographer and poet who eventually became a deputy in the Portuguese Cortes. Tenreiro, however, was not a *forro* but a mulatto with a Portuguese father, and as such was excluded from the inner circle of *forro* exiles.

In this respect, as in so many others, the experience of São Tomé and Príncipe was similar to that of the other larger colonies. The Portuguese imperial system, while allowing some access to the lower ranks of the administration to natives of the colonies, made no serious attempt to co-opt the intelligentsia, or the young educated Africans into the imperial structure. As a result men like Pinto da Costa, Trovoada and Graça felt alienated by a system that offered them no opportunities. It is not surprising that this group should have been attracted by the ideas of third world nationalism and negritude that were current at the time. Nevertheless São Tomé nationalism had a very weak base. Not only was political organization within the islands impossible, but abroad the numbers of São Tomeans involved in nationalist politics was tiny.

Encouraged by the rapid decolonization elsewhere in Africa and by the emergence of nationalist movements in the other Portuguese colonies, a group of São Tomean students on vacation in the islands formed the CLSTP in 1960 (Hodges and Newitt 1988: 91). This 'nationalist' movement had no supporting organization of any kind within the islands while the members who formed its core never amounted to more than a score or so in number.

In all the Portuguese colonies nationalist leadership emerged among the exile community and was self-appointed. In Mozambique and Guinea this leadership had to prove itself by organising an armed struggle against the Portuguese and was able to acquire some legitimacy through being better able than any its rivals to sustain the war. However, the self-appointed leaders of MPLA in Angola and the nationalists in São Tomé and Príncipe acquired their legitimacy prior to 1974 largely through gaining international recognition and by being supported by the CONCP, the closely-knit group of political parties representing the five lusophone African countries which was founded in 1961.

In São Tomé the leading *forro* families were all closely connected by marriage and the exiles who formed CLSTP were related to many of the leading figures in the islands. However, they never quite lost the aura of being a leadership that had been created by, and remained dependent on, the other African nationalist parties. Close families ties, of course, not only bind people together they can also define factions, and exile politics are notoriously prone to factional rivalries. These began to affect the CLSTP almost as soon as it had been formed and the small group split along lines of personality and regional support. Miguel Trovoada, as president of the newly formed CLSTP, set up offices in Libreville in Gabon in 1961 but by 1965 the movement had competing offices established in Accra and Gabon. The faction fighting led to the virtual extinction of the CLSTP as an active party and it was only reformed, this time as the MLSTP, in 1972 shortly before the Portuguese revolution. In an effort to unite the warring factions Manuel Pinto da Costa was elected president of the new party, which the following year was recognised by the OAU (Hodges and Newitt 1988: 93).

The connection with CONCP, of which it was a founder member, not only helped MLSTP gain recognition internationally but gave it vital diplomatic backing in its dealings with the Portuguese. It had other important implications as well. It meant that after independence, in common with MPLA, FRELIMO and PAIGC, the party would adopt the prevailing authoritarian Marxism and would seek to create a one-party state along marxist-leninist lines.

Decolonization

The general outline of the decolonization process following the April 1974 Revolution has been well established. Initially Spínola and his prime minister, Palma Carlos, tried to promote the idea of a political solution for the colonies that would stop short of full independence, would be phased over a number of years and would be secured through referenda. This stance was undermined in Lisbon and in the colonies by the radicals in the MFA, and it was particularly the army's unwillingness to hold the line in Africa and undertake any further military action that made Spínola's position untenable. By July Vasco Gonçalves had become prime minister, the colonies' right to independence had been recognised and negotiations had begun with FRELIMO and PAIGC, the two movements that were most obviously in a position to take power.

Divisions among the Portuguese politicians in Lisbon, which were building towards the crisis that saw Spínola toppled from power in September, the lack of any blueprint for decolonization and the unwillingness of the military to provide the Portuguese authorities with a bargaining position, encouraged FRELIMO and PAIGC to hold out for a total capitulation to their demands for unconditional independence. By 7 September the Portuguese had signed agreements for the transfer of power in Guinea and Mozambique – a transfer without elections and almost without conditions. Nothing was done to try to persuade Portuguese administrators, professionals or skilled workers to remain and they responded by leaving en masse. Nor was anything done to secure the position of those Africans who had supported or fought for the Portuguese. In Guinea independence was followed by widespread executions; in Mozambique by the flight of former soldiers and *assimilados* many of whom were soon to take up arms and form the core of the MNR (later RENAMO).

At the beginning of September 1974 the future of Cape Verde and São Tomé was still undecided. In the case of Cape Verde, although the PAIGC had a high profile and had already taken power in Guinea, there appeared to be some support for the idea that the islands should follow the route mapped out for Madeira and the Azores, which were to become autonomous provinces of Portugal. The future of São Tomé and Príncipe looked equally uncertain. At first it was considered unlikely that São Tomé and Príncipe would be decolonized as there were doubts about the viability of such a small community becoming an independent state and about the strength of the nationalist movement there. Various 'moderate' political parties were formed in the islands after April 1974 giving some credibility to Spínola's idea of creating a Portuguese Federation.

Prior to April 1974 the MLSTP had not been able to organise in the islands and even after April its leaders decided to remain abroad, but a radical movement allied to it, called the Associação Cívica Pró-MLSTP, was founded in São Tomé by radical students of an extreme left wing persuasion who returned to the islands and directed their agitation at *roça* workers, the lower ranks of the civil service and the local military. The Associação Cívica was able to instigate strikes and demonstrations, and to create an air of crisis sufficient to convince the Portuguese of the expediency of a quick settlement Hodges and Newitt 1988: 94). However, what ultimately decided the course of events in São Tomé and Príncipe was not so much developments in the islands as the shift to the left in the political situation in Lisbon and the stance taken by the rest of the world.

After the resignation of Spínola on 28 September 1974, the radicals in the MFA held a precarious ascendancy in Lisbon. Many of them shared the political perspective of the CONCP parties and they were anxious to get rid of all the African problems that remained which might serve to complicate the political situation in Portugal. They were, therefore, looking for the quickest and easiest way to complete the decolonization process.

At the same time the international community, headed by the UN, was encouraging Portugal not to delay the decolonising process. In the early 1970s the anti-colonial movement was still strong. No legitimate alternatives to complete independence were admitted and the tensions of the Cold War allowed radical leaders in the colonies to play off East against West in their search for international support. Neither the Eastern Bloc countries nor the West saw any advantage in recommending solutions that fell short of complete independence for former colonies.

Of course, alternative models for relations between small far flung communities and their former European colonial masters did exist. Denmark kept Greenland and the Faroes under a Danish sovereignty that covered security and international relations but allowed extensive internal autonomy; Britain and the Netherlands had a somewhat similar relationship with their small remaining island colonies; while the French had pursued a policy of total integration for their Caribbean possessions and for Réunion. Even Portugal itself provided alternative models as Madeira and the Azores did not move along the path of independence and remained part of Portugal but with the status of a Região Autonóma that allowed them considerable local freedom of action.

These models, which were not unrelated to Spínola's ideas about the future of a Portuguese community, would scarcely have been considered for the three mainland colonies but had considerable relevance for the Cape Verde Islands and São Tomé and Príncipe that in many respects shared a similar historical experience with Madeira and the Azores. However, the fact that the Salazar regime had claimed that it had implemented full integration of the colonies with Portugal and that it was against this supposed integration that the nationalist movements had campaigned for so long, meant that the status of an autonomous region held few attractions for those who remembered the devastating famines in Cape Verde or the Batepá massacres in São Tomé. Moreover there had been an understanding among the CONCP parties that they would support each other in claiming full independence and would show solidarity in not making any compromises with Portugal. If full and unconditional independence had been granted to Mozambique and Guinea, nothing less than full and unconditional independence could be entertained for Angola and the islands.

There was, therefore, a brief coming together of minds in the autumn of 1974 – the Portuguese leadership, the UN, the two sides in the Cold War, and the CONCP parties all pressed for independence and the transfer of power to a single party without any referendum – the quickest and easiest solution on offer, even if not necessarily the one with the best long term economic prospects.

Although Mário Soares had spoken informally with Trovoada, the first official negotiations between the MLSTP and the Portuguese government were held in Libreville between 28 September and 3 October. The Portuguese side accepted officially that MLSTP, which was strongly backed by the CONCP and incidentally by Gabon as well, was the only group with whom it could negotiate and abandoned all idea of a referendum before independence. The final negotiations took place in Algiers between 23 and 26 November with Jorge Campinos leading for Portugal and Miguel Trovoada for the MLSTP. The settlement reached was similar to that agreed for Mozambique. There was to be a six-month provisional government under a Portuguese High Commissioner but with a government of five ministers, four of whom would be drawn from MLSTP. However, unlike the situation in Mozambique and Guiné, it was agreed that elections for a constituent assembly would be held shortly before the final transfer of authority – the only condition that the Portuguese felt able to impose and one which the MLSTP tried hard to resist (MacQueen 1997: 115-8; Hodges and Newitt 1988: 94-5).

In Mozambique a good rapport had been established between the Portuguese high commissioner and the Frelimo authorities in the nine months leading to independence, but in São Tome the transitional period, which officially began on 21 December, was very disturbed. Tensions occurred because the Portuguese retained control of the armed forces and this gave the High Commissioner considerable authority, which seemed to run counter to the agreement to grant independence. Moreover the memories of Batepá and the ingrained hostility between the *forro* families and the Portuguese administration poisoned the atmosphere. However, the root of the conflict was a continuing struggle within the MLSTP leadership for control of the movement. Two radical ministers who had been among the founders of the Associação Cívica, tried to keep the revolutionary momentum of the previous year going by encouraging strikes and demonstrations, and by picking quarrels with the High Commissioner over the future of the islands' armed forces, while the other two MLSTP ministers remained loyal to Pinto da Costa and sought to achieve a smooth transition. At one point the High Commissioner threatened an immediate Portuguese withdrawal if the disturbances continued. In the end Pinto da Costa was persuaded to come to the island and in conjunction with the High Commissioner had the two offending ministers arrested and exiled. Independence day was brought forward to prevent the tense situation deteriorating further.

The action taken by the High Commissioner and Pinto da Costa undoubtedly restored calm to São Tomé but constituted in effect a firm Portuguese backing to Pinto da Costa's position as head of a one-party state. When elections for the constituent assembly were held, all the seats were won by the MLSTP, which was already the *de facto* government and was the only organization to put forward candidates.

In one respect the situation in São Tomé and Príncipe did resemble that in Mozambique – the exodus of the white settlers. The decolonization agreements had not offered any security to the Portuguese settlers or property owners, and plantation managers, administrators, skilled workers and professional people all started to leave. By independence most of the *roças* and other businesses in the islands had been effectively abandoned.

The establishment of the one party state

The first twenty-five years of São Tomé's independence were to expose the shortcomings of the decolonization process. The islands did not descend into violence, civil war and chaos, as did Guinea, Angola and Mozambique, on the other hand they became steadily poorer and more indebted until by the end of the century their inhabitants were among the poorest in the world. To a large extent developments during these 25 years were determined by the choices made at the time of the decolonization and by the nature of the process itself.

As explained above, the international circumstances of the time coupled with the political climate in Lisbon led to the self-appointed elite of the MLSTP being installed as the rulers of the islands. This elite had been fostered by the parties that formed CONCP and from the start Manuel Pinto da Costa depended heavily on support from this grouping, distancing himself from Gabon, which had befriended the movement since the early 1960s. At independence, São Tomé faced severe budgetary problems, an economy that had been plunged into chaos by the departure of the Portuguese and a shortage of professional expertise in almost every department of government. The president was aware that there were powerful neighbours who might try to influence its affairs, as well as rival factions among the *forro* families who resented his hijacking of the new state. Faced with these dangers Pinto da Costa had little choice but to seek a patron, a powerful ally on whom he could rely. Unlike Cape Verde, which sought a close relationship with the former colonial power, Pinto da Costa looked to the MPLA regime in Angola to provide this patronage.

The influence of the MPLA on São Tomé and Príncipe was to be of profound importance. Under its influence the islands adopted a marxist-style one party constitution in which power lay with the Political Bureau of the MLSTP. The party chose all candidates for election to the popular assembly and underpinned its position with special powers to legislate directly and to control the police and the tribunals (Hodges and Newitt 1988: 100). Like MPLA and FRELIMO, MLSTP declared itself a 'vanguard party' at its Congress in 1978 (FRELIMO had done this in 1977) and set up youth and women's organizations in direct imitation of its CONCP allies. However, Pinto da Costa received from MPLA more than just a model form of government. MPLA provided long term economic aid principally in the form of cheap oil so that at one time São Tomé was receiving oil at $4 a barrel when the world price was $18-20, and never paid even this amount, and, after 1978, a garrison of Angolan troops was stationed in the islands (Seibert 1999: 113). In return for this, MPLA, which was still not secure in its control of Angola, received unequivocal support from São Tomé in international affairs.

It can also be argued that it was MPLA influence that led Pinto da Costa to rely on Cuban advisers and to adopt an array of policies designed to establish a socialist style, centrally controlled economy. Soon after independence the president began the nationalization of the *roças* and established state run shops, *lojas do povo*. Later two state controlled companies were set up to handle imports and exports and internal distribution and sales. Banking and financial services were also nationalised. Pinto da Costa had been trained as an economist in East Germany and it is probable that he was ideologically disposed to adopt an East German style command economy. On the other hand it has been argued, as it has for Mozambique, that in the short term no alternative course of action was possible since the white settlers had all fled and the *roças* and other businesses had been abandoned. The decolonization process had not provided for the immediate needs of the new state and had made no provision for maintaining the economic infrastructure. According to this argument, the adoption of a centralised economy was not so much a matter of political choice as one of necessity.

In fact the close group around Pinto da Costa were not united in following the road to a command economy. It was strongly opposed by Carlos Graça who resigned from the government and went into exile as early as 1976, and by the Prime Minister, Miguel Trovoada, who favoured a more liberal, western oriented economy. Trovoada was accused of plotting a coup and was arrested and detained in 1979, finally going into exile in 1981 (Seibert 1999: 123-6). The following year, Leonel d'Alva, who had been prime minister of the interim government, and a number of other prominent political figures left the party and went into exile also objecting to the political and economic stance of the government.

By taking the line of least resistance during the independence negotiations the Portuguese had promoted the establishment of an authoritarian one-party state and had made no attempt to build political pluralism into the independence agreement. Differences of opinion had to be resolved within this structure and if this was not possible the only alternative was repression or exile. The MFA in Portugal had overthrown fascism and restored to the Portuguese the essential political and personal freedoms but it had not done the same for Africa and independence from

Portugal left the São Tomeans still subject to an authoritarian government and a secret police. Madeira and the Azores, on the other hand, by opting for Regional Autonomy, enjoyed the political benefits and personal freedoms brought by the fall of the fascist government in Lisbon.

By 1982 Pinto da Costa had lost all three of his principal allies of the early days and was becoming dangerously isolated. Just as the impossibility of organising political opposition to Salazar within the islands gave birth to the MLSTP as a party of exiles, so the impossibility of opposing Pinto da Costa spawned an exile opposition in Gabon. In 1981 Carlos Graça set up the FRNSTP in Libreville (Seibert 1999, 129-30).

The rule of Manuel Pinto da Costa, 1975-90

Manuel Pinto da Costa's gradual consolidation of his power within a marxist style one-party state, strongly backed by the Angolans, had three major consequences for São Tomé and Príncipe—it gave the islands fifteen years of internal stability, it entrenched a patrimonial style of politics and it led to years of economic stagnation and decline during which no effective measures were taken to reform the colonial inheritance or to encourage economic development.

For 15 years São Tomé and Príncipe were internally quiet and stable. There were no military coups, no seizure of power by mercenaries, no riots, no social breakdown. There was a 'mercenary scare' in 1978, the year when Bob Denard invaded the Comoros Islands and one pathetic attempt at a landing in 1988, which had been organised by exiles possibly with South African backing, failed ignominiously. São Tomé and Príncipe experienced neither the factional warfare of Guinea nor the regional and ethnic conflict of Angola nor the foreign-inspired banditry of Mozambique. In part this can be ascribed to the fact that Pinto da Costa was maintained in power by his MPLA backers and the Angolan garrison, but it should also be remembered that São Tomé and Príncipe was very different from most other African states. There were no strong ethnic divisions in the islands and the close-knit, interlinked *forro* families were unlikely to indulge in violence towards one another. The island minorities, the Angolares, the Cape Verdians and the other plantation workers, were isolated and in such small numbers that they would be unlikely to try any kind of bid for power. Moreover the lack of interest in the islands by the outside world was largely due to the fact that they had no wealth that any power covet, while their position threatened no sea routes and had no strategic importance. NATO apparently did not see the existence of a Russian-manned radar station, which Pinto da Costa allowed to be built at Monte Café, as any kind of threat. Moreover the islands were never attractive to exiles from other countries as they offered no opportunities for economic survival and their communications were so bad that any exiles would find themselves in effective isolation.

The stability of the islands therefore, although helped by the guarantees provided by Angola, had other causes and cannot be solely attributed to the Angolan connection (Seibert 1999).

The 15 years of Pinto da Costa's rule also saw the entrenchment of a patrimonial style of politics. The president used his position as head of the government and the party to create an elaborate power structure that sought to link a number of the major families and their dependants to his personal rule. The most important of these were his own family – his sister-in-law Alda do Espirito Santo, his brothers and his cousin Celestino Rocha da Costa all held important posts in the government, Celestino taking up the post of prime minister when Pinto da Costa relinquished it in 1988. Membership of the party was all-important for those wishing to receive patronage. It was not a mass party and its membership was estimated in 1978 to be 1,300 (Hodges and Newitt 1998: 101-11). The disappearance of the Portuguese had immediately created a large number of jobs in the government and the administration while the nationalization of the *roças*, the creation of state corporations and the government take-over of businesses provided a wide range of salaried posts in the gift of the MLSTP. Under Pinto da Costa's management the numbers employed in the civil service and the administration of economic institutions mushroomed, all of them paid directly out of state revenues. São Tomé, small as it was, became a typical example of the way in which successor regimes to the colonial governments created an elite who did not concern themselves with wealth creation but lived off the meagre assets of the state.

And there were other forms of patronage in the government's disposal. Missions abroad, for example, were eagerly sought after as it was only in Europe or the major African cities that consumer goods, health care, education and other aspects of the good life could be obtained. Rafael Branco, a minister and ambassador in the new state, commented on the way that anyone with any education was able to walk into a government job:

> ...the state has functioned as a form of 'primitive accumulation of capital', not only financial but also, and particularly the capital of contacts and knowledge generally situated abroad (Seibert 1999: 112).

And government service gave rise to opportunities for straightforward graft, corruption and embezzlement, which in an authoritarian one-party state went unchallenged and apparently unchecked.

In this way Pinto da Costa presided over a system of spoils politics in which the only means of advancement, and almost the only opportunity for employment, lay in supporting the president and the MLSTP.

Again it has been argued that this tradition of viewing politics as a means of gaining a share in the public wealth of the state had existed long before Pinto da Costa and independence. It resembled the way that the *forro* families had ruled the islands over two-and-one-half centuries between 1600 and 1850, and part of *forro* isolation from the rest of the world; resentment against the Portuguese had been due to the fact that the colonial regime had cut them off from the control of land and patronage. As Gerhard Seibert wrote of the establishment of the MLSTP in the offices of the town hall.

Historically the MLSTP's new accommodation symbolised the return of the *forro* elite to power. The same elite that had occupied offices in the town council contesting the power of the Catholic Church and the governor prior to the recolonization by the Portuguese, now returned to power on behalf of the ruling party (Seibert 1999: 109).

However, there can be little doubt that the establishment of a one party state in 1974, hardly needed from the point of view of nation building, and a command economy, where the opportunities for private business were so limited, made it necessary for the president continually to satisfy his main supporters with the distribution of state wealth as guarantees of their continued support.

The third characteristic of Pinto da Costa's rule was the failure to undertake any significant economic reform or to adopt any effective measure to halt economic decline. MLSTP had inherited what was in effect a monoculture. The islands produced only cocoa and imported virtually everything else – consumer goods, capital equipment, even food. Although the issue of the future management of the plantations had been raised during the discussions over decolonization, no firm agreements had been reached and São Tomé and Príncipe became independent without any long-term arrangements to sustain the colonial economy being made.

Before the country had become officially independent, the government had declared that it wished to diversify the economy and to increase food production through land reform, but virtually nothing was done to modernise the outdated Portuguese plantations (Eyzaguirre 1989: 671-8). When the Portuguese *roça* managers left, MLSTP had placed administrators in their place – usually people with no experience of cocoa production and with no incentive to make any improvements. The old wasteful methods of production continued with little or no investment in new plant or improved cultivation.

Regarding the estates, there was no book-keeping, their assets were not known, the bureaucracy did not function, the wages were in arrears for months, the soil was not fertilized, there was no shade management nor any phytosanitary control. Cocoa seedling nurseries had been abandoned... The cocoa rotted in the storehouses... because there were no sacks for transport (Mantero, cf. Seibert 1999: 139).

By 1984 the income from the *rocas* did not even cover their wages bill (Hodges and Newitt 1988: 135). Moreover no land reform was undertaken. The *roça* administrations still controlled large amounts of underused or wholly unused land, while the plantation workers continued to live in the poorest circumstances in the old servical barracks. In fact the government not only failed to distribute unused land but also actively discouraged the cultivation of small allotments (*lavras*) by the estate workers (Seibert 1999: 137). The reason for the lack of government action is not far to seek. The supporters of MLSTP had no reason to seek the emancipation or social advancement of the fifth of the population who were estate workers. Emancipated and educated workers might become politically active or compete with the *forros* for state resources. Moreover ownership of smallholdings was a *forro* privilege, a matter of status, not to be extended to immigrant workers. Although equality of all citizens had been a founding principle of the regime, it is significant that separate party structures were created for the populations on the plantations and for the traditional areas of *forro* settlement (Seibert 1999: 111).

Instead of encouraging peasant agriculture, the government committed itself to a policy of price subsidies for essential foods, fuel and consumer items most of which were imported – a subsidy paid by the state which did little to encourage productivity of the population.

Once again, it can be argued that Pinto da Costa had little choice. Although the world price for cocoa remained exceptionally high until 1980, it then underwent a collapse so that export earnings from the islands' tiny crop fell alarmingly and the *roças* moved further and further into debt, borrowing from the state bank in order to cover even their routine expenditure. Exports of cocoa, which had been 5,200 tonnes in 1975, had fallen to 3,400 tonnes by 1983, while income from exports, which had reached $24m in 1979, had fallen to $5.9m in 1981 (Hodges and Newitt 1988: 134). In these circumstances there were no funds available for investment or for social improvement on the *roças*.

The only effective response by the government to the widening trade and payments gap was to cut imports, which not only struck at the health and standard of living of the population but also deprived the economy of needed capital equipment and spare parts. Indeed there were fewer and fewer funds available to import anything, even to run the basic services of the government. Soon medicines were in short supply in the central hospital, malaria began to spread, there was no newsprint to publish newspapers and the shops were all empty.

In order to maintain the day-to-day running of the government and the supply of goods to support his patronage system Pinto da Costa resorted to borrowing. Individuals were allowed to 'borrow' from the state enterprises, industries and the *roças* borrowed from the state bank, while the treasury negotiated loans abroad. Indebtedness grew along with inflation while the official currency, the *dobra*, became hopelessly overvalued. In these circumstances, maintaining some sort of production on the *roças* was the only economic activity open to the islands and the reluctance of the government to interfere with this was understandable.

Of course, São Tomé and Príncipe was the victim of falling prices that were ruining the development plans and increasing the indebtedness of every country in Africa. However, unlike many other countries, the opportunities to diversify the economy seemed minimal and the chosen path of a Marxist one-party state actively discouraged overseas investors without providing a significant alternative flow of funds (although cheap Angolan oil remained hugely important). Once again the circumstances of decolonization – the flight of the Portuguese, the seizure of the *roças*, the lack of any long term economic settlement, the institution of a one-party state, the orientation towards and dependence on Angola – had trapped São Tomé and Príncipe in a pattern of political and economic development from which there was no easy way out. Under the Portuguese the greatest faults of the colonial regime had been the lack of freedom to criticise and inform; no free flow of information; isolation from the rest of the world; a lack of education and training for the local population; a discouragement of entrepreneurial talent; a relatively closed society with little social movement. Decolonization remedied none of these things. The swift and uncomplicated transfer of power in 1974-75, for which the UN and the CONCP parties pressed, for which the Lisbon government was prepared to settle and which the MLSTP grabbed with both hands, meant that one closed authoritarian regime was replaced by another. Ironically, by 1979 the MLSTP government was even being accused, like its Portuguese predecessor, of plotting to force the *forros* to undertake contract labour on the *roças*!

In 1984, faced with an inability to continue to finance his government and unable to pay for imports, Pinto da Costa began to change his hard-line approach to a state run economy. Liberalization began in the retail and trading sector of the economy and in the employment of private sector managers for the *roças*. In 1986 he approached the World Bank and Western European bilateral donors. The following year FRELIMO in Mozambique would take exactly the same course.

The result was a structural adjustment package to which the government had to agree in order to secure IMF funding and World Bank loans. The package was the same in its general outlines to that offered to other African countries – the removal of price subsidies, the reduction in the size of the civil service, devaluation (to boost exports and cut imports), the liberalization of commerce, privatization of state controlled business, including the *roças*, and land reform. The president also came under pressure to liberalise the constitution and to allow multi-party elections. These elections were eventually held in January 1991 and led to the MLSTP losing to a coalition headed by Miguel Trovoada who replaced Pinto da Costa as president.

Choices facing small island states[4]

São Tomé and Príncipe is the smallest independent state in Africa in terms geographical area and the second smallest in population – the Seychelles having a slightly smaller total number of people. Small states in general experience problems specific to their smallness – the size of their markets and limited opportunities for capital accumulation, security risks from powerful neighbours, the difficulty in sustaining the range of modern technical services from higher education to modern medicine. However, these problems become accentuated when one is dealing with small islands. Archipelagos often have highly dispersed populations, extremely expensive communications systems, and shortages of land and extreme environmental pressures, to add to the other problems of smallness.

Nevertheless small island states can find a successful formula for improving their living standards and modernising their societies within the confines of their limited geographical area and their relative isolation. Successful experiments have been conducted by Seychelles and Maldives to develop sustainable tourism; Mauritius has diversified its economy to tourism and industry as well as traditional plantation agriculture. Some island states have developed off shore banking and duty free ports, or have provided communication services, while a mixture of peasant agriculture and emigrant remittances have sustained others.

However, there are island states which have not been so fortunate – the Comoros Islands, for example, larger in land area and five times as populous as São Tomé, have not discovered the formula for success.

Although the circumstances of each island state are different, a great deal can be seen to depend on crucial choices that the governments make in terms of the path of development that they wish to follow. However, all these choices involve a well thought out strategy for developing links with regional neighbours and with richer economies. The choices made by São Tomé – to break with its colonial past and to seek development with the support of Angola, and to a lesser extent Cuba – rapidly collapsed when the world cocoa price fell after 1980. Since then São Tomé has failed to find a strategy to match that of more successful island microstates. Tourism has never been developed. Peasant agriculture has languished. No niche industrial development has taken place. Outside investment has been discouraged. Communications are poor and the islands have remained exceptionally isolated. Emigration by the poorer classes has never been a tradition, as it was in Madeira, the Azores and Cape Verde Islands, and the only emigrants of significance are the educated who leave the islands to attend universities overseas and frequently never return. Moreover São Tomé, although largely a peaceful and non-violent society, has acquired an unenviable reputation for being, in its own small way, among the most corrupt of African regimes.

In 1974 it chose the route of independence and in evaluating this choicea comparison can be made with the position in the world and the standard of living of the other Portuguese Atlantic islands – with Cape Verde which opted for independence but pursued successful development strategies, and with Azores and Madeira which opted for the status of Regional Autonomy instead of trying to sustain the near impossible burden of operating as an independent state and have benefited from the political freedoms and the massive investment that has come from Portugal's membership of the European Union.

Notes:

* Charles Boxer Professor, Department of Portuguese and Brazilian Studies, King's College, London.

[1] The classic account of São Tomé's geography and of the *roça* system is Tenreiro, F. (1961), *A Ilha de São Tomé*, Lisbon: Memórias de Junta de Investigações do Ultramar, No. 24.

[2] For the history of São Tomé see Garfield, R. (1992), *A history of São Tomé Island, 1470-1655: the key to Guinea*, San Francisco CA: Mellen Research University Press.

[3] An English version of the paper was published in the *International Journal of African Historical Studies*.

[4] See the Introduction to Newitt and Hintjens (1992).

4: Macau, Timor and Portuguese India in the context of Portugal's recent decolonization

Arnaldo M. A. Gonçalves[*]

The erroneous idea, cemented throughout the 40 year life of an authoritarian corporatist dictatorship, was of an Atlantic Portugal, with a universal overseas vocation; invested with a divine mission to spread Christian values and civilization; charged with a grandeur that was beyond its means and capabilities that nonetheless constituted the archetypical reference that had very little real reflection within the real nation.

25 April ended this manifestly unrealistic myth that had led to the African military adventures, the country's international isolation, and the series of military defeats, deaths and the human suffering that sacrificed an entire generation to a vain glory and left many wounded and exposed to the regime's propaganda, its mystifications and with its commiserations.

As Eduardo Lourenço noted majestically in *O labirinto da saudade*, it was necessary to introduce a profound trauma in the Portuguese collective consciousness before it was possible to re-evaluate the image that the Portuguese had of themselves and their place in the world. This re-evaluation did not happen, and the old empire fell into ruin, piece by piece, without leading to the perception that the Portuguese had 'lost' a part of themselves and without asking where it was going: what is Portugal's destiny?

The process of decolonization had unexpectedly begun in a way that was different from other similar processes, with great solemnity, as if the Portuguese own perception regarding their destiny would force them to 'come to terms with history' and return to the people with whom they shared their 'mirage' of multiculturalism and trans-nationalism: which were the slogans of their collective situation.

Save for the years that followed the decolonization of 1975 – years during which the return of the white colonists created social, community and professional tensions, as well as the confrontation of mentalities – it is possible to claim that the tearing down of the colonial political apparatus and the relatively peaceful military uprising, was simple, with no major resistance, without acrimony, and without any drama. Almost, according to Lourenço, an apotheosis. While others looked for neo-colonial means through which they could perpetuate Portugal's economic, technological and linguistic dominion over the people who had escaped from its colonialism, Portugal saw the writing on the wall and left, leaving the African movements free to call on the international community to recognise their political legitimacy to govern their respective countries.[1]

It is now possible to recognise that this process of liberation from the colonial shackles was only possible because during the opening of the political system to democracy, the exercise of pluralist liberty and increased civic participation, the leaders of the Armed Forces' Movement (MFA) were incapable of developing a vision for the colonial question. Even to the extent that the 'colonial question' was a point of friction within the politico-ideological leadership that organized and then led the *coup d'état*. The significant differences of opinion that existed between General Spínola and the leadership of the movement were expressed in the Captains' Movement's declaration that were later articulated in Law 7/74 of 26 July, which set out the necessary conditions for the transfer of sovereignty to the colonies (Mattoso 1998: 53-101; Ferreira 1986: 29).[2] It was these differences that, as a result of largely inorganic public pressure, led the leaders to pursue a popular revolution that would result in democracy and reject the neo-colonial ideals that were explicit in Spínola's book, *Portugal and the future*; ideals that did not appear to have any organized support in Portuguese society, let alone amongst the political forces that had emerged from the revolution and formed the constitutional arch.[3]

One important factor in these circumstances was the international pressure that was exerted from the earliest days of the revolution for the immediate opening of negotiations with the liberation movements and the early granting of independence.[4] This pressure substantially reduced the margins for manoeuvre available to those responsible for determining Portugal's foreign policy.[5]

It is relatively simple to conclude that no left-wing political line was being followed by the provisional governments appointed in the wake of the coup; while the MFA's shift to the left was, in the context of the options available to it, the only realistic alternative to a colonial situation that was political and militarily unsustainable in terms of both domestic and foreign policy.

The process of 'decolonization' of those territories that were integrated into Portugal's eastern empire (Portuguese India, Macao and Timor) was, for temporal, geopolitical and international reasons, manifestly peculiar to this logic of pre-eminence and urgency. Remote parts of an empire that began to collapse, first with the loss of Brazil, but which stubbornly continued to exist in Africa, these colonies were of very little significance in terms of Portugal's international obligations and privileges. Only inertia, in some cases, and the obstinacy of the dictator in others can explain their contradictory, and in the end happy unravelling.

International factors

When one analyses the decolonization process of Portugal's oriental colonies in comparison to that of Portuguese Africa, we can note a preponderance of exogenous factors exerting their influence on Portugal's foreign policy.

Exposed to the logic of decolonization that was the result of the agreement made between the four allied nations at Yalta, and which was made all the more urgent during the Cold War before finding its most explicit statement in UN General Assembly resolution 1314, Portugal's Asian colonial possessions were subjected to significant geo-strategic pressures. Goa, Damão and Diu (as well as Timor) were small territories, too remote from the imperial centre to be major influential factors in the determination of Portuguese foreign policy. Being small, they were of little concern in the balance of power between the two superpower blocs, yet they served as objects of some dispute between them as they each attempted to include them in their respective areas of influence. Goa and its possessions, being situated on the Indian subcontinent, were claimed by the Indian government that had only a few years earlier secured its independence from the United Kingdom to become the largest democracy in the whole of Asia.

Timor was both a diminutive part of the empire and its most remote outpost. Grafted onto the Muslim Indonesian archipelago, it was largely ignored by Salazar. Macao was a trading post and port of call on China's eastern seaboard. Its main use was as a centre for commerce and for Catholic missions – a *de facto* possession of Portugal that in time would be settled by both countries. While UN Resolution 1314 recognized both Portuguese India and Timor as Portuguese 'Dependent Territories', China refused to allow this status to be extended to Macao (Gonçalves 1993).

In the global decolonization process, Goa, Macao and Timor were largely of secondary importance, as they did not conform to the same logic that led the African colonies to gain their independence. None of the eastern territories were at war; there were no local liberation movements opposed to Portuguese rule; the military forces maintained in the territories were small, leaving them vulnerable to attack. They were not appetising morsels for the competing superpowers; they did not have reserves of important mineral resources; and they were of no strategic importance in terms of competing areas of influence.

Why then did the dictator resist placing them on the table for international agreement in such a way as would maintain the African 'jewels in the crown' intact?

To understand this, one must first understand Salazar's dogmatic personality and the nature of his authoritarian regime (Fernandes 2002). In order for his vision to prevail – that is, his inflexible ideas regarding the conception and prosecution of his political management – his regime fell back on the rhetoric of tradition, institutionalized rules, and long established practices, all of which were employed to prevent change and to vilify innovation. As Moisés Fernandes noted, 'this variable was, particularly, intensified by the nature of the Portuguese regime' now that one of the fundamental characteristics of Salazar's political system was the 'progressive concentration of practically limitless power'. When an initiative to open diplomatic relations was put forward by Franco Nogueira with Salazar's reluctant agreement, pressure from the regime's hardliners forced him to withdraw his support, stating that he 'was far too old to change'. With the fall of this initiative, the whole house of cards that was the Portuguese empire also collapsed.

Goa: from defeat and Salazar's stubbornness to recognition of a consummated fact

Goa had been the capital of Portugal's oriental empire. It was conquered by Afonso de Albuquerque in February 1510, and was to become an important centre for the diffusion of Christianity. It was also an significant entry point into the Indian subcontinent and a crossing point for the commercial shipping routes between the Indian Ocean and the South China Sea. The 'Portuguese State of India' was a collection of native communities governed by tribal chiefs with the consent of a colonial administration that was disposed to allow a great deal of religious and ethnic freedom, and which tolerated the continuation of local customs.[6] The colonial authorities made every effort not to interfere in community life, and it was not until the creation of the Goa Congress Committee in 1930 – a copy of the Indian National Congress – that there was any real opposition to the established colonial order.

The process that led to the independence of British India in August 1947 led to Portugal's colonial possessions on the subcontinent becoming involved in the protest movement that then swept India. Nehru, the Indian socialist leader, organized a rally in Margão in 1945 at which he demanded freedom of expression and of association for all Indians, claiming that Goa was a part of 'Mother India'. Salazar responded that 'if geographically Goa is Indian, then socially, religiously and culturally it is European. If there are westernized Indo-Portuguese and Indians, politically all are Portuguese citizens' (Coissoró 1979: 137-55).[7] From 1947 to 1953 the Indian government made several unsuccessful attempts to bring Portugal to the negotiating table. After the fall of Dadrá and Nagar Haveli to the Indian Union in July 1954, Indian military forces invaded the Portuguese territories of Goa, Damão and Diu in December 1961. Salazar refused to accept the loss of Goa and desperately sought to obtain a United Nations Security Council resolution condemning the invasion (Fernandes 2002: 562).[8] The United States, France, Turkey and the United Kingdom proposed the resolution, but its final approval was blocked by the Soviet Union's veto. In the meantime, the Indian parliament approved an amendment to the Indian constitution that enabled the incorporation of the former Portuguese territories as new member states of the Indian Union. For three months the Portuguese troops that had been taken prisoner during the invasion remained in Indian captivity. It was only in May 1962 – seven months after the invasion – that they were allowed to return to Portugal where the Governor of Goa, Vassalo e Silva, and several other colonial officials were accused of high treason and summarily dismissed for the defeat and surrender of the territories.

There were no diplomatic relations between Portugal and India when the new democratic Portuguese government received the dossier on Goa; however, relations between the two states were very quickly re-established in the wake of the 1974 coup. In September 1974, General Costa Gomes nominated a commission to review the cases of the officers that had been expelled in 1962, and to ensure their reintegration, with honour, into the Portuguese armed forces. Also in September, the Portuguese and Indian foreign ministers published a joint declaration at the 29th session of the United Nations, expressing their mutual desire to establish diplomatic and consular relations, and to cooperate in the preservation of Goa's historic and religious Indo-Portuguese relics. The constitutional law 9/74, dated 15 October, authorized the establishment of a permanent agreement between both parties. In December 1974, Mário Soares used his visit to New Delhi to sign a diplomatic agreement that recognized India's sovereignty over the former Portuguese territories.

Macao: a policy of realism

The Portuguese settlement of Macao probably dates back to 1557. Macao was the first European settlement in China, and was an important port of call for ships on the Lisbon to Nagasaki trade route.

For a long time, the legal status of this territory remained undetermined. Gonçalves Pereira states that it was a happy coincidence of circumstances that enabled Portugal to develop its policy of effective and continuous occupation of the territory – with the consent of the Chinese authorities – entrusting it not only to practise commerce that was adapted to local conditions, but also to construct a unique form of political organization in the Macao Senate (Kramer 1995). Other authors have noted the absence of modern documents on the exact terms of the settlement, with the result that the occupation of Macao was simply a *de facto* situation legitimized by the payment, dating from 1573, of a ground rent to the Chinese emperor, and the simultaneous construction by the Chinese authorities of the first territorial frontier, the *Portas do Cerco*, and the stationing of Chinese troops on the other side of this border in order to control the movement of people and goods. The ground rent was paid regularly until the middle of the nineteenth century, justifying its description as being of mixed jurisdiction (Edmonds 1993; MacQueen 1985: 167-9; Rayner 1987: 199-206; Keaton 1969).

Portugal's presence in Macao did not lead to the territory being considered a true colony, since it had not been taken by force from another sovereign power. Rather, its occupation was legitimized through the tacit consent of the imperial Chinese authorities in Canton with 'an understanding of the special nature and the limitations to the powers that may be used by the Portuguese in its establishment' (Saldanha 1996). The city had always admitted to a double responsibility, a compromise by both the authorities in Lisbon and the Chinese Government. The establishment of a Chinese Customs house in Macao in 1688, through which the Chinese authorities exercised their fiscal jurisdiction, and the foundation in 1736 of a local mandarinate with powers to prosecute criminals and impose penalties, clearly emphasise this mixed jurisdiction. It was only following the surrender of Hong Kong to the United Kingdom following China's defeat in the Opium Wars that, in December 1887, the Treaty of Friendship and Commerce was signed (ratified in April 1888) through which China recognized the occupation of Macao by Portugal, and its government of this territory in perpetuity, and also acknowledged that the territories under *de facto* occupation by Portugal would remain under Portuguese jurisdiction, while Portugal agreed that it would never alienate the territory without China's prior agreement. The 1933 Colonial Act integrated Macao into the Portuguese colonial empire, while the 1951 constitutional revision described it as an 'overseas province'.

The territory's Portuguese status was never threatened during the New State (Fernandes 2002). Following the establishment of the People's Republic, all activities by the nationalist Kuomintang were prohibited, while Communist activities were tolerated – albeit under the ever-watchful eyes of Portugal's overseas authorities. Salazar knew that China would seize Macao should the territory be allowed to be used as a base for anti-Chinese activities, or if Portugal should attempt to use military force to incorporate the territory into its empire. With great ill humour, Portugal administered the territory through governors appointed by Lisbon whose decisions were subject to the consensus of the Macaense (Sino-Portuguese) population, or through the intermediation of the powerful Macao Commercial Association (Associação Comercial de Macau) – the unofficial representatives of the Beijing Government in Macao.

The consensus between the two sovereign powers was reinforced with the 1974 coup. In September 1974, three delegates from the National Salvation Committee (the provisional authority after the 25 April *coup d'état*) were sent to Macao to assure China's semi-official representative, Ho Yin, that relations between Portugal and China had not changed and Portugal would not seek to seize the territory. Almeida Santos, then Minister for Inter-territorial Coordination, states that Macao was a 'special case', and that the policy of decolonization was determined by the need to resolve problems and relieve tensions and could not be applied to territories 'where understanding prevails'.[10] The Constitutional Law 7/74, of 27 July 1974, vested the President of the Republic with the necessary powers to conclude agreements relating to the exercise of the right of self-determination of Portugal's territories, after consultation with the institutional authorities.

On 6 January 1975, the Portuguese government issued a diplomatic note recognising Taiwan as an integral part of China, and the government of the People's Republic of China as the 'sole representative of the Chinese people'. Decree Law 1/76, of 17 September 1976, granted Macao an even more special status that approved its 'Organic Statute', while article 306 of the Portuguese constitution defined Macao as 'territory under Portuguese administration'.

Between 1976 and 1979 a series of informal negotiations were held between Portugal and China with the aim of establishing diplomatic relations between the two countries. The final communiqué made no mention of Macao, although a secret appendix probably established an obligation on the part of the Portuguese authorities to negotiate the return of Macao to China, to respect Chinese nationals and prohibiting acts hostile to the People's Republic (Martins 191: 433-57; Fernandes 2000: 363-4).

On 13 April 1987 Portugal and China reached an understanding whereby Macao would be restored to Chinese sovereignty in 1999. The Joint Declaration of the Governments of the Portuguese Republic and the People's Republic of China established their obligations during the transitional period, outlined the terms by which the future Basic Law (the mini-Constitution) of the Special Administrative Region of Macao would be applied, and guaranteed the continuation of capitalism, the rule of law and original social practices in Macao for a period of 50 years.

On 20 December 1999 Macao became one of China's Special Administrative Regions in accordance with the Joint Luso-Chinese Declaration of 1987 and by means of article 2 of the Region's Basic Law (Gonçalves 1996; Magalhães 1998).[11] With the formal transfer of power from Portugal to the People's Republic, Edmund Ho, the former vice-president of Macao's Legislative Assembly, became the first Chief Executive of the Special Region, answerable directly to the Chinese central government.

The logic of realism had prevailed.

East Timor: from revolutionary agitation to Indonesian occupation. The legitimization of the self-determination process by UN

Timor is an island situated to the east of Lesser Sunda Island between the Timor and Savu Seas. The Portuguese established a trading post on Timor in 1590, while the Dutch took control of the western part of the island that was occupied by the British in 1812 for two years. Two treaties, signed in 1860 and 1914, authorized the island's partition between the two occupying European powers and established their common border. Dili, on the northeast coast, became the capital and principal port of Portuguese East Timor, which was extended to include the islands of Ataúro and Jaco.

East Timor was a colony for much of its history, and remained economically backwards. The main occupation was subsistence agriculture based on coffee plantations and other exotic primary products. From the political and administrative points of view the Portuguese colonial administration existed only formally, and not through an efficient British style colonial apparatus. It simply adjusted itself to suit the local structures of tributary power and the feudal relations of a traditional society (Gunn 1999).

During the New State, the absence of freedom of expression and of association that was typical of the regime were extended to East Timor; consequently, during the 1960s a new educated elite – made up mainly of students who had attended universities in Portugal – emerged and developed a new national consciousness of a Timorese identity, and used the local Catholic press to appeal for more cultural and social openness in Timorese society.

Following the 1974 Revolution, General Lemos Pires was appointed Governor of the territory. He arrived in Dili in November 1974 without any clear mandate from the political authorities in Lisbon, or any idea of what the island's destiny was to be (Mattoso 1998: 35-101). As the MFA's representative in East Timor, the Governor's mission was to maintain order and discipline and to ensure the operational readiness of the Portuguese garrison until its surrender could be organized. However, this did not happen until March 1975 and, according to several sources, this delay, and the circumstances that led the Portuguese troops to become embroiled in local party politics and factional struggles, resulted in the outbreak of violence between armed pro- and anti-independence forces. The Portuguese authorities rapidly lost control of the situation as an anarchic civil war broke out.

During the summer of 1975, East Timor was every bit as politically unstable as Portugal. In July, the Assembly of the Republic approved Law 7/75 which granted the people of East Timor the right of self-determination, and set the third Sunday of October 1976 as the date for the election of a Popular Timorese Assembly 'with the objective of defining, by majority in a direct and secret ballot, East Timor's political and administrative status'. During August there were a number of violent clashes between factions of the East Timor Revolutionary Front (FRETILIN) and the Timor Democratic Union (UDT). On 10 August, the UDT, with the aid of some troops from the Portuguese garrison, staged an attempted coup. Ten days later, militias loyal to FRETILIN occupied the Portuguese barracks and freed those Portuguese officials who had in the meantime been taken prisoner by the UDT. On 26 August, the Governor and his staff fled to Ataúro, letting power fall into the streets, while leaving FRETILIN in control.

In the aftermath of this development, Portugal's Foreign Minister met his Indonesian counterpart in Rome at the beginning of November to discuss the future of the territory. On 28 November, FRETILIN issued a unilateral declaration of independence and the establishment of a socialist state. The remaining East Timorese political forces, the UDT, APODETI, and two minor factions, the Klibur Oan Timor Aswain (KOTI) and the Labour Party, responded by issuing their own call for Timor to be integrated into Indonesia and appealed for the overthrow of the FRETILIN regime. Portugal rejected both declarations, but the flight of its Governor to Ataúro left it with no negotiating power. A few days later, the Indonesian president visited Washington where he met President Ford and his Secretary of State, Henry Kissinger. It was there that plans were made for Indonesia to resolve the East Timor question by force.

In June 1976 a contingent of Indonesia's armed forces invaded East Timor, transforming it into the country's 27th Province. Portugal immediately cut diplomatic relations with Indonesia and used diplomatic channels to condemn it and try to force its withdrawal from the eastern part of the island. According to Indonesian sources, during the six years that followed the invasion and occupation, around 300,000 people were killed and all rights of expression and association were brutally withdrawn. Indonesia's military occupied the territory and implemented martial law, pushing anti-Indonesian guerrilla forces into the mountains. The territory was subjected to a forced programme of 'Indonesianization'. After the initial waves of repression, and the news that the Australian Prime Minister had eschewed his country's support for an independent East Timor, the resistance forces in the mountains and in exile – which were concentrated around the two main political parties, FRETILIN and the UDP – organized themselves into the East Timor National Resistance Council (CNRT) under the leadership of Nicolau Lobato. Following Lobato's death in combat in 1981, Xanana Gusmão became the leader of the resistance movement (Carascalão 2002; Gusmão 1994; Horta 1994; Barata 1998).

During the intervening period, the United Nations' Security Council, under diplomatic pressure from Portugal, approved several resolutions recognising the right of the East Timorese to self-determination and condemning Indonesia's continued occupation; this international pressure, however, was half-hearted at best – if not actually hypocritical (Magalhães 1999: 117ff). It was only the events of 12 November 1991 that brought the plight of East Timor to international attention when a young Australian journalist brought images of 250 massacred youths in Dili's Santa Cruz cemetery to the world's television screens. One year later, Xanana Gusmão was captured by Indonesian forces and taken to Jakarta where he used his trial and the international media coverage it attracted to denounce the situation in East Timor. Xanana was sentenced to life imprisonment, although this sentence was later reduced to 20 years hard labour. In 1996, Bishop Jimenes Belo, and the political activist José Ramos Horta – who was responsible for the creation of East Timor opposition coalition – were both awarded the Nobel Peace Prize, adding a new visibility to the Timor issue. During 1998, and as a consequence of the Asian economic collapse, Suharto's Indonesian regime became the target of violent street protests in that nation's capital. The demonstrations very quickly assumed a political nature as the crowds demanded Suharto's resignation and the introduction of democracy.

Suharto was replaced by his Vice-President, B. J. Habibie, who introduced some political reforms, released some political prisoners, and gave signals that he was about to embark of a programme of domestic democratization that could lead the way to the concession of autonomous status to East Timor. These signs of opening did not satisfy the leaders of the resistance, however, and they continued their demand for independence. On 27 January 1999, Indonesia's Information Minister declared that his country was ready to leave East Timor and grant its people independence should they reject the Jakarta government's proposals for increased autonomy.

The Indonesian and Portuguese Foreign Ministers, Ali Alatas and Jaime Gama respectively, signed an agreement on 30 August 1999 that set out the consultation process and governed the procedures for the referendum to be held under the auspices of the United Nations. More than 80 percent of the East Timorese electorate participated in the referendum, with 78.5 percent of these voting for independence. Despite this unequivocal result, four hours after the decision had been officially announced, pro-integration militias, with the support – both tacit and implicit – of the Indonesian government embarked on a terrifying process of 'cleansing' pro-independence supporters. Many East Timorese were killed in this wave of terror, and 500,000 were forced to flee their homes to the western side of the island. On 5 and 6 September, the majority of international observers, journalists and UNAMET officials (the international officials that supervised the referendum) were evacuated. On the night of 6 September, the United Nations' Security Council refused Portugal and its allies' request to send in a peacekeeping force. The Indonesians declared that they were capable of restoring peace, but would not provide any guarantees to that effect. In the meantime the cleansing and killing continued. The Security Council eventually agreed to dispatch a fact-finding mission to Timor that would prepare a report on the situation and the Indonesian government finally agreed to accept the assistance of the international community.

UN resolution 1264 condemned the orgy of violence against the East Timorese people and approved the creation of a peace keeping force, UNAMET, under Australian command, set up base in Dili on 28 September 1999 (*Economist* 1999). On 19 October the Indonesian parliament recognized the result of the East Timor referendum, while six days later, UN resolution 1272 established the United Nations Transitional Administration of East Timor (UNTAET), which had overall responsibility for the security and government of the territory until independence. Although there were some minor complaints, East Timor's leaders were involved in every stage of this process, which was led by the UN's administrator, the Brazilian Sérgio Vieira de Mello. Following a peaceful ballot in East Timor's first ever free legislative elections held on 30 August 2001, FRETILIN won 55 of the 88 seats (57.37 percent) in the Constitutional Assembly. After six months of internal debate and popular consultations, this Assembly approved East Timor's constitution. Elections for the country's presidency were held on 14 April 2002, and were won by the former FRETILIN leader, now running as an independent, Xanana Gusmão.[12]

On 20 May 2002, the official ceremonies celebrating the transfer of sovereignty to the new state were held under the auspices of the UN's Secretary General in the presence of the Portuguese President, Jorge Sampaio, and his Prime Minister, Durão Barroso, the President of Indonesia, Megawati Sukarnoputri, the Australian Prime Minister, and the former US President, Bill Clinton.

Portugal's colonial responsibilities had come to an end with this ceremony that marked the end of 28 years of decolonization that had begun with the 1974 revolution that brought democracy and peace to the country. With the creation of this new state of East Timor, the colonial era that had been brought into question from beyond the democratic political institutions finally came to an end, and Portugal could finally embrace the European destiny it had previously rejected.

Postscript

For over one-quarter of a century after Portugal rediscovered its democratic and European vocation, the country has implemented and concluded the final processes of decolonization; or better, it has overseen the emancipation of those territories that formed part of its colonial empire for 500 years.

It has achieved this with impeccable disinterest, with a sense of the times and with feelings of solidarity with the several peoples with which, at certain moments in their history, it shared a common experience.

On balance, and recognising that mistakes were made along the way, Portugal fulfilled its obligations as both a European power and a newly democratic nation towards the African and Asian people with which it maintains shared emotions. The small group of territories that were claimed during the era of Vasco de Gama: Goa, Macao and East Timor, have followed their own distinct destinies that have, in some cases, been determined by their individual circumstances, and, in others, by the will of their people.

Today, Goa is part of India, and experiences the challenges to progress and development that are the result of globalization and the spread of international trade within one of the most important democracies in the whole of Asia; yet it is doing this without breaking its links with its Portuguese heritage, remaining the crucible and melting-pot of European culture within the cradle of Hinduism.

Macao has become a part of a modern China, and shares in its very promising future. Instead of becoming a socialist society in 2049, Macao probably will lead the way to China's transformation from an economic dragon to a reliable democratic society making real the desires of Deng Xiao Ping, without leaving behind the 400 years during which it shared a very special relationship with Portugal. It is highly probable that the special administrative system therough which it is to be governed until 2049 will come to be a model and a reference for the profound political, social and economic transformations that destiny has in store for China, its people and its leaders. Its neighbour, Shanghai, has become the new twenty-first century Asian megalopolis from where, perhaps as in the past, the winds of change will blow, leading to a new political era in China.

East Timor chose another destiny in its refusal to be forcibly incorporated into its giant neighbour, Indonesia. While this incorporation was imposed upon the East Timorese people, this was desperately opposed. The broad autonomy that was offered within a state that was so much larger, so much richer and so much more powerful was seen to be impossible, if not even farcical. Of the three examples discussed here, East Timor is the case that raises major concerns. The East Timorese people were persistent in their claims to exist in their own right without being ruled by others, they were consistent in their expressions of their right to self-determination and freedom from colonialism in accordance with the United Nations' Declaration of the Right of Self-Determination of Colonized Countries and People that was published on 14 September 1960: 'the subjection of people to foreign oppression, domination and exploitation constitutes a denial of fundamental human rights, is contrary to the United Nations' Charter and places the cause of peace and global cooperation in peril; all people have the right to free choice; in virtue of this right, they may freely choose their political constitution and to freely pursue economic, social and cultural progress' (Ribeiro and Saldanha 1995).

Many important observers have predicted the failure of this experience (*Far Eastern Economic Review* 1999; 2000; *OneWorld.net* 2002), with the absence of natural resources,[13] with its persistently backwards economy and society exacerbated by centuries of colonial domination and Indonesian occupation, and by the proximity of its gigantic neighbour upon which it depends for its primary materials, equipment and commerce in order to survive.[14] Although some minor incidents happened recently between its civilian population and its government, the future of East Timor as a nation and the East Timorese as an independent people will depend on their ability to develop their economy and to export Timor's produce to the other nations within its geographical sphere and thus to stabilise its fragile democratic system.

Portugal's imperial destiny in Portuguese India, Macao and East Timor has reached its conclusion. Now it is time to face the challenges of a new enlarged and diversified Europe.

Notes:

* Assistant Professor of International Relations, Lisbon International University.

[1] We share a collective responsibility for the manner of our decolonization, and for our typically Portuguese attitude that 'there was nothing else we could do' and 'these territories were not ours'. We must face our rather shameful attitude that 'the past is over' and confront a situation for which we were collectively responsible.

[2] This sentiment was expressed in his book, *Portugal and the future*, which outlined the political and psychological conditions necessary to end the rebellion and overthrow the authoritarian regime. The greatest consequence of the wars in Africa was the dependence of the civil authorities on the military apparatus and the extent of the defeats and victories in the conflicts. The unity of the regime was retained only because the cohesion of the two strata (the bellicose and the civilian) resisted all internal differences, the personal quarrels and the senility of a political elite that was incapable of recognising the winds of change and adapting themselves to them. This allowed the development of a 'critical mass' to Marcello's timid attempts at liberalization. The regime was getting old and tired, and fell as a result of the decrepit degeneration of its own political corps that had been manipulated by Salazar to whom they owed their obedience, loyalty and their complicity.

[3] Neither the Socialist Party (PS) nor the Popular Democratic Party (PPD, later PSD), both of which were to develop during the years following the revolution, had a clear vision of the path to follow in relation to the colonies. Their priority was to open political negotiations with the African guerrilla leaders, and to silence the guns at the front. It was perhaps only the Communist Party (PCP) and the extreme left who had were openly in favour of Portugal's immediate withdrawal from the colonies. The Social Democratic Centre (CDS) did not have any clear doctrine; its principal concern was with its own survival, surrounded as it was by the radical forces of the extreme left, and threatened with possible banning.

[4] These pressures began to be felt even before Spínola took office as President. Kurt Waldheim, the then UN Secretary General, sent a message to the UN's Permanent Mission in Portugal that stated his expectation 'that the new government will recognise the right of self-determination and independence before it begins negotiations with the African liberation movements in order that peace may be established without delay'. See Mattoso (1998: 53-101).

[5] In an interview published in *Der Spiegel* on 6 May 1974, later published in Soares, M. (1982), *Democratização e descolonização: 10 meses de Governo Provisório,* Lisbon: Dom Quixote, p. 35, the reply to the question merited an affirmation that Spínola had proposed in his book that the colonies could be granted autonomy within a type of Commonwealth. Soares retorted that the African liberation movements 'demand immediate independence, and they are right to do so', and that his party 'also demand this'. On 23 September 1974, Soares reiterated this opinion at the 29th Session of the United Nations' General Assembly. Soares later acknowledged that Kurt Waldheim's visit to Portugal had 'contributed to the acceleration of the process'

[6] During the nineteenth century, some discontent was to emerge towards the apostolic activities of the Jesuits who had been established there as a consequence of a treaty of

1855, and which granted this religious order the traditional tribal *ranes* prerogatives. The local population, however, only obtained limited representation in the colonial administration in 1917, following a revolution in Lisbon, when some of their representatives were elected to the Government Council that was led by the Governor General

[7] Extract of a speech to the National Assembly. This rhetorical exercise revealed Salazar's unwillingness to even consider any solution that did not maintain the empire at any and all costs.

[8] In his extensive report to Salazar, dated 13 January 1962, Franco Nogueira recognized the reorientation of Portuguese foreign and colonial policy as a means of minimising Portugal's international isolation. This document recognized that the principal objective of the anti-colonial movement was the political, rather then the military defeat of the regime, and that Portugal did not possess the political, economic or military means to maintain its isolationist policy.

[9] Evidently during the events of 1952 and 1966, when communist agitation (during the second Cultural Revolution) perturbed the small enclave's peace as a result of a direct order from Mao Tse-tung.

[10] Said during the swearing into office of Macao's new governor, Garcia Leandro.

[11] In accordance with article 2 of the Basic Law, which states: 'The National People's Assembly of the People's Republic of China authorises the Special Administrative Region of Macao to exercise a high degree of autonomy and the enjoyment of independent executive, legislative and judicial powers, up to and including supreme judicial power'. Article 12 established that 'The Special Administrative Region of Macao will enjoy an elevated degree of autonomy while remaining directly subordinate to the People's Central Government.'

[12] On 20 March 2000, Xanana gave an interview to *Time*, in which he revealed his reservations in becoming President of the new country that he had helped liberate. The reservations of this old guerrilla leader did not disappear and it was only as a result of pressure from both the international community and his resistance colleagues and the Portuguese government that convinced him to accept his position. See *Time* (2000).

[13] Australia and East Timor signed a treaty in May 2002 to divide all profits from any oil and gas that may be discovered in the Timor and Arafura Seas separating the two countries. East Timor was not completely satisfied with the terms of this treaty, however. See *AP World Politics* (2002).

[14] The archipelago, which includes 13,000 islands and has a population of 210 million, is riven by ethnic and racial tensions and conflicts. Even now, four years after the fall of the Suharto dictatorship, and one year into the weak presidency of his successor, Abdurrahman Wahid, the current President, Megawati Sukarnoputri is having difficulty implementing the promised democratic reforms in any meaningful manner, nor has he managed to remove the military's influence from Indonesian politics.

PART III

Portugal and the PALOPs

5: Portugal and the CPLP: heightened expectations, unfounded disillusions

Luís António Santos

> 'The CPLP is a disaster, and for that I blame the Portuguese government.'
> Mário Soares, Universidade do Minho, Braga, 28 June 2000

> 'The CPLP appears not only to have been born of a 'caesarean section' but it also suffers from a very considerable 'ideal deficit'. In fact, it undoubtedly seems to have started out with the wrong ideal.'
> Michel Cahen, 'Des caravelles pour le futur?', Lusotopie, 1997

Portugal's relation with the *Comunidade dos Países de Língua Portuguesa* (CPLP) has been uneasy from the start. Although proposals for the creation of a new institutionalised relation with its former African colonies and Brazil had been put forward at least since 1983, several different factors concurred to prevent any serious undertaking until the end of the 1980s: first and foremost, pre-1989 international involvement in Angola and – to a lesser extent – in Mozambique, greatly reduced both Portugal's diplomatic leeway and the new countries' interest in a new entity. Secondly, Portugal's own internal political life was going through a time-consuming state of instability until 1987, leaving governments very little scope for dealing with less than immediate concerns. Finally, less than 15 years after decolonization, Lisbon's position regarding its former African colonies was still very much determined by a fear of neo-colonialism accusations. By the same token, relevant sectors of the African single party regimes' were weary of any political or diplomatic option that might even hint at any Portuguese prominence.

Portugal's role in the Angolan peace process, and its insistence on maintaining some degree of intervention in the Mozambican peace discussions appeared to be instrumental in changing its own perception of what the new relationship could amount to, and also in gradually securing a level of mutual trust especially with these two countries.[1] The political wrangling which followed the debacle of the Angolan peace process, and particularly the length and the periodic susceptibilities of the ensuing process of creation of the CPLP would nevertheless come to prove that doubt, suspicion, and resentment remained an integral part of the relation, and were thus inevitably both integrated in the genetic code of the new organization and conditioning Portugal's role.

Four years after the formal institutionalization of the CPLP, Portugal maintains a cautious position, based on the same structuring premise – the necessity to shy away from almost every 'leading role' opportunity for fear of neo-colonial accusation – and on more down to earth reasons like the limited availability of funds.

Should we thus infer that the empty shell like existence of the CPLP derives from such a Portuguese attitude? Should we alternatively argue that the demise of the Community is linked to its 'Lusotropical emanation' beginnings?

We would submit that even if both these queries did get favourable answers, another dimension should be added to the debate – a discussion on the level of expectations. Indeed, both those who defend that Portugal should have had a more prominent role in the organization from the start, and those who instead argue that a new relationship framework should be in place before the CPLP could work, seem to share the notion that a great deal more could be attained.

In this paper we would like to propose that such readings seem to compare their own (sometimes very elaborate) specific notions on what the CPLP should be like with actual plans and achievements, invariably drawing negative conclusions on the organization/community's performance.

An ambiguous start

The idea of a Community anchored on a shared linguistic background has been hovering over Portuguese politics at least since the mid-1950s. The first enunciators of such proposals were undoubtedly influenced by the writings of Gilberto Freyre on the singularity of a Lusotropical culture.[2] Agostinho da Silva would write in 1956 that Portugal or Brazil should take it upon themselves the task of creating a linguistically based association in order to develop the 'common cultural affection' (quoted in Domingues 1999: 4). Nearly a decade latter, one of the staunchest defenders of Portugal's strategic turning to the Atlantic, Adriano Moreira, would organise the First Portuguese Culture Community Congress in Lisbon. A second gathering, in Mozambique, would follow it and two organizations would emerge as a result: the Union of Portuguese Culture Communities, and the Portuguese Culture International Academy.

Not being our purpose to analyse in detail these organizations and initiatives, two remarks should be nevertheless be made; firstly, they were somewhat contradictory in purpose, by taking on board Freyre's notions on the added value of cultural interplay, yet at the same time clearly stating their metropolitan-centred nature;

secondly, their creation – ostensibly parting from the reality of an ongoing war – should be interpreted more as an indication that they were part of the proposed alternative path on colonial matters for a very particular group within the regime than as an objective and, especially, viable proposition (Graham 1973: 32-3). Their importance as creators of a particular framework that would demarcate the debate henceforth should not however be in any way diminished by the previous comments. Indeed, the longevity of some basic notions – the pivotal role of the Portuguese language and the proposed cultural prominence – advises against any hasty dismissals, and the existence of ambiguities in the past if anything reinforces the link with the foundation and initial wavering of the CPLP itself.

It would take nearly two decades for the theme to resurface in Portuguese politics. The so-called 'spirit of Bissau'[3] had formally initiated a period of more open contacts between Portugal and its former African colonies, and Jaime Gama (Foreign Affairs minister in 1983) would venture the possibility of institutionalising this strengthening of ties. The aim was to 'bring consistency and decentralization' to the Portuguese Language tri-continental dialogue, *via* a biannual summit of Heads of State and government, annual meetings at ministerial level, and frequent consultations between Foreign Affairs Ministry representatives. A permanent secretariat ('ideally located in Cape Verde') would secure the management of this 'new dynamic' (Gama 1983).

The carefully selected wording of the project, and its ostensive focus on mutually beneficial diplomatic actions would not however be sufficient to promote its materialization. It could generally be argued that Portugal's post-colonial relations with the African Portuguese speaking countries had not yet reached 'the state of friendliness which such a move required' (Venâncio and Chan 1996: 47), although some very particular but intertwined factors could be presented as major contributors to such a scenario: Portugal's political instability, the emergence of distinct approaches to the question of relations with the former colonies, the limitations still imposed by an international bipolar division, and also the new African countries' continued (if somewhat dimmed) suspicion of Portuguese intentions (Reis 1994: 74-89).

In a period of no more than a decade, democratic Portugal had had very distinct approaches to the relationship with its former colonies, and relevantly, they very seldom reflected a 'national' strategy, agreed upon by government, Presidency, political parties, and military. President Eanes – who sought for himself an intervening role in this particular area of external relations – believed in a pragmatic (though personalised) approach, hoping to enhance Portugal's economic and political presence in Africa. In essence, this strategy was shared by the Social Democrats, led by Sá Carneiro, although they believed these matters should not be in the hands of the President. The Socialists, led by Mário Soares, were more permeable to both American intentions and the pressures of interest groups and African anti-governmental organizations. The alternation of Social Democrats and Socialists in power had clear reflections on political attitudes towards Africa, and also on the African posture towards Portugal. The fact that Jaime Gama's proposals were not followed by any concrete measures hence tells us very little about their specific validity. If reasons are to be sought, they rather lay in the demise of the Socialist lead Central Bloc government, in the expression of Angola and Mozambique's by now chronic misgivings towards Soares' inspired initiatives (Venâncio and McMillan 1993: 101-4), and also in the ostensive non-involvement of Brazil in any type of discussions on the matter.

By 1989 conditions had considerably changed. In Portugal, Cavaco Silva's majority Social-Democrat government assumed that relations with Portuguese speaking African countries were strategically important, and that concrete confidence building and cooperation measures were needed.[4] A strategic plan, elaborated by diplomats and officials at the Foreign Affairs ministry in March 1988, foresaw Portugal's active involvement in the search for peace both in Angola and Mozambique, following a process which entailed the promotion of state to state relations, and the cessation of contacts and imposition of circulation restrictions to Angolan and Mozambican rebel movements (Interview with A. Monteiro, 19 July 2000). At the economic level, Portugal's proposal on the existence of assistance programmes for countries without geographical continuity was accepted during the Lome IV discussions, thus allowing the five Portuguese speaking African countries to be treated as a 'regional group'. Much in the manner previously envisaged by Eanes and especially Sá Carneiro, this *rapprochement* was linked to the perception that Portugal's role within Europe would be enhanced.[5] Importantly, Constitutional revisions had by now clearly established governmental prominence over the conduct of foreign affairs, reducing the risks of Presidential 'interference', and promoting an external image of greater unity on these matters.

A specific set of conditions led Angola to interpret Portugal's commitment with less suspicion than in the past. Indeed, Soviet effective retreat from Africa under Gorbatchev, a severe economic crisis, a desire to further relations with the EC, and significantly an intention to establish a new relation with the United States, secured Luanda's adhesion to a mutually beneficial political and diplomatic convergence, nudged forward by 'confidence building' measures, like the curtailment of UNITA's activities in Lisbon and the symbolic refusal of an entry visa to its leader, the late Jonas Savimbi.

Ravaged by a succession of natural catastrophes and by a paralysing civil war, Mozambique was also receptive to Portugal's renewed attentions. The intensification of economic and, especially, military cooperation was enshrined in a series of agreements signed in 1988, and the political emphasis was given by Cavaco Silva's official visit to Maputo in 1989. Having initiated a delicate process of peace negotiations with Renamo, the Mozambican government also sought to secure Portugal's help in convincing the Portuguese Community in South Africa to both terminate their support for Renamo, and initiate an investment oriented return to the country.

Possibly due to the lack of post-colonial internal conflicts, lesser international involvement, and the exiguity of self-sufficiency resources, Cape Verde, São Tomé and Príncipe, and Guinea-Bissau all opted from a non-confrontational relation with Portugal since 1974. The fact that Portugal was now an EC member if anything increased their interest in strengthening that link.

Finally, a democratic yet economically debilitated Brazil, also started to recognise the advantages of closer contacts with Portugal and the Portuguese speaking African countries. The historic affinity and the existence of a 700,000 strong Portuguese community in Brazil had never managed to ignite a substantive relation between the two countries. Caricature images of each other were, until the late 1980's, the reflection of such a steady aloofness. Portugal's adhesion to the EC was instrumental in the inversion of that trend; Portugal sought to strengthen its image as a worthy interlocutor not only in Africa but also in Latin America, and Brazil was keen on reinforcing its relation with the European Community. From Africa, Brazil expected an expansion of its cultural products market, but also – particularly in the case of Angola – a spill over effect into other areas.

More than ever before, conditions were hence appropriate to the establishment of a new type of relationship between Portugal, Brazil, and the new African states. The first summit of Portuguese speaking Heads of State – which took place in São Luis do Maranhão (Brazil), on November 1989 – nevertheless resulted in no more than the formal creation of the Portuguese Language International Institute (PLII). Under pressure from distinct internal conditions, and in the absence of clear leadership, the 'seven' were only able to vaguely agree on the defence and promotion of a common linguistic heritage.

Whilst the Portuguese President, Mário Soares, seemed to share with his Brazilian counterpart, José Sarney, and with the Brazilian Culture minister, José Aparecido de Oliveira, an enthusiasm over the evolution towards a more encompassing entity (Avillez 1996: 53), Angola's failed peace process, and delays in achieving a settlement in Mozambique advised the Portuguese government against any hasty protagonism (Briosa e Gala, Interview, 19 February 1997). In the name of 'a long term national interest policy', but also as an indirect acknowledgement of its own limitations, the Portuguese government opted for the safety of an incremental approach, through an engagement in concrete sectorial '5+1' meetings.[6]

The arrival of Itamar Franco at the Presidency, would definitely thrust Brazil into a leading role. Its ambassador in Lisbon, Aparecido de Oliveira, would in March 1993 (some three months after the EC had become the European Union) present a concrete proposal for the creation of the Comunidade dos Países de Língua Portuguesa. Confirming the support of all seven Heads of State, a meeting of Foreign Affairs ministers – held in February 1994, in Brasília – would state the 'spontaneous' nature of a project that was based on the 'special relationships' forged by a common language.

Two failed dates for the formalization of the CPLP – 28 June 1994, and 29 November 1994 – would however expose the political frailties of such a special relationship, and hint at the continued stress between different objectives, and importantly, possible oscillations in member states' interest for the project. Itamar Franco's last minute unavailability for the proposed June meeting was[7] – despite Portuguese diplomatic efforts[8] – interpreted by the African countries as a political snub. Hence their immediate (and joint) decision to stay away from the planned event. Despite numerous reassurances to the contrary (Bernardes 1994; *Jornal de Letras* 23 November 1994), the second attempt would also run into problems when Angola's President decided to announce his absence, as a result of the perceived interference of his Portuguese counterpart in Luanda's 'internal matters'.[9] A total collapse was avoided by intense diplomatic activity, which would nevertheless only produce results more than a year latter. What Mozambican President, Joaquim Chissano, would (rather euphemistically) describe as a 'natural maturation process' (Domingues 1999: 7) finally resulted in the July 1996 Heads of State summit, not without a last reminder of how fragile the whole construct was – Angola's insistence on appointing a former prime-minister as the CPLP's first Executive Secretary,[10] revealed that susceptibilities were still very high, and that not all countries had the same posture towards the new organization. Indeed, if Angola can be – on this particular occasion – singled out for taking advantage of a tense situation, it should be noted that Brazil's acceptance of such a demand was decisive. In fact, Brazil's new President, Fernando Henrique Cardoso, and (especially) his Foreign Affairs minister, Luis Filipe Lampreia, were not entirely in accordance with Aparecido de Oliveira's ideas on the nature and purpose of the organization, and Angola's demand was an opportunity to solve a potencially damaging internal problem. Not proposing Aparecido de Oliveira, could hence be presented as a goodwill measure, with the purpose of cementing trust among all member states.

Besides the solemnity of the occasion, the Lisbon summit produced a series of generic undertakings, on the defence of the common language, on the progressive affirmation of a Portuguese Language block in the international *fora*, and on mutual solidarity and cooperation (CPLP 1996b). As the final communiqué so clearly shows, the new organization was however very much an empty shell, awaiting its 'mechanisms and instruments', 'a list of priorities and projects', and 'strategic guidelines' (CPLP 1996c).

In essence, the CPLP had an Executive Secretary imposed by one Member State, no head office, no staff, no clear orientation, and – despite Brazil's last minute offer of US$4m – an insufficient and erratic supply of financial means. Its members all admitted an interest in the organization, although their purposes were not coincidental. If Portugal's caution advised it against going much further than to hope for a 'means to project the language', and for the development of a genuine new understanding: 'We thus actualise a secular familiarity, punctuated by light and shadow, but now assumed in its entirety and without complexes... Our heritage belongs to us all, and we must all enrich it. The rules are quite clear: equality, solidarity, and mutual respect. Not forgetting that this community is marked by our own reading of universalism' (Sampaio 1996: 2, 6-7). Brazil was much more straightforward in the expression of its political and economic goals: 'we will be presenting some concrete cooperation projects that we would like to see prosper. They are realistic projects, simple but goal oriented initiatives' (Cardoso 1996: 2). Brazil's strenuous appeal for a 'sense of realism' was seconded by the African member states, even if relating to different purposes. As Angolan President, José Eduardo dos Santos, put it, the new States were seeking 'new ways to fight exclusion' in the international arena, thus hoping for less 'grandiloquence, and sentimental rhetoric', and more 'effective solidarity' (economic, political, technical, but also in sensible areas like migratory policy) (Santos, J. E. 1996: 1).

Less than six months later, Brazil's Foreign Affairs minister, Luis Filipe Lampreia, would make no effort to hide his personal lack of confidence in a structure like the CPLP, by stating that his country's first interest was to strengthen ties with the European Union (presumably with Portugal's help), and that Brazil could very well be in Africa without the CPLP (Sousa 1996: 8). The natural follow up to such statements would be the early 1997 internal devaluation of the CPLP, in terms of Brazilian Foreign Affairs priorities.[11] On the first anniversary of the organization, the Executive under secretary, Rafael Branco, admitted its chronic shortcomings: the oscillations in member states' commitment,[12] the lack of a concrete progression strategy,[13] and the exiguity of funds (Silva 1997: 5).[14] In 1998, he would add that the organization still lived 'in a sea of ambiguity', and that it had not yet managed to become 'a relevant consideration in each member state's decision-making process on foreign policy' (Abecassis 1998: 18).

Some three years (and two Heads of State summits) latter, the CPLP has not yet been able to assert its existence in full, and – significantly – it has not managed to escape the immobility trap. Tentative efforts in the diplomatic arena (as was the case during the 1998 coup in Guinea-Bissau), or the sponsoring of cultural and scientific events and meetings do not seem to be enough to justify the existence of the organization itself. Lack of political autonomy and financial resources have rendered it powerless in the face of catastrophes (as was the case during the 1999 Mozambican floods), and silent in the face of human rights violations (particularly in matters relating to Angola).

The Heads of State 2000 summit, held in Maputo, has apparently attempted to kick-start a new, more cultural oriented organization. The choice of an academic for the position of Executive Secretary could be interpreted as an attempt to isolate the CPLP from political interference, thus creating some (until now non-existent) room for manoeuvre. Still, if compared with the initial proposals on greater political, diplomatic, and economic harmonization, this change cannot but be interpreted as a downgrading of member states individual and collective hopes. It could be argued that conditions are finally in place for the affirmation of a flexible language Community but it could as much be said that a dimming of members' interest signals the demise of the organization.

Interpretations and their weight

Such a troubled and historically attached past, and such problems in its initial years have had profound effects on the CPLP's image. Indeed, criticism of the organization itself and of particular member states (for their perceived 'responsibilities') has been constant, with the added peculiarity of uniting politicians from distinct (and sometimes opposing) persuasions, writers, diplomats, and academics.

Notwithstanding the fact that specific positions have distinct nuances (which are often seen as relevant differences by their holders), it could be argued that criticism has revolved along two broad arguments. The first one departs from the notion that Portugal is historically responsible, and therefore should play a more active role in all matters concerning the CPLP. Portugal having hence failed to fulfil its duties, the CPLP could not but be an incomplete (at best) or failed (at worst) project.[15] The second argumentative line, departs from the notion that a Lusophone Community should develop from open and egalitarian exchanges between member states. The CPLP's undoubted Lusotropical origins imposed ideological, and even structural constraints, which have definitely contributed to some member states' mistrust, and concomitant deflation of the project.

The first position's most recognisable proponent is former Portuguese President, Mário Soares. Whilst recently stating that the CPLP is 'a disaster', he blamed the Portuguese government for not being able to go beyond what he considered a 'poor formulation' (Lima 2000: 11). Committed from the start to a Brazilian led,[16] eminently cultural, and politically autonomous project – that personified by Aparecido de Oliveira – Soares no doubt shares Almeida Santos' (his long term friend and political ally) notion that Portugal has always 'played defensively' for fear of 'public opinion's reactions which never occur' (1993: 20). In essence, Soares seems to regret that an over-cautious Portuguese attitude (which has been constant in the last decade, irrespective of the party in power) transformed a 'people's project' into no more than a political instrument. This notion is complemented by the former Foreign Affairs minister and European Commissioner, João de Deus Pinheiro: 'while the CPLP is seen as a "governments' thing" ...it will be able to do very little... To have nominated a former Angolan prime minister for the top job was, I believe, an enormous political mistake... "civilian" was needed, capable of making the organization as "civilian" as possible' (Nóbrega 2000: 25).

Notwithstanding the obvious fuel provided to these positions by a tense relation with some African leaders (namely in the Angolan government), the fact is that they are supported by a series of assumptions on what the Portuguese foreign affairs attitude towards both the CPLP and its members should be: political assertiveness, commitment to the upholding of human rights and civil liberties, and concrete economic investment. Ranging from the prudent: 'The Portugal that has come out of 25 April is not neo-colonialist, and should thus not squat, always begging forgiveness for the help it provides' (Vasconcelos 1998: 32) – to the hyperbolic: 'Portugal should assume the right of interference' (Tavares 1999: 13) – supporting comments all embody the notion that opportunities are being lost, either due to unnecessary complexes or overzealous *real politik*.

The second position's scepticism derives from one main premise – the CPLP's ideological origins are embedded in a time resistant Lusotropical discourse, and it embodies the fanciful self-esteem constructions of a predominantly white Brazilian community whilst providing an 'imagined' sustenance to Portugal's national identity. This 'adaptation of paternalism to modernity', as Michel Cahen calls it (1997: 431), could not but create suspicion among the African countries, thus preparing the ground for an uneven commitment and, ultimately, for a growing disinterest in the organization. The fact that the organization is sometimes referred to as 'lusophone' hints at the existence of an invisible centre/periphery construct, which can seldom be either flattering or beneficial to members other than Portugal.

Even if positions might slightly diverge on what Portugal does get from this fundamentally discursive insistence on the 'community of affections' – the Angolan historian, Carlos Pacheco, would stress a straightforward economic interest ('Questions related to Africa are still dealt with in the backyard. Always in the hope some quick profit might be made. Just profit. As it was in the past' (1996: 15)),[17] whilst Mozambican writer, Filimone Meigos, would rather focus on the self-perceptive value of institutionalising the global projection of a language that defines the Portuguese nation: 'A country like Portugal, periphery of the periphery, now wants a leading role in a process already closed by History' (Cahen 1997: 410) – the shared understanding is that the CPLP proves Lisbon's still problematic relation with its colonial past.

Disinterest in the reality of African affairs is – again according to Pacheco – 'soaked up by ignorance and disguised with folkloric propaganda,' hence leading some politicians to 'mingle knowledge of Africa with personal friendships and political complicities forged in PIDE's gaols, the Students of the Empire's House, and the exile in Algeria, with Africans which belonged to a very specific socio-cultural universe – the urban one' (1996: 15). The CPLP is, thus, no more than part of that folklore, serving the dual purpose of guaranteeing some singularity to a country that feels increasingly diluted in Europe and 'invaded' by Spain, whilst attempting to cement old self-assurance notions, like the 'unique ability to interplay with other cultures', or the 'non-racist character' of the Portuguese people.

Heightened expectations

Apparently opposing, as they may seem, these two broad argumentative lines share the assumption that the CPLP could have been much different from what it is at the present. If the first position envisaged an active cultural community, under clear leadership, jointly strengthening its ties on the basis of a mutual linguistic heritage, the second one expected a much looser entity, without any centre, acting as a partial cooperation tool between an heterogeneous but mutually respectful group of states. Irrespective of their intrinsic value, these proposals should not, however, be used in isolation when evaluating the concrete actions and purpose of the four year old organization. Departing from a high level of expectations, they do bluntly expose some of the most obvious problems of the CPLP, yet precisely that departure point hampers fairness in comment, leaving very little room for a discussion on the expected fluid nature of an organization like the CPLP.

The first position is in fact the inheritor of more than 40 years of mostly Lusophone centred discussions on the creation of a Community. Its weight has been felt especially during the pre-institutionalization phase, although it becomes very difficult to read this fact as a somewhat premeditated initiative to 're-subjugate' the former African colonies.

As we tried to show in the first part of this paper, two models of association were debated over for a lengthy period, with oscillations in their relative prominence deriving in essence from the result of internal political disputes, both in Portugal and Brazil. A less ambitious and progressive evolution of the 5+1+1 understanding at different levels, was the preferred option of Portuguese Social-Democrats and also of Fernando Henrique Cardoso's presidency, whilst a more symbolically appealing community, sharing a language and proposing to strengthen cultural, political, and economic ties, was argued for by both José Sarney, Itamar Franco, and their Portuguese counterpart, Mário Soares. It should be added that throughout only the smaller African states showed some genuine interest in either project, with internal problems conditioning both Angola and Mozambique's commitment.

The fact that the CPLP resulted in an ambiguous construct – appearing to democratise some of the ideological trappings of the Lusotropical vision (Cabral 1996), whilst also enshrining structural anti-centralization measures, like the fact that important questions are solely decided by unanimity, at the Heads of State summits—does indicate that a deliberate effort to cater for all sensibilities was very much present. The formalization of a 'minimum common denominator' association (interview with A. Monteiro, 19 July 2000), although appealing to neither the supporters of greater Portuguese intervention nor to those hoping for a cleansed egalitarian association, was the only politically consensual option available. It seems as hard to imagine African concessions to a monolithic 'Portuguese Culture valorization' project, as it does to expect Brazil and Portugal not to have their specific goals and perceptions. In the same manner as a Mozambican finds it difficult to see the relevance of belonging (even if by proxy) to the 'União Latina' (to appropriate one of Michel Cahen's most telling examples), a Portuguese fails to see any problem in the intertwining of Lusophony and the mythology of the CPLP under one single totality, even if each of its components is characterised by a distinct culture. A project of association between such distinct readings could never exist unless some concessions were not made.

What the first position fails to realise is that such a language derived Portuguese centrality 'should not have any other dimension besides the genealogical one' (Lourenço 1999: 179). When appeals are made for greater Portuguese intervention in African state's affairs, or for a more politically assertive CPLP, this position inevitably attracts support from more conservative quarters,[18] with the twofold effect of heightening African apprehensions and giving added value to an ideological discourse which – in fairness – has long been effectively deflated.

The core problem of the second position is precisely the fact that it takes at almost face value such a discourse, by inference assuming that Portugal could only aspire to construct a centralised, and culturally coated preferential trade arrangement such as France and Britain have with their former colonies. We would rather argue that Portugal does (and cannot afford not to) have a political and geostrategic affirmation policy – where the language plays a pivotal role – although there is very little indication that a neo-colonial attitude is implied. Portugal's economic and cultural presence in its former colonies results much less from governmental guidance than from private initiative, and it could hardly be described as intense (Teixeira 1995; Dias, A. S. 1995). Its official political posture in the last decade tends to privilege the maintenance of state-to-state relations, sometimes at the blunt expense of principles that it so strenuously wants to uphold in other situations.

The fact that Portugal undoubtedly uses the geographic extension of its own language as a self-image booster should not be read as more than just that. To use Moura's expression: 'The end of the Empire was compensated by the transfer of a frustrated imperial vocation to the linguistic level. Not being a very intelligent attitude, it nevertheless is pretty much harmless... It is a formula like any other, useful for some speeches and to proclaim more or less superficial fraternities' (2000: 25).

Another significant frailty of the second position is to assume that the African states have been passive observers of a primarily Brazilian-Portuguese construction. Besides being historically innacurate, this position denotes a predisposition to consider that, to the exclusion of some elite clusters, Africans tend to consider their colonial heritage – including the language of the coloniser – as a malefice. Even if some particular states (or their leaders) do indeed still appear to be so attached to the colonial past to the point of episodically being so emphatic in their 'exorcism' attempts,[19] the fact is that African input has been at least as relevant as individual states wanted it to be. Besides the fact that for the first four years of its existence two African politicians managed the CPLP, some of its most relevant initiatives (particularly in areas related to professional proficiency) have taken place in African countries. The CPLP was, hence, as much a foreign affairs tool to Angola and Mozambique, as it was for Portugal and Brazil. The obvious existing differences are, surely, much more in terms of degree than substance.

Ideologically conceived as a depurated version of the Lusotropical dream, structurally attached to an ostensibly centre-less framework, financially and politically constrained, an organization like the CPLP could never be the autonomous embodiment of an active cultural community, not could it be the light, informal, egalitarian shared expression of individual identities. Portugal's active formal disengagement, Brazil's ostensive preference (from the start) for little else than a vehicle for preferential trade (especially in cultural products), Angola's wavering allied to an internal absorbing situation, and Mozambique rather more survival related priorities have all contributed to the feeble, pale, dream-like *façade* nature of the organization. In a sense, it could even be argued that by reflecting the general lack of commitment of its founding members, their disparate levels of development (hence their dissimilar needs), and relevantly, their general lack of mutual knowledge which seldom goes past folkloric references, the CPLP has become the only possible association of these seven countries, at this particular moment.

To fuel a debate based on high and specifically oriented expectations is useful only insofar as it projects different views on the nature and objectives of the CPLP. To assume it in any way as a scale might lead us to hasty and inaccurate conclusions.

Conclusion

Some four years after its official launching, the CPLP is often presented as a stillborn. Among those committed to the debate on its nature and role, the only consensual note is precisely on the aura of failure that surrounds the institution. Those who perceive it as an opportunity for Portugal's international projection rise against the evident lack of political commitment, and concomitant lack of strategic goals and funding. Those who instead interpret it as an emanation of Lusotropical ideas – hence retrograde, and irreversibly attached to the authoritarian past – argue that such a departing point runs against the nature of a true community. If we look beyond the emotional charge of the debate – both at the political and academic levels – we should concur that these postures, whilst highlighting obvious failings in members' commitment, and in the running of the organization, all seem to depart from exaggerated levels of expectations, hence inducing partial conclusions on its nature and performance.

It is our contention that both these positions hold some validity if we are to consider them in tandem with some important caveats. Firstly, they should not be taken as mutually exclusive interpretations. Secondly, they should be stripped of some of their most obvious oversimplified assumptions. The high level of expectations of these two positions however seems to indicate that, with or without the CPLP, a broad consensus exists on the idea that a language based community is a viable formula to both strengthen internal ties, and create an anti-globalization barrier.

Irrespective of what might be made of the CPLP, Portugal's interest in such an ostensibly non neo-colonial organization is high. Not discarding the importance for certain sectors of the Portuguese economy of traditionally receptive markets, and by the same token not diminishing the relevance of an effective political alliance in the international fora, this link with the former colonies is still vital for Portugal's self-image. That explains the fact that, as it did for a considerable part of the authoritarian period, the attachment cuts across political barriers, creating odd alliances and unique partnerships. It might also help to explain the emotional charge of the debate. As Lourenço so aptly put it: 'Lusophony is an obscure or voluntarily obscured jungle', marked by the uneasy 'coexistence of readings, and unconfessed or unconfessable intentions, all of which expressing particular contexts, situations, and cultural mythologies, definitely non-homologous and, only at best, analogous. This is the reality of things, and as such we must all assume it' (1999: 179)

Notes:

[1] Post-1974 relations with Guinea-Bissau, Cape Verde, and São Tomé and Principe were never haunted by severe disputes, thus allowing for an incremental build up of bilateral trust. However, in questions relating to the formation of the CPLP, these small Portuguese-speaking countries have always tended to follow the lead of Angola and Mozambique. Such a procedure was self-evident when Angola decided to boycott the constitutive summit of the organization, initially arranged for November 1994.

[2] The broad analytical area of Portuguese relations with the Africans has clearly been exposed to political appropriation by both those who argued in defence of some sort of singularity, and those who have strenuously attempted to prove quite the opposite. Gilberto Freyre's theoretical postulations on the existence of a distinct Lusotropical culture, resulting form the specifically characteristic Portuguese interplay with other populations, were (and still are) at the core of these discussions. A predominantly cultural focused construct thus acquired a unexpected prominence and notoriety, which in turn limited the possibilities of non-militant discussions. For an evaluation of the limits still imposed on the debate by the two opposing views on the subject see Neto (1997) and Macedo (1989). For a more balanced reading of *Lusotropicalismo* see Barreto and Mónica (1999: 391-4), and for a tentative analysis of the reasons why it remains such a sensitive topic see José Carlos Venâncio (1996).

[3] As the result of the combination of two movements – President Eanes' intention to promote a national interest geared policy for Africa, and the European Economic Community's indication that Portugal's prospective adhesion might benefit from its historical link with the five new African countries (significantly, all under some degree of non-Western influence) – Portugal initiated a *rapprochement* with Africa soon after decolonization. The most serious problem being the relation with the ruling Angolan party, the MPLA, Eanes sought regional help – namely from Cape Verde and Guinea Bissau – to establish initial contacts. Success resulted in the August 1978 Bissau summit, between Ramalho Eanes and Agostinho Neto, where all the major problems were alleviated. The ensuing new phase in relations between Portugal and its former African colonies would henceforth be attributed to the 'spirit of Bissau' (for more details see Antunes (1990: 110-6) and Venâncio and Chan (1996: 42-3)).

[4] Cavaco Silva would say: 'Before I took office, the climate was still very much one of intense suspicion. African leaders were tired of "political talk" and wanted concrete plans and actions' (Interview 20 April 1998).

[5] '...Portugal's ties with its former colonies, Brazil, and other areas of the World are indeed trump cards which increase our relative weight in the Community' (Silva 1988); 'If we are "less important" in Africa, then we will also be worth less in Europe. We cease to have something of our own' (Interview 20 April 1998).

[6] Although less formal meetings between the five African countries and Portugal had occurred previously, the '5+1' format was officially a reality since the November 1990 meeting of Foreign Affairs ministers, held in Bissau. In a period of five years, at least 56 specific high-level sectorial meetings would take place, relating to areas as distinct as Electoral Administration, Social Security, Justice, Customs, Environment, or Finance

(MNE 1995: 130-4).

[7] It has been argued that in the wake of his nephew's sudden death, Itamar Franco was advised by Mário Soares to miss the constitutive summit (Meireles and Guardiola 1994: 22).

[8] Portugal's diplomacy attempted to divert attentions (thus avoiding further damage), by insinuating that bureaucratic communication deficiencies were to blame (Albino 1994: 10).

[9] Symptomatic of an increasing rift with the Portuguese government's official policy towards Angola, President Soares had recently made some comments on the Lusaka negotiations, appealing for national reconciliation, but also criticising the Angolan government for its duplicity – whilst discussing peace, they were also attacking Huambo. Portugal's Foreign Affairs minister at the time, Durão Barroso, has recently revealed that henceforth two (undisclosed) African countries decided they would not participate in any type of organization while President Soares remained in office (Monteiro 2000: 13).

[10] One week before the Foreign Affairs ministers meeting in Maputo, ambassadors from the seven member countries had agreed upon the name of Aparecido de Oliveira for the task. Besides representing the biggest Member State, he was generally acknowledged as the 'father' of the CPLP. Angola put it to the others that – either resulting from a set consensus or from the adoption of a rotational alphabetic order – the first Executive Secretary had to be an Angolan.

[11] Leading Aparecido de Oliveira to write an article that started as follows: 'How goes the CPLP? Very poorly, despite Brazilian rhetoric' (1997: 12).

[12] The above-mentioned Brazilian downgrading of the CPLP in its own external relations' priorities list was perhaps the most relevant. Notwithstanding, by June 1997 a strategic re-orientation was already perceptible. In an extensive interview, Presidente Fernando Henrique Cardoso would admit that 'mistakes' had been made, whilst promising a 'more active involvement' henceforth (Avillez 1997: 46-56).

[13] 'I have lived these eight months under a lot of pressure. I would sometimes think that people were right when they accused us of doing nothing. Our attitude was – for a period – defensive, to the point of doing things just to counter that notion. An organization must know what it wants, where it wants to go, and must stick to that. If, after this first year, we can come up with concrete ideas, it will not be so bad' (Silva 1996: 7).

[14] An estimated first budget prediction of US$506,000 was partly covered by the fixed member states' contributions of US$30,000 each. The remainder was dependent on the goodwill of those who could afford a supplementary contribution – Brazil and Portugal provided US$100,000 each, and Angola gave US$50,000. Concrete cooperation activities were financed by a separate fund, also dependent on voluntary contributions from member states (Silva 1997: 6). Relevantly, the CPLP only managed to occupy its head office – a building in Lisbon, ceded by the Portuguese Foreign Office – two weeks short of the first anniversary

[15] If we substitute 'Portugal' for 'Brazil' in this argument, we find that a similar position is shared by prominent (if in the minority) Brazilian diplomats, writers, and academics. The most visible face of this informal group, Aparecido de Oliveira, already spoke of the need

to reformat the whole project as early as February 1998 (Oliveira 1998: 20). For the purposes of this specific paper we will devote greater attention to the Portuguese version of the argument.

[16] The suggestion has been made that in fact Soares was behind the whole project from the start, yet he 'used' Brazil as a vehicle to present it, as if by procuration (Cahen 1997: 398).

[17] On this matter, another academic would write that fashionable constructions like the numerous triangular variants (Portugal-Brazil-Africa, Portugal-US-Africa, Portugal-EU-Africa) often run into 'reality': 'the problem with these builders of strategic triangles is that they seldom know what those situated at the other extremities really think' (Soares, A. 1997: 22).

[18] See Dias's strategic consideration on Portugal's need to safeguard its own sovereignty through an overseas extension: 'As it once was, we will not find in Europe a basis for our freedom and prosperity' (1998: 22).

[19] As was the case in October 1997 when Eduardo dos Santos ostensibly delayed (for half an hour) a meeting with the Portuguese Prime Minister, António Guterres, who was on a scheduled official visit to Luanda (Madrinha 1997: 2).

6: What good is Portugal to an African?

Michel Cahen

In addition to studying Portuguese-African relations, it is also useful to try and see the image and impressions Portugal conveys to the leaders and citizens of the PALOP (Países africanos de língua oficial portuguesa – African countries whose official language is Portuguese). To explore this topic fully would require serious groundwork dependent on the country, the place, and the social/religious/ethnic environment, as well as the particular historical development each has undergone: the present attitude towards the former colonizer obviously depends not only on the experiences lived through at the time of colonization (notably the late colonization of the 1960s and 1970s), but also the ways in which the present political leaderships have manipulated them. Quite clearly we shall not be venturing that far in this paper, but merely seeking to point out the major tendencies. We shall therefore be considering each of the PALOP countries, with an occasional incursion into the heart of 'metropolitan' Portugal itself, placing the main emphasis on Angola, since this is the country where the present situation is most tragic and it is absolutely imperative that we spend most time commenting upon it.

The first element to discuss, if only to set it aside as not being the main thrust of this analysis, is the economic dimension: obviously commercial and financial relationships heavily influence the way Africans (in particular the ruling classes) view Portugal.

Africa is not Brazil

From this point of view, there is a striking contrast between the relationships between Portugal and Brazil and Portugal and Africa. For a long time throughout the twentieth-entury, the former were maintained at a very low level, as if the numerous family ties and the common language scarcely had any effect on trade and direct investment. But, over the last ten years, the internationalization of the Brazilian economy, along with privatization and the age of multimedia which makes language (and therefore the common language) a commodity, have all begun to cause trading relations and bilateral direct investment to take off. It is a little too soon to know whether this improvement will continue to produce stability of growth, but for a decade now it has been very real (Silva 1999). Besides, it is clear that the common language has not been the source of the phenomenon and neither Portugal nor Brazil are the main direct investor in each other's country nor their key business partner, far from it. The real root is liberalization and privatization in both countries allowing for the international globalization of their economies. But on this basis, either by happy coincidence or the 'comparative advantage' open to the people of both countries, their common language and all the myths attached to it have managed to play a role in convincing both investors and traders alike.

Nevertheless, certain processes have taken place in Africa that can in principle allow comparison – at least in some sectors – starting in 1985 and accelerating after 1990. And yet, the importance of the PALOP (and even Africa in general) in Portuguese foreign trade remains disappointingly marginal – even in the best years, it hovers around the 2 per cent mark of total imports-exports (Cahen 2001a):

Table 6.1:
Position of PALOPs in Portuguese exports and imports, 1973-98 (%)

	Exports	Imports
1973	14.6	9.7
1975	8.2	4.8
1977	6.5	1.1
1979	5.1	0.9
1981	7.6	0.4
1983	4.4	0.5
1985	3.9	1.2
1987	2.0	0.4
1989	3.4	0.4
1991	4.2	0.5
1993	3.1	0.1
1995	2.8	0.2
1997	2.9	0.3
1998	2.6	0.2
1999	2.3	0.18

Source: Banco de Portugal, *Evolução das economias dos PALOP, 1996-97*, Lisbon, September 1997, p. 163; *Evolução das economias dos PALOP,* 1999-2000, http://www.bportugal.pt/

The relative values are obviously going to vary depending on the country – Cape Verde for example has a disproportionate status within Portugal's trade with Africa, in terms of its GNP – and this general weakness stems from the state of permanent crisis of the African economies. These factors, however, ought to be evenly balanced between all the western countries in their trade with Africa: yet western countries outstrip Portugal, by a wide margin, in their commercial trade with the PALOPs.

Table 6.2:
Position of Portugal in PALOPs foreign trade, 1990-97 (%)

	Exports	Imports
Angola	1.1	23.7
Guinea-Bissau	8.2	35.5
Cape Verde	72.4	39.9
Mozambique	8.6	6.4
São Tomé and Príncipe	4.4	34.7

Source: Banco de Portugal, *Evolução das economias dos PALOP, 1999-2000*, http://www.bportugal.pt/

This can be seen much more starkly when one examines commercial trade, this time as a share of foreign trade with other African countries: Portugal is only a decisive element in the case of Cape Verde (Dias 1996). It is interesting to note that imports from Portugal nearly always outweigh exports to Portugal (except Mozambique[1]): this reflects the 'sociological' weight of the importation of consumer goods by the Portuguese-influenced elite (wines, fabrics, etc.), often transacted by Portuguese traders on the ground.

Spain and France, however, are just as much ahead of Portugal in terms of exports from Angola (2.3 per cent and 5.0 per cent respectively) – not to mention the US (61.9 per cent). Spain (19.1 per cent), South Africa (16.8 per cent) and Japan (9.4 per cent) are equally ahead of Portugal in exports when one looks at Mozambique. And one should not be surprised to learn that the principal destination of exports from Guinea-Bissau, not just in one year, but on average throughout all the years of 1990-1999, is India (82.5 per cent, due clearly to the boom in cashew nuts exported whole without local shelling[2]). Contrary to what one might imagine, given the new 'Francophone' allegiance of Guinea-Bissau, France (1.1 per cent) lags far behind Portugal and its position hardly seems credible.

Portugal, on the other hand, dominates at the level of PALOP imports, for the reasons explained earlier, except for Mozambique, which makes 28.6 per cent of its purchases in South Africa and 6.9 per cent in France. Furthermore, the old coloniser is an important investor in the PALOPs (in particular Cape Verde and Mozambique), which shows that the flow of money doesn't always follow the same routes as trading relations.

Naturally, it is important to compare like with like, and Portuguese investment capacity will always stay lower than that of the United States or even France. But these countries do not invest in the PALOPs alone, whereas Portugal is virtually absent from the rest of Africa (with the exception of South Africa): at least in the *Cinco* (the 'Five'), Portugal could be much more influential than the more powerful countries. It is all very well and good for a certain cosiness to exist or a reluctance on the part of Portugal to take risks in unstable countries: might this be a case of typical banking behaviour, or alternatively short-term trading habits, rather than just traditional Portuguese capitalism at work? There is also no doubt that, despite diplomatic pleasantries, a certain opposition continues to exist on the part of governments and African administrators in charge of affairs within the PALOPs towards investment and trade from the very country which was formerly the coloniser and is still not seen as just 'one of the rest'.

In spite of everything, these obstacles clearly strain the image and standing of Portugal within the politics of the PALOPs. It is also true that one must guard against being economical in one's analysis of Afro-Portuguese relations: if so, one will fail to understand their still passionate and often controversial aspects.

'African of Portuguese expression' did I hear you say?

From the above perspective, we should begin with a very simple observation, namely the title which the new States emerging from Portuguese colonization have adopted for themselves: PALOP, African Countries whose Official Language is Portuguese. Not much attention is attached to the phrase in Portugal, nor even in France, where people shamelessly use the absurd formula 'African countries of French expression'. The nationalists who, in 1975, took over power in the *Cinco*, wished to show that their choice of the Portuguese language as the official language of the state did not mean that it had become a national language, merely a linguistic tool for national unity when confronted with a context in which the diversity of ethnic cultures was often seen as tribalism. 'Decolonising the colonial language', they certainly used Portuguese, but only as a form of *African* expression. Now of course one can, and one must, analyse in a critical manner this 'paradoxical nationalism' (Cahen 2001b; Chabal 1996), which produced a very strong non-Portuguese mode of expression but which, in practice, has done more for the dissemination of Portuguese in Africa than 'five centuries of Portuguese colonization'. The fact remains that, at the level of political definition, they wished to use the most neutral formula possible at the level of lusophone identity: *the minimal*.

This is also very important for an understanding, very often simplistic or muddled, of what constitutes 'Lusophone'. The fate of spoken Portuguese does not lie in Portugal, nor in Brazil, but in Africa as well as marginally – if only of symbolic importance – in Asia (especially Timor Loro Sae[3]). In fact the concept of '-phone' (be it Anglo-, Franco-, Hispano-, Luso-, etc.) is a catch-all phrase, which, in a prejudicial way, mixes together the very different *social statuses* of the language and communities involved.

There is hardly any sense in saying that a French person is francophone, precisely because French is the mother tongue that gives him or her, his or her identity. On the other hand, one is franco*phone* if one 'hears' and 'understands' French and is capable of using it as a *tool* in one's daily life. This is the case of many Africans. But French is not their language of identity; it does not have anything to do with their main social identity. All too often one confuses the social statuses of a language and includes, from a perspective of power, the States who 'share the use of French' (according to the standard official formula) and one ends up under-estimating those comunities which are actually 'French-speaking' in terms of their mother tongue, since they carry with them neither a supporting voice at the UN nor juicy contracts: it is fine to train the presidential guard of such and such an African head of state ('on the road to democracy' of course), yet for the very same price there is nobody prepared to create a French university for the Manitobans of Winnipeg or the Cajuns of Louisiana who could well do with fortifying their French identity amidst an ocean of English-speakers (Cahen 1998).

There are therefore francophone and lusophone Africans, but that does not define in any way a sphere of linguistic identity: the notion of a 'cultural zone', which infallibly is measured merely by the colonial language ('francophone Africa', 'lusophone Africa', etc.) to the detriment of otherwise vibrant languages ('bantu-phone Africa'), should not be rejected if it is conceived as a relatively secondary pallette where available identities can be mixed. The 'language as means', or 'second language', is only one of the multiple palettes of identity still in play and certainly not the main one, as is the case in traditional linguistic heartlands.

Consequently the lusophone world (just as the francophone and anglophone ones) cannot be defined nor regarded by Africans as a community of language identity, they can only energetically refute the formula used so tellingly by Fernando Pessoa: *a língua é a minha pátria* (my language is my country), which, quoted out of context, makes 'Portuguese-speaking' (*lusofonia*) an extension of 'Portugueseness' (*lusitanidade*).

In fact the PALOPs are only minimally lusophone – even under the very restrictive definition I have given the various '*phonenesses*'. In Mozambique, 1.23 per cent of inhabitants had Portuguese as their mother tongue (and hence identity) in 1980; in 1997, at the time of the second census, this percentage had risen to 6.2, whereas 8.9 per cent of Mozambicans declared having Portuguese as 'the main language spoken at home', and 32.5 per cent declared they could 'understand' it (but at what level?). In the case of Angola, we don't have equivalent statistics but it is very likely that the penetration of the Portuguese language is stronger, expressing the stronger historical presence of assimilated and Creole groupings. In Cape Verde, Guinea-Bissau and São Tomé and Principe, it is infinitely weaker and practically nobody speaks Portuguese due to the extent of the 'luso-creoles'. But on the other hand, it cannot be denied that Portuguese-rooted Creoles maintain a solid relationship with Portuguese and contribute to their 'tuning in' to Brazilian and Portuguese media broadcasts.

These reservations and nuances do not mean, however, that the Portuguese language, and all the other aspects bequeathed by the history of the Luso-Brazilian expansion, have no influence on identity: Lusophonie must thus be defined not primarily in terms of Portuguese language, but rather as a 'specific area of intersection with other identities'.[4]

The contradictions of Portuguese-speaking African nationalism

One must, nevertheless, point out the contradictions in African nationalism for, despite their insistence on 'non-Portugueseness' and their own deep reservations about the concept of lusophonie, the PALOP elites have done more in 25 years of independence for the linguistic 'Portuguese-ization' of their countries than Portugal in 'five centuries of colonization'. The states they have created are totally Portuguese in their written language even if they are hardly at all Portuguese in their spoken language. In particular, with the exception of certain pilot projects, they have refused to teach the primary school years in the mother tongue, precisely when the mechanisms of literacy are acquired – with the self-same aim later on of learning Portuguese more thoroughly. The fact is that, somehow, their image of modernity and of nationhood is rooted in Portuguese, in concrete and in town.

But with this very contradiction in mind, it is quite understandable that the ideology that presided over the creation of the CPLP (Community of Portuguese Language Countries) on 27 July 1996 in Lisbon, has merely succeeded in upsetting the Africans: how could they accept the speech of Mario Soares or of José Aparecido de Oliveira on the 'common origins', the 'centuries of conviviality' and their 'common blood' (Cahen 1997)?

On the other hand, although the Portuguese speech and the speeches from the Brazilian side – both of which lent authority to the CPLP – were virtually identical, it is curious to note that the African condemnation was specifically directed against Portugal. One can see that the Portuguese position still remains a greater bone of contention than that of Brazil, clearly due to the still recent colonial past.

In fact, the ideological burden of the CPLP has been heavy: don't forget, the CPLP was not 'created' in Lisbon, but simply 'institutionalized', as if it 'had always existed', 'naturally', in the name of the so-called 'common origins' and, dare we say it, 'blood' as well. Therefore, what has been created is not an 'organization of states where Portuguese is the official language', just as other state organizations exist, but a 'Community'; and not a state community, but one of 'countries'; and not a 'community where Portuguese is the official language' but 'of the Portuguese language', full stop. So, Marcelino Moco, the first Secretary General of the institution, was well disposed to turn this ideological position in favour of the Africans and say that at the heart of the 'community', visas should be abandoned, free circulation assured, even a common passport issued. In the age of Schengen...

It is clear that a yawning gap has quickly opened up between the limited sphere of action of such a community and the ideological burden it has to bear on its baptismal foundations. This has obscured the fact that, for the PALOPs, the CPLP was an instrumental body, just one more mechanism amongst many others for international cooperation, exactly like the integration of Guinea-Bissau and Cape Verde into the Francophonie and Mozambique into the Commonwealth.

I think myself – and this is a personal conjecture – that this ideological burden has put in danger the acceptance of the CPLP by the PALOPs – along with other factors to which I shall return later. They could not obviously accept those speeches about 'common origins' and 'common culture', etc. But this emphasised above all the 'internal problems' of the PALOPs, for behind the CPLP, it wasn't so much the Portuguese-speaking world that was at stake, but the relationship with Portugal itself. Now this also singled out from amongst the PALOP peoples certain minorities suspected of being 'more Portuguese', those whom I would generally describe as 'Creoles', whatever the colour (white, mixed, or black) of their skin. I mean exactly that when I say 'it singled them out', and not that they themselves felt implicated.

But the debate on the CPLP and Portugal has also contaminated the discussion on identity, on being Angolan or Mozambican as opposed to African, or on being a Creole suspected of being a foreigner, as against being African. The situation has nevertheless been quite different depending on the countries involved and, before discussing in depth the Angolan case, we must examine the individual cases of each of the other PALOP countries.

Far-off Mozambique

In Mozambique, the debate on the CPLP and the speaking of Portuguese is not much of an issue, which does not mean that the Portuguese language is in danger. It remains an important means of self-definition for Mozambique, which hardly enters into each person's identity, but rightly defines that specific area of intersection with other identities. Mozambique is without a doubt, due to the very weakness of penetration of the Portuguese language, a good example not of Lusophonie but of 'Portuguese heritage' (*lusotopie*), a place fashioned by the history of the Portuguese expansion no matter what its 'speech'.

But in Mozambique, the tensions surrounding the notion of Creole identity are much lower than in Angola, since those who could claim to be Creole, namely those who genuinely have a Portuguese mother-tongue culture, never describe themselves as such – they see it only from the standpoint of a total all-embracing 'nation' with no residual Bantu ethnicity (that does not rule out, of course, secret ethno-clientelist behaviours) (Cahen 1994). The mixed groups themselves have since colonial times always been less numerous than in Angola, and also more regionally dispersed (Maputo, compared with Luanda, is not the densest mixed-race area in Mozambique).

Guinea-Bissau or 'intermediary Creole identity' as shown by the war.

Guinea-Bissau is not a Creole nation, unlike Cape Verde or São Tomé and Principe, but a country where the Creole language is spoken by roughly one-third of the population and no doubt understood by two-thirds. The internal situation of the country has hardly permitted a true debate to develop on Creole identity.

Certainly, when need be, president 'Nino' Vieira would allow anti-*burmedju*[5] feelings free rein, but that was never allowed to go so far as overt racism, which would have been to officially deny Amílcar Cabral, a racism that had no mass society basis.

Clearly, Nino Vieira was let down by Portugal when he requested the monetary integration of the peso into the Portuguese escudo zone – something that Portugal did do in 1998 for the Cape Verdean escudo. Nino, as we know, went to call on France who received him without too much fuss. The commercial ties of Guinea-Bissau with Portugal, especially on the level of imports, remained strong however. It is quite evident that Portugal has a specific interest in Guinea-Bissau: a small country marooned in an ocean of French-speakers, looked upon from above by Senegal (even before the 1998 war), its ties with Portugal serve to maintain the political identity of the state and the country (but not the ethnic identity).

This has been illustrated to a certain extent by the recent war: the entry of the Senegalese has swung the population, originally in favour of a wait-and-see policy, towards the side of the rebels of Ansumane Mané, for Senegal was associated with the social problems stemming from the country's entry into the CFA franc zone – inflation, competition from Senegalese traders, etc. The attitude of France itself has done the rest and one should not be surprised if this kind of francophone politics has led straight to the burning down of the French cultural centre in Bissau. But we should not rewrite history any further and see two distinct camps: in reality, the French and Portuguese governments have maintained Nino Vieira for years, closing their eyes to nepotism, corruption, violations of the constitution and have done so for as long as they felt they could get away with it.

But the fact remains that the Portuguese media and public opinion very quickly took the side of the rebels. The Portuguese motives for this were twofold:

On the one hand, the rebellion – initially a simple internal crisis for the PAIGC – was seen as a means of getting rid of a long-discredited President. *This represents the democratic tendency of pro-rebel sympathy within Portuguese public opinion;*

On the other hand, very rapidly and indissociably linked, there appeared the notion of Nino Vieira as the 'pillar of francophonie'—this was ostensibly 'proved' by his request for Senegalese military intervention—whereas the rebels defended the 'Portugueseness' of Guinea-Bissau. Articles even appeared presenting the MFDC (Democratic Forces Movement of Casamance)[6] as a movement of resistance against French-speaking Senegal, lamenting the good old days when Zinguinchor was Portuguese! *This represented the Portuguese-nationalist tendency,* emerging very rapidly from the 'defence of democracy'. The same Portuguese press that buzzed with sympathy for the defence of Portuguese-speaking Bissau or even Casamance, paid little attention however to the fact that Ansumane Mané, chief of the insurgents, did not after 'five centuries of colonization' even know any Portuguese.

The fact remains that, with France having sustained Nino Vieira beyond the limits of the possible, this 'Portuguese-Guinea complex' objectively served to reaffirm the political identity of the Guinean State. In the longer term, one might nevertheless think that French will continue to make inroads into Guinea-Bissau, notably in the public services, which from now on will benefit from French plans for training. But that would not mean automatically that Portuguese is going to die out. Portugal will still remain a resource for Guinean political identity.[7]

Portuguese Cape Verde?

Cape Verde, albeit as 'French-speaking' as Guinea-Bissau, has taken much clearer strategic choices. Not only have the MpD, like the PAICV,[8] maintained their teaching of basic literacy in the Portuguese language when the relative linguistic unity of Creole would have greatly facilitated doing so in the mother tongue, but also the present tendency is towards an unprecedented tightening of ties with Portugal. This is illustrated particularly by economic and financial policy. On 17 March 1998, the Cape Verdean currency was to all intents and purposes 'pegged' to the Portuguese escudo (itself integrated within the Euro from 1 January 1999 onwards). This linkage produced a liberalization of the flow of capital, merchandise and goods of all types and the lifting of limits on currency outflows. With the backing of the Portuguese escudo, there is quite obviously an organic link to the Euro's future from 2002, but this link will still be subject to the guarantee of the Portuguese Treasury. Mario Soares' old dream of according the Cape Verde Islands the same status as that given by the EU to the French DOM-TOM ('Ultra-peripheral European Regions') will in this way be broadly realized. The other aspect to this choice of direction concerns the privatization of Cape Verdean public enterprise. It is quite evident that these have mainly benefited Portugal which has developed a real 'leverage' when it comes to tendering, often offering four times as much as its competitors in order to win bids, an even greater political pressure than that generally coming from public Portuguese enterprise (Caixa Geral de Depósitos, etc.). In at least one case – the privatization of CV Telecom – it brought about a political crisis. In effect, the Cape Verdean telecom company was handed over to Portugal lock, stock and barrel, both the telephone end as well as the Internet, which means nowadays that the whole of the country's telecommunications network depends entirely on an outside country. Several members of the MpD rejected it and three ministers were dismissed.

It is absolutely clear that the Cape Verde government had realized that, as far as it was concerned, Portugal was the safest and most practicable way into Europe. From a Portuguese perspective, however, this is the exception that proves the rule: in fact, in all other cases, the Portuguese attempts to 'sell' Lisbon to the EU as the 'Gateway to Africa' failed completely, merely because any company in France, Britain, Italy, or any country come to that, have absolutely no need whatsoever to go 'through' Lisbon in order to invest in Angola or Mozambique. From the Cape Verdean viewpoint, it is worth noting that the real objective is Europe, not Portugal: Portugal is merely the price to be paid for getting into Europe. In fact even in 2002 when the Euro became the general currency, there was be no 'Euro zone' in Africa – at least not immediately – since that would imply bringing African economies under the financial umbrella of the Central Bank in Frankfurt:

the CFA franc, and now the Cape Verdean escudo, are not considered by the EU as currencies, but rather marginal 'excrescences' of the French and Portuguese Treasuries which merely guarantee their convertibility. Yet the reality of that conversion is still the Euro.

Cape Verde is therefore structurally dependent on Portugal, and therefore indirectly to Europe. It is a choice of long-term economic policy, but it is also a complete cultural split with the Africanist tradition of the PAICV, the PAIGC and Amilcar Cabral.

Implacable Angola

Angola represents a far more complex, sad and shameful situation, whichever way one tries to look at things.[9] As was already mentioned, the link with Portugal and, by extension, to the CPLP, directly challenges the identity of the former Angolan Creole elites or, at any rate, called their identity into question from the perspective of the debate on Angolan identity versus African identity, or put more crudely on the difference between *filhos de português* (descendents of Portuguese) versus *genuinidade* (indigenous natives, authenticity). But all these debates and all these values which are also worthy of serious discussion, are *extremely manipulated*, and *strategically exploited*.

In fact, for quite different reasons, there is an endless stream of criticism issuing from Angola against Portugal, whether it be from the MPLA camp or UNITA,[10] as if every one were against Portugal, *as if something important were at stake for Angola*.

Now, if Angola is very important to Portugal, Portugal is not in the least important to Angola. How then are we to explain all this criticism, instead of what should be merely polite indifference? Well, one must distinguish between what happens at a government level and what happens at the level of society.

Portugal 'with Angola'
The Bicesse process had been entirely orchestrated by the United States who were counting on a UNITA victory (seen at the time as the 'champion of democracy'), but negotiations had been well received in Portugal which had developed an active political presence. Consequently, after the process stalled, the three countries that made up the 'troika' (the US, Portugal and Russia) went over to giving military support to the MPLA government, and presented the sanctions against UNITA as having the aim of 'encouraging dialogue'. Also, in 1998, the political opposition to the UNITA war was quite visible when it broke off all contacts with the troika accusing it of partiality. Nevertheless during the whole of 1999 and even the beginning of 2000, the arguing did not stop between Portugal and the MPLA government, the latter demanding again and again a full alignment by Portugal with its own position. *Now Portugal has always taken the line of showing that it was 'on the Angolan side', and in practice that was translated as "on the Angolan government side", something increasingly out of step with the Angolan civilian population which demanded peace and dialogue.* The root of the problem is that Portugal is obsessed with selling

to Europe its role within Africa as a 'gateway'. Obviously, the Cape Verde case isn't sufficient for that and the strategic Portuguese axis therefore passes through Angola. A consensus exists within the Portuguese 'central block' (PS-PSD) on this issue.

In a way, the more odious the Angolan government became the more Portugal wanted to show it was with them. UNITA summed up this astonishing attitude saying: 'Russia wishes to reduce Angola's debt by selling it new arms;[11] the US wants Angola's oil. And Portugal wants to be humiliated.' I do not share this punchy line from UNITA, but there remains no doubt that the basic result of the Portuguese attitude until fairly recently has been an almost total and humiliating alignment with the Angolan position.

So there we have it, everybody arms the Angolan government, but nobody says so, except Portugal who often says so to show 'it is on the Angolan side'. Portugal trains the Angolan commandos, just as the Spanish Civil Guard trained the military police *ninjas*. Almeida Santos (president of the Assembly) visited Angola unofficially in 1999 and returned saying that 'there was no other *solution* for the war' [my emphasis], at the same moment the Catholic Church demanded further negotiations. Durrão Barboso was more moderate in his expressions, but he did not deny that 'there are moments when war is inevitable'.

This very clearly compliant attitude of the Portuguese towards the Angolan government is turned more and more to the latter's own advantage. In January 2000, the total Angolan public and commercial debt with Portugal was US$1.5bn: almost all Portuguese journeys to Angola have this issue as their main agenda, yet the envoys return financially empty-handed and politically compliant. Even though part of the debt is covered by oil, Angola often suspends its output, as it did at the end of 1998.

In fact, Portugal falls in perfectly with the Angolan government's plan, deeply set in concrete in the Futungo,[12] of not letting itself be outdone by France, Spain or the US, in order to continue to make a credible selling point within the EU of its role as 'European gateway to Africa'.

The paralysis of public opinion

In Portugal itself, the only entity to question this compliance – apart from the pro-UNITA lobbies – was the courageous stand by the Portuguese daily, the *Público*. For a long while it stood alone. When the report of Global Witness, *A crude awakening*, came out describing item by item the cleptocracy of the nomenclaturist Angolan power, for three days the *Jornal de Notícias* said nothing, and the *Diário de Notícias* said nothing also. They only began to do so when Paulo Portas, leader of the Partido Popular, at the time the party of the Portuguese right in favour of UNITA, began to ask questions. The Portuguese Secretary of State for Cooperation then said: 'We are not going to change our policy merely because a report on corruption is published'.

In fact, be it at government level or in the media, Angolan questions are treated as Portuguese domestic political issues, a situation nurtured even more by the hundred and one personal links maintained for example by former leaders of the MFA[13] who also maintain private dealings with Angola (Rosa Coutinho, Pezzarat Correia...).

Nevertheless, there is one frontier that Portuguese diplomacy has never dared to cross, and one that merits Angolan scorn. President Eduardo dos Santos effectively dubbed Jonas Savimbi a war criminal and, as a consequence no agreement with UNITA was made possible or legal. But since at the same time he had to show that the 'process of peace was continuing', he fabricated his own UNITA with very little dissidence, the UNITA-Renovada. Now the fact is Portugal did not recognise UNITA-R nor declare that Jonas Savimbi was a war criminal – unlike Brazil, the People's Republic of China, the CPLP, the SADC[14] or the OAU. The UN didn't either: but since the only concrete action it is authorized to carry out is the imposing of sanctions against UNITA, it all comes down to the same thing. The Fowler Report by the Sanctions Committee even called for sanctions against political support for UNITA: will the next step be the sanctioning of Paulo Portas?

This Portuguese attitude of compliance – not total, as one can see, but strong nevertheless – has been matched by a paralysis of Portuguese public opinion. This is in total contrast to the attitude held by the same public opinion at the time of the Timor Loro Sa'e (East Timor) affair. The two wars were taking place at the same time; there were far more deaths and famine in Angola, but everybody kept mum. It is clear that if Angola produces governmental acquiescence, it does not on the other hand provoke a consensus of public opinion. And that is exactly why things began to shift at the end of 1999.

Creole identity: 'son of a colonist' or 'anti-Portuguese'?

But before analysing this glimpse of a change in Portugal, one must return to Angolan society itself. It is racked by debates which all overlap without really influencing each other. So it is that, on the FNLA[15] and UNITA side (even today), they oppose the *genuinos* and the *filhos de colonos* (they avoid saying white or mixed race). But quite obviously, the MPLA does not define itself as the party of the 'children of Portugal', therefore it is reproached for another form of highly political affiliation: 'Portugal has handed power over to the MPLA'.

Nevertheless, from the standpoint of *MPLA society* – the social milieus who to a greater or lesser extent recognise themselves in it and live within its domain – the former truly assimilated people, the former truly Creole people are politically the *Argelinos* ('Algerians', because of their long stay in that country during the war of liberation) and these have always been violently anti-Portuguese! They despise Portugal and would have preferred to be colonized by others! So those whom the FNLA and UNITA stigmatise as being 'children of the Portuguese' are the most anti-Portuguese, so much so, that they prefer the US – whose great-grandparents at the end of the nineteenth-century also called for a change of coloniser.

These are *not* only words. These former Creoles were amongst the few and the very last to take up a Portuguese passport, whereas there were many amongst the black *nomenklatura* who privately took up such a passport.

So, on an identity level, those who claim Angolan identity over an African one and consequently are stigmatized as children of colonists or the quartermasters of Portugal are actually the most anti-Portuguese. The result is a confused compartmentalization of opinion, so much so that often a *genuino* party (like the residual FNLA) collaborates against the MPLA, with a very *claro* (fair/mixed-race) party (like the FpD), distant heirs to the OCA![16]

So when Filomeno Vieira Lopes (the FpD's 'Filó') was arrested, there was immediately a general outcry in Lisbon and, whether it was the PS (Socialist Party) or the Bloco de Esquerda[17] (Left Bloc), the entire old OCA network went into action! He was released in a matter of hours.

Portuguese civilian society and Angolan state strategy

In Portugal, after the courageous but solitary stand taken by the *Público*, what began to unlock the situation was the systematic intervention of the Bloco de Esquerda in parliament – especially during the incident involving the arrest of the journalist Rafael Marques[18] and then when Mario Soares was accused by the Angolan powers of being an ivory trafficker! At the vote on the BE motion, the Socialist Party and Social-Democratic Party abstained at the first reading while the Portuguese Communist Party left the chamber! Even so to refuse to defend an imprisoned journalist and the honour of the former (socialist) president of the Republic was bad style and a fortnight later a watered-down motion was voted through. But Angola was wild with rage.

Wild with rage also when Mario Soares, now in the European parliament,[19] succeeded in getting a laudible motion passed on the freedom of the press. The Angolan government then unleashed its venom, declaring Mario Soares and his son João Soares amongst the principal beneficiaries of diamond and ivory trafficking. The Portuguese government did nothing and didn't even summon the Angolan ambassador. But in response the Portuguese newspapers did react and it was no longer just the *Público*. The question was: 'But what is this regime doing making such accusations against such a person and how come our government doesn't respond?' The Left Bloc proposed a motion, which, amended by the PS, was voted through.

And so the Angolan debate on the Portuguese side begins to be 'civil'-ized (in the sense of becoming a question for 'civil'-ian society). This tends no longer to be 'whose side are we on?', but 'what's the problem with Angola?' and 'what is Portugal's policy regarding this problem?' The turning point is far from being reached, but there are now signs, such as recent developments surrounding the Elf scandal,[20] the failed boycott of the OAU summit in Togo,[21] as well as the holding in Luanda itself of a congress for peace in July 2000 at the initiative of the Episcopal Conference of Angola in the presence of the community of Santo Egidio,[22] that can only nudge things in that direction.

On the Angolan side, opinion has much less ease of expression and it is the Catholic Church, which is leading the fight against a war it has officially described as illegitimate. But in addition to repression, there is also the fact that the Angolan government strategically controls all aspects of the links with Portugal, including the CPLP. Its aim is an analogous position to that of Sierra Leone, a country where the RUF also has diamonds. It is all a question of taking the war into the courtroom, dragging Savimbi to the International Court of Justice, at the same time as getting UNITA-R recognized as a valid interlocutor.

This strategic vision is further illustrated by the following episode: amongst the stumbling blocks and reservations in Africa at the time of the creation of the CPLP, which I pointed out at the beginning of this paper, there is one that has not yet been mentioned: the former minister Durrão Barroso recently revealed that Angola and another African country (probably São Tomé and Principe) did not want the CPLP while Mário Soares was president of the Portuguese Republic. This shows that, in its dealings with other countries, and even more so with Portugal, Angola has no state-to-state relations, merely ally-to-ally.

★★★

One can clearly see, when we consider Cape Verde's strategic choice of Portugal as its European partner; Guinea-Bissau's 'Portuguese leveraging'; São Tomé's skilful equidistancing of itself between France and Portugal, Gabon and Angola; Mozambique's polite self-distancing; and Angola's relationship tightly determined by war, that the PALOPs as they are today present quite different agendas from Portugal.

From the perspective of a geopolitical grouping, 'Portuguese-speaking Africa' does not really exist. But, make no mistake about it, there are many things that only exist in the imagination and yet are talked about for thousands of years.

Notes:

* Paris, 18-19 May and 31 August 2000. I would like to thank Christine Messiant for her contribution to my reflections on Angola.

[1] We should not be fooled into viewing the apparently 'strong' Cape Verdean percentage in absolute terms, especially as it is a fairly weak export figure overall.

[2] The incredibly low labour costs of Indian women make it (financially) less costly to export cashews in their unprocessed form than to shell them locally. This is an even more controversial issue in Mozambique where local processing is the subject of an intense hostile argument with the World Bank. The latter has since 'presented its apologies' for the error, but nobody knows whether it has paid out any damages for the bankrupcy of the processing factories specifically set up for this purpose in Mozambique.

[3] There is every reason to believe that the Portuguese language has no more of a future in Macao than it had in Goa after 1961. Even if numerous Portuguese works and even Atlases persist in colouring in the state of Goa on pretty maps as 'Portuguese-speaking' on a par with Portugal and Brazil, it is time to take cognisance of the fact that *absolutely nobody* speaks Portuguese in every-day life in Panaji (nor in the surrounding countryside) and that there are more students of German than Portuguese at Goa university. That does not mean to say that Portugal is absent: it remains visible at every turn (in the names of streets and businesses, the names of people, architecture, a Catholic minority stronger than anywhere else) and the Goans themselves say quite openly in Konkani or in English: 'The Portuguese people were nice, the political system was bad'. Panaji-Goa is the typical example of a non-Portuguese-speaking 'Lusotopia'. In contrast, there are still Portuguese-Creoles in Malacca, Flores and Sri Lanka. The fact is the Portuguese-Creole language there possesses a social identity, which is not the case in Macao apart from among very rare mixed-race families (the Macanists, as distinguished from the general Macanese).

[4] As you will have noticed, in this context I fully support the analysis of Eduardo Lourenço, or indeed that recently expressed by Tabbuchi.

[5] *Burmedju*, in Creole, *vermelho* (red) in Portuguese, refers to 'red skin' i.e. mixed race. But the word has more of a socio-cultural than 'racial' connotation and a Black can perfectly well be *burmedju*.

[6] MFDC: Democratic Forces Movement of Casamance, a rebel movement who fight for the independence of Casamance from Senegal, and whose fighters often seek refuge in Guinea-Bissau.

[7] The comparison often made with the Philippines, rapidly de-Hispanized after the Hispano-American war, is not in my opinion valid: having Spanish or English as a dominant colonial language changed nothing for Philippine identity within the larger context of a South-East Asia divided into various colonial zones (British, Dutch, French, Portuguese).

[8] The MpD (Movement for Democracy) defeated the PAICV (African Party for Cape Verdean Independence), the former single party, after the elections of 1991.

[9] Editor's note: please bear in mind that this article was written before the military defeat

of Unita and the death of Jonas Savimbi.

[10] MPLA, Popular Movement for the Liberation of Angola, the former single party still in power; UNITA, National Union for the Total Independence of Angola, the rebel movement for a long time supported by South Africa.

[11] The Angolan debt with Russia is six billion dollars!

[12] The Futungo is the presidential residence where all the real power is concentrated.

[13] The Armed Forces Movement that ousted the Portuguese dictatorship on 25 April 1974.

[14] The Southern African Development Conference, which brings together all the countries of Southern Africa.

[15] FNLA, National Front for the Liberation of Angola, ally of Zaire and the US at the time of the first civil war of 1975-1977. The FNLA mainly recruited amongst the bacongo tribes of Northern Angola and developed a violent political diatribe against the 'mixed races' and the 'children of colonists' of the MPLA. Militarily defeated, it has since been reintegrated into Angolan political life. It is today a small party with a few deputies.

[16] FpD, Front for Democracy, a small party formed especially from escapees of the OCA, the Angolan communist organization, pro-Albanian Maoist group destroyed in 1977. The OCA certainly had black militants, but also numerous mixed-race and white.

[17] The Bloco de Esquerda is a small extreme-left coalition that gained two deputies in the 1998 Portuguese legislative elections. If its direct political voice is restricted, it has an undeniable influence on the left as a whole, as well as in the parliament.

[18] Rafael Marques is an Angolan journalist who was imprisoned for several months after accusing the President of corruption. His case was widely publicized in the media because he is the correspondent in Angola for the *Forum for an Open Society* of the billionaire, George Soros.

[19] He had expected to become president.

[20] The French oil company Elf acknowledged having paid millions of dollars to the Angolan president and to members of his family.

[21] Angola had appealed for the boycotting of this summit, accusing Togo and Burkina Fasso of aiding in the smuggling of UNITA diamonds.

[22] The community of Santo Egidio steered the negotiations that led to peace in Mozambique. It represents the secular arm of Vatican diplomacy.

7: Portugal's lusophone African immigrants: colonial legacy in a contemporary labour market

Martin Eaton[*]

Migratory movement of people has been a fundamental component of Portuguese society for hundreds of years. Traditionally, therefore, the international movements of both the country's domestic and foreign populations have shaped the economy of the country. During the 1980s and 1990s, in particular, Portugal moved from a country associated with emigration to one typified by immigration (Céu Esteves 1991; Rocha-Trindade 1995; Guibentif 1996). This shift in the migration pattern has had profound impacts resulting in the emergence of a new spatial division of labour. Dual labour markets have developed covering the formal and informal sectors of economic activity, and both are increasingly fuelled by the employment of foreign, and particularly, ex-colonial, often Portuguese-speaking, immigrant workers.

At the end of 1999, Portugal's legally resident foreign community numbered almost 191,000, representing an estimated 2 per cent share of the national population.[1] However, the 'real' figure is believed to be much higher given the largely undocumented prevalence of illegal immigrants now living in the country. Foreign workers entering Portugal reflect a mixture of ethnically and culturally diverse peoples, and yet at the same time, many possess a strong post-colonial dimension (Dupraz 1999). They include relatively large groups of lusophone-Africans, South Americans, and Asians, as well as more recently, North and East Europeans. Many are engaged in jobs ranging from the menial in construction and domestic service industries through to skilled employees in financial, education, and medical services, as well as professional sporting activities.

At the same time, relatively little research has been carried out that assesses the contribution made by these *estrangeiros* (foreigners). Methodological penetration of elements that are clandestine is, of course, extremely difficult. Moreover, any examination of members of ethnic communities, even if they are officially registered, can suffer from problems associated with suspicion, fear, and refusal to co-operate. It is not a section of society that lends itself easily to theoretical consideration nor empirical investigation and we should be aware of such limitations and their impact upon this study. Indeed, what follows is largely tentative in its assumptions and designed to stimulate additional research into the twilight economies afforded by the immigrant communities in Portugal.

With these reservations in mind, this chapter, first, introduces the theoretical framework associated with the dual labour market process that is now emerging in this part of southern Europe; second, and by drawing upon published statistical data, it outlines the general nature of Portugal's recent (post-1960) immigration patterns; third, and in conjunction with a renascent literature, it examines the influx of a specific ex-colonial immigrant group; the Lusophone-Africans. Fourth, the article assesses the labour market experiences of selected national groupings by focusing upon Cape Verdean, Guinea-Bissauan, and Mozambican communities, in the light of their contributions to contemporary Portuguese society, before concluding with a discussion of lusophone-Africans' positions upon a conceptual pyramid of socio-economic well being.

Dual labour markets

Immigration patterns into Southern Europe are now characterized by features that bear little resemblance to the traditional guest worker or post-colonial flows of the 1950s, 1960s and 1970s. Baldwin-Edwards (1999) identifies the diverse nationalities and educational attainments, the illegality of entry, the use of recruitment agents and traffickers, the paucity of social and legal rights, and the important role played by the informal economy. New immigration centres have subsequently emerged (in Greece, Italy, Spain, and now Portugal) where the labour market has been shaped (to varying degrees) by the employment of immigrant labour (King et al. 1997). Increased unemployment in Southern Europe since the 1980s has coincided with a general level of reduced investment and attendant recession. In turn, native Southern European populations have often preferred joblessness or longer periods spent in (further and higher) education, rather than collecting low wages in the menial jobs that remained. Consequently, domestic demands for labour grew dramatically in those economic sectors that were characterized by low remuneration and low productivity. Such activities could not realistically raise wage levels because of the danger of them becoming uncompetitive. As a result, the very survival of these Southern European economies has become dependent upon the work of (often illegal and) cheap immigrant labour (Baldwin-Edwards 1999: 3). Moreover, the attraction of a large underground economy capable of supporting immigrants has become one of the main 'pull' factors for many of the newer immigrants now entering Southern Europe, although the 'push' from relative poverty and economic hardship continues to exert an influence.

Within this theoretical context, Portugal offers an interesting case study, not least because spatially segmented labour markets have emerged. Conventionally, labour markets can be divided into two or more segments, and movements between them (because of the temporal and financial costs involved) may be limited. A dual labour market, for example, can be segmented on the basis of skilled and unskilled workers, and spatially divided to a point whereby workers in the latter category are unable to compete for jobs in the former. In Portugal, the labour market is further divided on the basis of legal foreign residents and illegal immigrants being employed in the formal and informal sectors of the economy. The two sectors often exist in parallel, especially in the construction and public works industries. This stems from the increased globalization of Portugal's immigrant markets, the lowering of costs with respect to transport and communications systems, and a series of relatively relaxed border controls at its international airports and land frontiers.

Portuguese migration patterns

The transitory movements of people both into and out of Portugal have been endemic features of the country's demographic settlement patterns. The Portuguese have a long association with emigration and this outward movement continues, albeit on a vastly reduced scale (Baganha 1998a). The diaspora of Portuguese out-migration reached a peak in the final years (1960-1974) of the Salazar/Caetano dictatorships. At that time, many thousands of Portuguese fled austerity and repression at home to make new lives for themselves in Northern Europe. France, Germany and Switzerland were (and still are) their main destinations, and many of those who left Portugal found employment in the lower end of the Euro-destination job markets.

Immigration into Portugal, on the other hand, started to evolve in earnest in the 1960s when state policy on foreigners entering the country was relaxed. This was a time of manpower shortages resulting from economic expansion, domestic development, the previously mentioned intensive out-migration of Portuguese nationals, as well as military requirements stemming from the colonial wars of independence being fought in Africa. The shortfall altered as Lusophone-African immigrants began supporting the physical and economic development of Portugal through the provision of their relatively cheap, but at the same time, highly industrious labour (Machado 1994; 1997). Cape Verdeans, for example, have traditionally entered to fill gaps in the lower end of the Portuguese job market; jobs which the Portuguese themselves refused to undertake (Filho 1996). Many were pushed into emigrating as much by poverty, drought and civil instability at home, as by any heightened sense (or 'pull') of economic opportunity in Portugal, or by any greater affinity with the Portuguese language and culture (Brookshaw 1992; Cahen 1999). This pattern has continued up to the present although the: 'dominance of Cape Verdeans among foreigners from the [former Portuguese speaking African countries, which] was very marked in 1986 (more than 70 per cent), ...had fallen to a little over 50 per cent a decade later' (Corkill and Eaton 1998: 154). Therefore, and while Cape

Verdeans continue to dominate in aggregated terms, their relative influence within the overall immigrant structure in Portugal has waned considerably. Nevertheless, the longer established settlement history of the Cape Verde islanders means that they have a generally higher level of integration. They are racially more assimilated with the white Portuguese population and not as spatially concentrated as other more recent arrivals from Africa who tend to congregate in highly localized areas. Furthermore, the Cape Verdeans have their own *Associações* (community centres), dance halls, restaurants, bars, and nightclubs scattered throughout Lisbon, for example, and are recognized as making a particularly strong contribution to the capital's contemporary cultural landscape.

In the 1970s, however, immigration remained relatively stable and emigration declined dramatically after the Portuguese Revolution took place in 1974. The main movement of persons into Portugal at this time related to a group that did not appear in the official statistics; namely, the growth in numbers of *retornados* (returning Portuguese nationals) (Rule 1996). In the mid-1970s, between 600,000 and 800,000 returnees from the former colonies (mainly Angola, Guinea-Bissau, and Mozambique) were reintegrated into mainstream Portuguese society. Heralded as: 'one of the... unsung achievements of Portugal's precarious infant democracy', (Corkill 1999: 172) large numbers of (poor, and initially, disenchanted) returnees were successfully reassimilated. While there is surprisingly little documented evidence available on this group, many were helped by the government to find work, housing, and in some cases, to set up their own businesses. Moreover, some were helped to re-emigrate and the majority went to seek new lives for themselves in Brazil (Lewis and Williams 1985).

In addition to the *retornados*, significant numbers of Angolan and Mozambican nationals began migrating to Portugal in the late-1970s as each country was engulfed in civil war. Many arrived as refugees, traumatized by their experiences but keen to settle in their former colonial homeland. A large number were enrolled as students who travelled to be educated in Portugal's tertiary level institutions but who subsequently experienced hardship as their grants were suspended or withheld as a result of the chaotic conditions in their homelands. It is, of course, one of the great ironies of this post colonial issue to realise that in this situation many Portuguese professional workers now conduct their business in buildings constructed and offices cleaned by individuals who originally trained as doctors, surgeons and accountants in their source regions of Lusophone Africa.

In the 1980s and 1990s there was a significant turnaround in the country's overall migratory balance. Indeed, Portugal now offers a potentially lucrative destination for growing numbers of Lusophone-African, South American, North European, Asian, and more recently still, East European immigrants to travel to (Eaton 1999; Costa 2002). While the overall migratory balance remains in a state of flux, it is clear that Portugal offers a fairly 'soft' target for increasingly large numbers of immigrants seeking permanent and temporary work in both the legal and twilight sectors of the host economy.

The process of integration for these types of immigrant is, however, a complicated one. For example, many immigrants enter the country by air-transit and utilise valid tourist and/or student visas for a short time before remaining illegally in the country after their permits have expired. Others, with the help of intermediaries, quickly disappear into 'safe houses' located in shanty dwellings scattered around the major towns. More recently, they have been housed in resettlement accommodation blocks built specifically to rehouse the shanty-dwellers in the suburbs of Lisbon. These workers then move on to become part of a complex and often illegal network that is characterized by numerous and virtually impenetrable layers of subcontracting firms. Agents 'sell' workers to these 'subbing' companies who, in turn, secretly transport the illegal workers to building sites and factories located throughout the rest of the country (Malheiros 1998). Here they live in compounds adjacent to their workplaces, rarely venturing beyond the confines of the construction yard and working fourteen hour shifts, seven days a week, with little recourse to health and safety considerations nor social security payments. It is a precarious but, as we shall see, a fairly rewarding existence.

At the same time, opportunities have arisen in the domestic service industries where female immigrants, in particular, have been required for office, household, and similar types of work in the hygiene field (Fonseca 1997). Again, illegals offer distinct advantages because informal verbal contracts are typical, and the hiring and firing of domestic servants, in particular, is commonplace. However, and in spite of the migrant's vulnerable position, the authorities appear reluctant to intervene in what has now become a highly organized but an unregulated segment of the Portuguese labour market.

Lusophone-African immigration

Table One demonstrates the changes in immigration flows that took place in Portugal during the 1990s. While foreigners remained a small part of the total population, it is equally apparent that their relative position and numbers have grown. Overall, immigrant numbers increased by 65 per cent between 1990 and 1998, and while there was a slowdown in the second half of the decade it is fair to assume that legally resident foreigners (LRF's) will continue to be an increasingly important feature of Portuguese society. This is particularly true in areas found on the margins of major cities, in the *bairros de lata* (tin/shanty towns) and around transitional, low cost, rented accommodation blocks, where strong national community-based networks and natural human gregariousness tends to lead immigrants to congregate (Branco 1999). This is important because where this resettlement pattern occurs; the immigrant groups can transcend their normal insignificance, and rapidly become visible and (potentially) very influential communities at the local scale.

National immigrant groupings entering Portugal are structurally and spatially tied, in that, first, and as we have seen, they have a strong post-colonial dimension, and second, distinctive spatial settlement patterns have emerged. The links with the former colonies are reflected in the classical migratory channels that have been established, particularly with respect to the lusophone-African countries, and also

Table 7.1:
Change in the number of legally resident foreigners in Portugal, 1990-98

Country of origin	LRF Totals			Variation (Number and Percentage)					
	1990	1994	1998	1990-94		1994-98		1990-98	
Cape Verde	28 796	36 560	40 093	7 764	+30	3 533	+10	11 297	+39
Angola	5 306	13 589	16 487	8 283	+156	2 898	+21	11 181	+211
Guinea-Bissau	3 986	10 828	12 894	6 842	+172	2 066	+19	8 908	+223
Mozambique	3 175	4 186	4 429	1 011	+32	243	+6	1 254	+39
São Tomé and Príncipe	2 034	3 782	4 388	1 748	+86	606	+16	2 354	+116
Other Africa	1 958	3 685	4 176	1 727	+88	491	+13	2 218	+113
United Kingdom	8 457	10 731	12 680	2 274	+27	1 949	+18	4 223	+50
Spain	7 462	8 531	10 191	1 069	+14	1 660	+19	2 729	+36
Germany	4 845	6 773	8 846	1 928	+40	2 073	+31	4 001	+82
France	3 239	4 415	5 804	1 176	+36	1 389	+31	2 565	+79
Netherlands	1 827	2 530	3 302	703	+38	772	+30	1 475	+81
Other Europe	5 580	8 839	11 284	3 259	+58	2 445	+28	5 704	+102
Brazil	11 413	18 612	19 860	7 199	+63	1 248	+7	8 447	+74
Other Latin America	5 963	6 203	4 868	240	+4	-1 335	-21	-1 095	-18
United States	6 935	8 352	8 065	1 417	+20	-287	-3	1 130	+16
Canada	2 058	2 388	2 083	329	+16	-304	-13	25	+1
Asia	4 154	6 322	7 887	2 168	+52	1 565	+25	3 733	+90
Total	107 767	157 073	177 774	49 306	+46	20 701	+13	70 007	+65

Source: INE (1991: 165); INE (1996: 167); INE (1999: 153)

Table 7.2:
Occupational structure of lusophone–African workers in Portugal, 1998

Country of Origin	Tot	AP	% total	0/1	% AP	2	% AP	3	% AP	4	% AP	5	% AP	6	% AP	7/8/9	% AP	NAP	% total
Angola	16 084	8 177	50.8	597	7.3	16	0.2	187	2.3	241	2.9	1 078	13.2	48	0.6	6 010	73.5	7 907	49.2
Cape Verde	39 153	21 936	56.1	353	1.6	15	0.1	649	2.9	170	0.8	1 995	9.1	125	0.6	18 629	84.9	17 217	43.9
Guinea-Bissau	11 397	7 215	63.3	433	6.1	14	0.2	131	1.8	127	1.8	581	8.1	85	1.2	5 884	80.9	4 182	36.7
Mozambique	4 321	1 900	43.9	259	13.6	59	3.1	149	7.8	458	24.1	156	8.2	5	0.3	814	42.8	2 421	56.1
São Tomé and Príncipe	4 334	1 940	44.8	193	9.9	6	0.3	92	4.7	70	3.6	443	22.8	7	0.4	1 129	58.2	2 394	55.2
Others	3 715	1 973	53.1	443	22.4	242	1.2	51	2.6	374	18.9	81	4.1	21	1.1	761	38.6	1 742	46.9
Africa	79 004	43 141	54.6	2 278	5.2	352	0.8	1 259	2.9	1 440	3.3	4 334	10.1	291	0.7	33 187	76.9	35 863	45.4

Source: INE (1999: 58)

Key:
AP=Active Population; NAP=Non-active Population
Active population includes employees and those seeking work
Non-active population includes domestic house-persons, students and retired

Professions:
0/1 Professional, scientific, technical, self-employed and related
2   Executive, administrative and managerial occupations (public and private sectors)
3   Clerical and office workers
4   Commercial sales
5   Service sector
6   Agriculture, animal husbandry, forestry, fisheries, hunting and related
7/8/9 Industrial production and related (in manufacturing), transport equipment and manual labour (building and construction)

with parts of South America. Consequently, it is interesting to note that Portugal has one of the highest proportions of African immigrants in the whole of the European Union. Indeed, in 1999, Lusophone-African immigrants dominated the overall picture in Portugal representing over 42 per cent of the total number of LRF's. The largest and most established community to be found was that of the Cape Verdeans (almost 44,000 strong and representing more than one in five of all immigrants residing in the country). They were followed by Brazilians (11 per cent of the total number of LRF's), Angolans (9 per cent), and Guinea-Bissauans (7 per cent). This structure is not surprising given the close relationships based upon a common language and culture and the prevalence of flows and counter-flows of migrants moving between the countries mentioned. Typically, business and job information is rapidly disseminated along these trails, and familial networks are swiftly established and then maintained, making the migratory transition an outwardly easy, and indeed, 'attractive' proposition for many of these immigrants.

Table One also shows that, during the 1990s, the numerical dominance of the Cape Verdean community was challenged. Increasing numbers of immigrants from Angola and Guinea-Bissau, and to a lesser extent, from the São Tomé Islands settled in Portugal. Of note, the Guinea-Bissauan community grew by a remarkable 223 per cent between 1990 and 1998. Moreover, Machado suggests that part of this central West African group is relatively well educated, often entering teaching, medical, scientific and technical professions in Portugal (Machado 1997). In reality, figures from INE (1999: 158) suggest that what Machado terms as professional immigrants (Machado 1997) accounted for only 6 per cent of the total economically active population (EAP) for this national grouping. While they do not conform quite as easily, therefore, to the common notion of the unskilled and uneducated lusophone-African worker entering Portugal, they are, nonetheless, a minor, but, as we shall see, an important part of the overall working population.

Lusophone-African labour market insertions

Figure One illustrates the spatially polarized nature of immigration into Portugal with, first, the focus of settlement being the coastal littoral margin, and second, the dominance of the capital – Lisbon, and to a lesser extent, the district of Setúbal. The settlement pattern clearly reflects the underlying unevenness of the economic development process in Portugal and its emphasis on a relatively small number of regional foci in the west of the country. Most lusophone-Africans have been attracted to a band of coastal *distritos* (counties) running in a northwest to south direction from Oporto towards Aveiro, Coimbra, Lisbon, Setúbal and then on to Faro in the Algarve. By contrast, the eastern interior margin along the Spanish border is virtually ignored by immigrant settlers.[3] This is a direct response to the real (and just as importantly, the perceived) availability of work and to the major infra-structural construction projects that typified the socioeconomic development of Portugal in the mid to late-1990s. Large-scale schemes (co-financed by the EU and the State), such as the building of the World Expo '98 site, the Vasco da Gama Bridge across the River Tagus, the Colombo shopping mall in the capital's suburb of Benfica, and the extensions to the Lisbon metro system, as well as the construction of underground car parks in the capital, all fostered a high demand for construction workers. Consequently, a constant flow of relatively unskilled Lusophone-African workers helped to satisfy this building site demand. Significantly, there is little sign of a let up, with projects such as a second Lisbon airport at Ota, the construction of the Alqueva Dam in the Alentejo, the Oporto underground railway system, and building and rejuvenation of stadia associated with the 2004 European football championships all likely to necessitate an input of manual labour in the future.

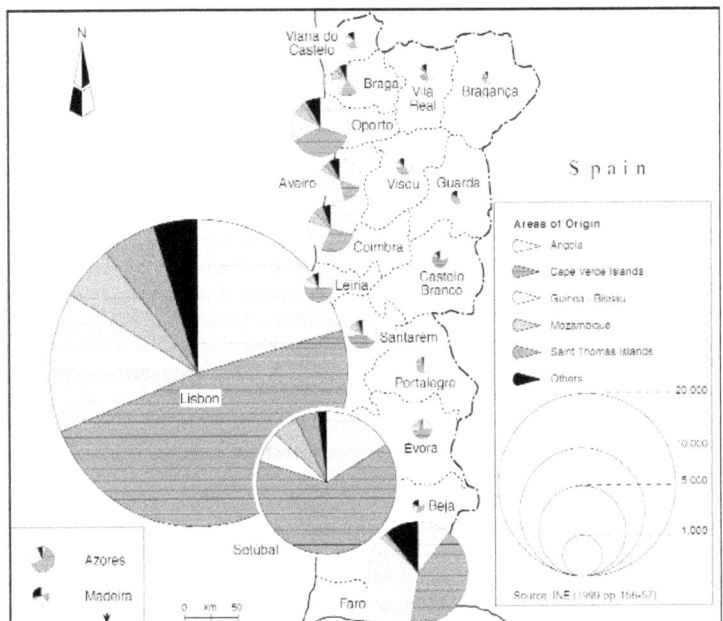

Figure 1: Distribution of Luso-African Immigrants in Portugal, 1998.

The key motivating factor for the majority of legal immigrants entering Portugal is, therefore, obvious and is related to the base demand for labour. The prospects of securing employment in the country's (formal or informal) labour markets are high. Moreover, this process carries the likelihood of remuneration and the chance to improve an individual's quality of life increases significantly. The relatively high remittance value of wages means that there is the added incentive of being able to convert part of a salary into a local (or home) currency 'fortune', thus improving the conditions endured by the migrant's family in the country of origin. This combination of opportunities encourages many immigrants to tacitly accept the social and economic parameters that impinge upon their lives. These include relatively precarious working conditions; low pay; abuse and exploitation by sometimes unscrupulous employers; occasional racial prejudice; sporadic racist violence; discrimination in the arenas of housing, education and criminal justice, and the attendant (and sometimes heavy-handed) monitoring by the Portuguese authorities (Corkill 1996; Eaton 1998). Indeed, the capacity for many lusophone-African immigrants to accept these conditions of 'semi-slavery', and their propensity to allow themselves to be 'self-exploited' makes them a very competitive and extremely flexible addition to the national workforce. In turn, they represent: 'human commodities in an unregulated market - which paradoxically guarantees their employability and... [their] survival' (Veiga 1999: 127).

Meanwhile, the problems experienced by LRF's are compounded further in the informal sector. As we have seen, illegality often equates with cheapness and both employers and employees appear content to allow a 'low pay, long hours' pattern to be fostered. Many illegals live in poor conditions close to their place of work and often they are bonded workers in the sense that employers will retain their personal documents (passports, birth certificates, ID-cards, etc.) as security against desertion. The workers are thereby obliged to cooperate given the inherent danger of being revealed to the authorities, and in extreme instances, deportation. The consequence of this situation is that Portugal's burgeoning underground economy can be effectively maintained with minimal government intervention (Baganha 1998b). There is also a suggestion that the state colludes with this activity in that it tacitly condones the developmental fruits of the clandestine workforce's efforts. Privately, it appears that the authorities adopt the attitude that if the illegals do not cause problems then they should be left alone. The willingness on the part of the immigrant to accept a measure of 'self-exploitation', and an assumption of toleration (with respect to their illegal presence) on the part of the government, have, therefore, combined to produce a grey area in the labour market but one that is having a significant impact on the nation as a whole.

The official Portuguese immigrant labour market situation is shown in Table Two. It indicates the occupational structures associated with Lusophone-African workers and highlights a series of national scale differences. Economic activity rates (EAR's) were generally high in 1998 with some 55 per cent of all lusophone-Africans having a job compared to only 45 per cent for the domestic Portuguese population (Eurostat, 1997). However, national EARs range from the Guinea-Bissauans (63 per cent of the total in work) to the Angolans (51 per cent) and the Mozambicans (44 per cent).

Over three-quarters (77 per cent) of Lusophone-African immigrant workers were engaged in the manual and relatively unskilled professions such as those found, particularly, in the construction trades and manufacturing production. This is not surprising given the substituting effect of immigration in Portugal (Fonseca 1997: 7) that has been highlighted, and the fact that Cape Verdeans (85 per cent of the total), Guinea Bissauans (81 per cent) and Angolans (73 per cent), especially, are prominent in these lower, working-class sectors. The second largest area of activity is that of the service sector (including tourism) with around one in ten of ex-colonial immigrants employed here. At the opposite extreme, only 5 per cent of lusophone-African immigrants are either employed or self-employed in the professional, scientific and technical sectors. Equally, employment is low (and even negligible) in the sectors of commercial sales (just over 3 per cent of all lusophone-African workers), and farming (less than 1 per cent). There is a clear duality, therefore, in terms of the positions of most legally resident lusophone-African immigrants on Portugal's occupational ladder.

The general pattern of employment illustrated in Table Two is, however, complicated by the fact that a number of national groupings have now established themselves in niche rôles within specific sectors of the Portuguese economy. Indeed, some lusophone-African individuals have achieved relatively prosperous and prestigious positions; among them the Mozambicans who are a small group in absolute terms (around 4,500 legal residents in 1999) with a generally low economic activity rate. However, relatively large proportions of Mozambicans can be found in commercial sales (24 per cent of EAP), in technical professions (14 per cent), in clerical positions (8 per cent) and in executive management arenas (3 per cent). Almost one half of this group are, therefore, employed in more professional arenas. On the other hand, 43 per cent of the Mozambican group are still employed in the manual building and industrial manufacturing sectors, and a further 8 per cent in the local service sector (with refuse collection and street cleaning being common occupations). It is clear, therefore, that in addition to substituting for labour at the lower end, the Mozambicans are also beginning to complement domestic workers at the higher and more specialized end of the labour market. This may not indicate a sea change in attitudes but does suggest that opportunities exist for suitably qualified and highly motivated indivduals to be integrated into more professionally based employment activities in Portugal.

Conclusion

The investigation shows that the dual nature of the Portuguese labour market has led to Lusophone-African workers occupying different points on a conceptual pyramid of social and economic conditions. Moreover, the segmentation that has occurred on the occupational ladder has meant that some national groups have established themselves in niche rôles, which do not necessarily conform to the general rule. Nevertheless, majorities of Cape Verdeans, Guinea-Bissauans and Angolans lie towards the elongated base of this conceptual pyramid for immigrants living in Portugal. The base of this pyramid, in turn, consists of (relatively) low wages (in a EU and Portuguese context), combined with poor living conditions, limited quality of life, and usually, employment in manual ('blue collar') jobs.

In contrast, over one half of Mozambicans (around 57 per cent of the economically active population) have established themselves in the non-manual ('white-collar') professions. Of these, almost six out of ten are on the much narrower mid to upper echelons of the pyramid where socioeconomic conditions are generally better. While this conceptualization includes a number of assumptions, it appears to show a gradual improvement for some sections of the Mozambican immigrant community. In spite of this change, however, a great deal still remains for Portugal to undertake and manage in order to integrate larger proportions of the lusophone-African communities into more influential sections of mainstream life. It is a challenging task, and one that should not be underestimated nor ignored given the significant contributions that Portugal's ex-colonial communities are now making (quite literally) to the physical construction and economic expansion of the country.

At the top of this pyramid's apex lie many of the skilled and professional (as well as the international retiree – Williams and Patterson, 1998) North European, North American and Brazilian immigrants (Nunes 2000). These groups have become more prominent in recent years on the back of inverse migration trails, globalization processes, the internationalization of the Portuguese economy, and the commoditization of the retirement product, for footloose migrants. The impact of foreign direct investment, privatization of industry and services, and influxes of European Union funding have all precipitated a demand for mobile and professional workers. Equally, of course, this same process has continued to spawn a demand for the lusophone-African manual construction worker to help build the physical infrastructures that are fundamental to continued growth in the economy. Many foreign immigrants in Portugal (irrespective of their origin and their polarized positions) are, therefore, part of the same economic development process. The socioeconomic differences between them are pronounced, however, and their differential insertions into the occupational pyramid (and underpinned in both the formal and informal sectors) are marked. Given the escalation in numbers of foreigners seeking to legalise their residency status, and the difficulties associated with tracing illegal immigrants, it appears unlikely that this situation will change as we traverse the new millennium.

Notes:

*Lecturer in European Regional Development, School of Biological and Environmental Sciences, University of Ulster at Coleraine, Northern Ireland, BT52 1SA. Email: M.Eaton@ulst.ac.uk

[1] http://www.ine.pt/ (2002).

[2] While Portuguese is the official language of eight countries that make up the CPLP (Commonwealth of Portuguese Speaking Countries) it is only spoken by majorities of the host populations in two countries; Portugal and Brazil.

[3] In some African nations such as Angola, Portuguese is spoken by around 60 per cent of the population, in Guinea-Bissau by just 2 per cent (Silva, 2002), and in the Cape Verde Islands, Creole is the first language.

[4] More recently, there have been suggestions that immigrant settlement is starting to decentralise towards the interior of Portugal. Here, immigrants are being employed in the agricultural industries where an ageing domestic population bereft of its young working population (many of whom have emigrated) has struggled to cope with labour shortages (Costa, 2002).

PART IV

Testimonies

8: Portugal, Africa and the future

Douglas L. Wheeler*

Discussing intelligently the future of Portuguese Africa might well loom as academic mission impossible in subject where the past can paralyse observers. We know little about the past there, not much about the present, and the future seems out of reach. The Portuguese are not the only to suffer past shock. If we have some basic works now on Portuguese Africa, American scholars still tend to entertain stereotypes about the Portuguese, policies and actions. A notion of changelessness persists, a concept of stereotyped response. The facetious might propose that Portugal would respond with a second, handy, '500-year plan'. Some might characterize Portugal as a kind of Iberian rose of Washington Square: she 'has no future but oh, what past!'

Serious students who ponder the Portuguese African future must do so with a clear caveat: the track record of futurologists is particularly *poor* on Portuguese Africa, and casualty rates for prophets here are high.[1] After predictions of early independence due to overwhelming pressures, after 13 years of war in Angola, the Portuguese regime remains firmly entrenched.

Certain elite groups in Portugal recently demonstrated their concern about the future in Portuguese Africa. They hired the ultimate futurologist, Herman Kahn of the Hudson Institute, to conjure up visions of the future and policy alternatives. A two-week study in 1969 was prepared by Kahn's staff and paid for by the Portuguese super-conglomerate 'CUF' (Companhia União Fabril).

After a flying trip of two weeks to Africa, Kahn and team became instant lusologists; their two volume friendly recommendation was that Portugal chooses an option of 'rapid economic development'. Kahn based the work on quantitative studies, but added a final warning that all his assumptions could be undermined if home opinion turned against the war. Rapid economic development would, in his words, 'improve the Portuguese world image' and solidify home opinion in support of the wars in Africa.[2]

Kahn hypothesised five ways in which Portugal's control of its African territories could end:

> Due to spreading insurgency, military defeat would occur.
>
> Portuguese home opinion would turn against the war.
>
> An alliance of black states would invade and win.
>
> (A) neglected territory(ies) would secede due to conservative development policies.
>
> A prosperous colony (the report was mainly, Angola) would secede following Brazil's example of 1822.

In my view, none of these scenarios is imminent, but a combination of them might in time become possible. If I were to make a meaningful comparison with another former colony whose past may resemble something of Portuguese Africa's future, I would rather discuss *Algeria* than Brazil.

Kahn's rather uncritical and superficial study is weak for two main reasons: one, it is based on too brief an effort of analysis; two, it fails to take into account an intimate knowledge of the Portuguese culture and past. Professor Lynn White in his Presidential address for this year's American Historical Association meetings put his criticism of this kind of 'Technology assessment' quite succinctly.

White pointed out that two major defects of this kind of exercise are a lack of sense of depth in time and a failure to consider cultural analysis. It is interesting to note, too, that Professor White describes one of the two main defects in technology assessment as 'the Hudson Institute syndrome'.[3]

Failure to perceive the shape of the Portuguese African future is not limited to the last thirteen years. In the last two decades of the nineteenth century, leading Africanists in South Africa and the United Kingdom, including the explorer Henry Norton Stanley, predicted that Portugal's control over her African territories was marked for early destruction; certainly few non-Portuguese experts at the time believed that Portugal could survive British ambition, African hostility or German power plots. A possible exception was Sir Harry Johnston, who believed that Portugal could hang on indefinitely. But few at the time of the British Ultimatum in 1890 saw that this episode would increase rather then dampen Portugal's determination to survive.

What might have been concluded by prescient observers in 1890 might have some application today: among a proud and highly nationalistic people an external pressure may not work the desired change; but internal divisions and pressures in the long run may have a more *meaningful* effect.

If we were to assess the possible shape of the future, we must study the recent past and present. One of the problems in learning much reliable news about current Portuguese Africa is not only Portuguese propaganda and censorship, but also

African nationalist propaganda, and the increasingly shallow and superficial analysis of facts found in recent United Nations reports on this area. In Portuguese Africa, three areas of concern deserve discussion: the wars; the economy; political factors, and the African masses.

The wars continue at uneven paces. In general in all three territories, a military stalemate continues, but in two territories this situation may be gradually altering. In Guinea-Bissau, the war was heated up in the last year and a half, due probably to several factors: the main nationalists party, PAIGC has changed tactics to employ mass attacks on interior Portuguese installations and forts: the use of heavier anti-aircraft and anti-personnel weaponry which have resulted in heavier Portuguese losses in personnel and unprecedented losses in aircraft. In May 1973, the Governor-General and commander in Guinea General Antonio de Spínola returned to Portugal, where he apparently informed Lisbon of the worsening situation; he resigned his post, remained in Lisbon, and began to do all in his power to make public aware of the worsening military situation. After a term as chief Portuguese official in Guinea since May 1968, Spínola resigned well before his second four-year term was up. This remarkable general returned tired, probably discouraged, but a powerful individual in Armed Forces circle, most important in a country where Generals have had such potential power, he was temporarily unemployed until the Government found a special position, created just for him, as Vice-Chief of Staff in January 1974. The wars had created an 'African hero'.

Other factors should be noted in Guinea-Bissau – Senegal appears to be more involved in aiding the PAIGC than previously; more arms than ever are pouring into the area; and the Portuguese have continued a massive Africanization of their armed forces. In Guinea – Portugal has at least 30,000 and possibly 35,000 troops from Portugal, not counting local forces. Portuguese economic stakes in Guinea have been reduced; CUF has largely de-camped, has sold land to African villagers and with heavy industrial investments, is fishing for new profits in Angola and Mozambique. In short, with little or no settler pressures or private economic stake in Guinea, Portugal's commitment to remain in Guinea is more problematical than in her other African territories.

In Angola, the war is now not quite as threatening as it appears to be in Guinea-Bissau and in Mozambique. The fronts in Cabinda, Congo, eastern and southern Angola seem fairly stable, thought the MPLA (the strongest Angolan nationalist party) is still active in the east. The economic situation is changing: there is an increase in oil revenues due to world price rise and the boycott; increasing industrialization through massive new Portuguese and foreign investments; a Government import-export control policy which is gradually ending the traditional easy market situation in Angola for Portuguese manufacturers. With new duties on wines and textiles, Portuguese merchants must end their dependence on the Angolan market and seek markets in Europe and North America. Local industries are being encouraged. An increase in the Portuguese population of Angola (it is now possibly as high as 450,000), a rise in the wages and standard of living of Angolans must be balanced against black-white job and housing competition and an erosion of African land-ownership and uneven agricultural production. Despite Government reforms in housing, education, welfare, and labor, with current conditions of inflation, centralised Government control, and increased political discussions, it is likely that African mass discontent has increased. Although there is more local autonomy after the 1971 Constitutional Revisions and the March 1973 provincial elections, there is some war-weariness, and observers in Angola are concerned about troubles in Portugal recently, and the heated up wars in Guinea-Bissau and in Mozambique. Further pressure in another war front, can have direct effects on other territories. The Government has recently transferred possibly 10,000 troops (or one-sixth of the regular forces in Angola) from Angola to Mozambique. A worsened situation in eastern Africa can thus reduce Portuguese armed force in Angola. Could this process encourage increased nationalist action in east Angola? Politics is now more important in Angola; 1973 elections brought a European majority to the new Legislative Assembly (53 strong); but it is significant the famous book by General Spínola sold out in Luanda as well as in Lisbon in the last weeks. Angolans, too, are pondering an uncertain future; despite greater local autonomy in this economy, discontent is increasing.

In Mozambique the situation is more complex. There another 'African General' (General Kaúlza de Arriaga) endeavored to make a big political reputation for his own future in Lisbon. Like Spínola he attempted to profit from mistakes of his failed predecessors; launching massive offensives, new programs of local reform, Arriaga spent four years as Commander; his reputation cannot equal Spínola's since when he left Mozambique this summer to retire to Lisbon, he left a more divided and troubled Mozambique. As in Angola, the rural resettlement programs are not shortening but are prolonging the war, and the African discontent engendered by re-grouping and the economic dislocation resulting from 'a strategic hamlet' syndrome is serious. Despite some FRELIMO (the main Mozambique nationalist party) defections to the Portuguese in the north, the real crisis area is at the Zambezi and south of it.

The worsened Portuguese position hinges on growing FRELIMO infiltration in the area of the construction of the Cabora Bassa dam; considerable fighting has occurred there in the last year, although the dam opening apparently will go on schedule late this year or 1975. South of this area, between the port of Beira and the Rhodesian border at Umtali, railroad line and the area near Vila Pery have in the past five months come under increasing attack by FRELIMO units. Three developments suggest that the Portuguese leadership is seriously concerned with central Mozambique: one, the transfer of a significant number of troops from Angola to Mozambique; two, severe criticism of Portuguese military failures and tactics by white Rhodesian sources in Salsibury and beyond; and, finally, evidence of intensive conflicts between Portuguese settlers and the Army in central Mozambique as a result of the FRELIMO attacks near Vila Pery which resulted in the deaths of Portuguese in areas formerly considered as 'safe' regions. The opening of divisiveness between Army elements, the DGS (secret police), settlers and the Rhodesians over war in Mozambique is significant; if this manifest disunity grows, FRELIMO may well be able to take advantage of it. That there is increasing polarisation over the war effort concerning Mozambique is openly referred to in the Lisbon moderate press; *Expresso*, a weekly paper financed by fairly liberal business and industrial interests has referred to a speech by officials calling for 'unity' in Mozambique in the face of new threats.

In the Portuguese Army in Mozambique, as in Guinea-Bissau, there is a sign of more war-weariness, increased but still modest desertion rates so far, and resentment of competition from other military elements such as the powerful DGS, the secret police outfit, which is equipping its own para-military African units. A recent report in Africa Report suggests that there are 'three wars' in Mozambique: the war with FRELIMO, the war between Army and DGS, and the war between the Army, DGS and the Lisbon Government.4 Further evidence suggests that FRELIMO is also changing tactics to increase the use of mass attacks; and its armament is increasing in quantity and quality.

The 1973 Legislative Assembly elections in Mozambique resulted in the election of a majority of African delegates (in Guinea – the Legislative Assembly reportedly, is all African). A heavy voter turnout – heavier than in Portugal – suggests that the official party of the Caetano regime, the ANP (National Popular Action) has organised locally well beyond what Salazar's National Union did in previous decades. Signs of internal opposition are few; it is worth noting, however, that in 1972-73, there were opposition activities among students at the University of Lourenço Marques, which now grants its own degrees, there was a banning of the University student association, and the arrest of students.

When one analyses the economics of Angola and Mozambique, it is clear that the highly publicised improvements are uneven. In 1972, both Angola and Mozambique had budget surpluses for the first time in 12 years. Their economies are experiencing impressive growth rates of between 11 and 14 percent a year; Portugal's average growth rate has recently been 7-8 percent, well above that of many western states. Most impressive is industrial and manufacturing growth; local economic self-dependence is growing. In 1971, Mozambique's per capita domestic product was US$216, which is respectable in terms of African independent states' incomes today. What is unclear is the impact on the people of the adverse factors; high inflation, educational bottlenecks which prevent Africans getting enough education to obtain good jobs; European competition, for the newly created jobs; and continuing dependence on European imports. Unlike Angola, Mozambique still has not located her mineral eldorado; and part of the Cabindan oil is now being shipped to Mozambique to help maintain fuel supplies.

There is an economic 'boom' in Mozambique and in Angola, to a greater extent; but it is difficult to assess the impact. Although wages and living conditions in general are probably higher than ever before in history, the result may *not* be *counter-revolutionary*, but revolutionary. Perhaps students may be reminded of Crane Brinton's analysis in his *The anatomy of revolutions* where: in the four revolutions discussed,

> ...these were all societies on the upgrade economically before the revolution came, and the revolutionary movements seem to originate in the discontents of not unprosperous people who feel restraint, cramp, annoyance, rather than downright crushing oppression.[5]

I am not suggesting that many Portuguese Africans are 'not unprosperous'; I do suggest that presently the revolutionary potential in Angola and Mozambique lies more among Europeans on the rise, who may be moved to commit revolutionary acts if present trends continue. Significant groups of Portuguese residents of these areas are increasingly distressed with their lack of control of the economy and policy; the changes of the Caetano regime since 1968 have both encouraged and frustrated them; the 1971 constitutional changes gave them a little but not enough and perhaps too late.

A brief look at war, economy and politics in Portuguese Africa would be incomplete without a discussion of internal affairs in Portugal. The Caetano regime began with some promising liberal gestures in 1968-69, and then retrenched. As a joke in Lisbon recently put it, Caetano, signaled left but turned right. The reasons for this increasingly conservative hue to the regime lie in the continued power of the internal forces which supported Salazar for 36 years as a civilian premier, managing but not ruling the armed forces. There is *continuidade* (continuity), and continued *immobilismo* (stagnation) among the roots of that support: in the conservative elements of the officer corps; high banking and finance; large corporations; a conservative wing of the Catholic Church and the remnants of an apparently disappearing breed, the large landowners in central-south Portugal, the *latifundistas*. Through some strange political alchemy based on intrigue, threats and monetary power, they have held on. The Caetano regime has attempted to create a Third Republic, or its own second act of the Estado Novo (New State). Caetano has appointed his own men at key positions from local to national levels; has written his own 1971 constitution, which gives more power to the National Assembly, reduces book censorship, widens local autonomy in Africa; he has supported some liberal economists to introduce innovations in a backward economy, but by early 1973 his honeymoon with the moderate and liberal elements was finished; and his truce with the Rightist powers was fast ending. Right wing forces have pressured him to clamp down on opposition, as under the Salazar regime, to continue press censorship; to continue a traditional African policy, albeit with some reforms and autonomy; to make the 1973 National Assembly elections a *tour of force* for the only legal party, his own. When I was in Lisbon last year, several of this writer's friends swore that the Generals were now ruling Caetano, that the heady days of 1968-69 were gone and that he had been under virtual house arrest a year or two ago. Others suggested that Caetano had great prestige and could manage the Generals nicely, that soldiers had now become civil servants who would be obedient to the lawyer-Premier.

Whatever the truth, there is increased polarisation over the wars in Africa and greater opposition to them among key elements of the elite: in the Church, the armed forces, business circles and intellectuals. What liberals there were among Caetano's legislative delegates have resigned; the cabinet reshuffles have placed conservative, Salazaristas in key positions again, and in the crucial position of Defense Minister Silva Cunha, a veteran conservative, civilian ex-Minister of Overseas, is in command of the Generals. For Caetano, opposition to the wars, and to his regime has seriously increased among the University population, which is growing in influence and size; next year four new universities, with four new university populations will be in operation, some of them in the provinces. In spite of gerrymandering, official support and planning, the city of Lisbon remains a focus of opposition or hostile indifference to Caetano's regime; in the 1973 elections, the Lisbon voter turnout was the lowest in continental Portugal. In a future crisis, the cockpit of conflict will again be Lisbon, the urban key to Portuguese politics.

The crisis of March that made world front-page news (*New York Time*) is an important one to analyse. It began with the return to Lisbon of the leading African Generals and their colleagues from the worsening wars in Guinea and Mozambique; by summer, both Spínola and Kaúlza de Arriaga were unemployed. The regime especially feared these two men with the most important records and best senior command reputations. Kaúlza is a hardline Portuguese cold-warrior conservative, whose political ideas are much closer to those of the right wing establishment than those of Spínola. Kaúlza has been anxious to play Portuguese strategic possessions in the Atlantic and Indian Oceans to the hilt in order to obtain Western aid for Portugal in the African wars. His reform plans for Mozambique were not very original, and were very cautious. Kaúlza feared too much development too fast and suggested increasing white immigration to offset the growth in numbers of assimilated Africans.

Spínola is a special phenomenon, and his record and ideas are worthy of special study. Now 64 years old, Spínola is a robust, energetic General who gained an early reputation in Portugal and the Azores as an efficient bright young officer with original ideas; an internationally known horseman and cavalry officer, he was commandant of the Azores at the end of World War II and, briefly, Minister of War in a 1945 Salazar cabinet. He had all the credentials of a New State loyalist and veteran alumnus. Spínola drops from sight until the Angolan war in 1963-68, when he serves in the north as a Lt. Colonel of combat troops steeped in the latest counter-insurgency. From Angola in 1968, he moved to be Governor-General of Guinea, where he gained a 'miracle man' reputation as the man who could stop PAIGC infiltration, stem the red tide, as he would call it, and win the African masses to Portugal's side. If any leader Portugal had could do it, perhaps Spínola could and in 1971-72 he came close to it. But the factors I mentioned above caused a deterioration in the Portuguese position in 1973. When Spínola returned from Guinea, his mission over but not completed, he was given Portugal highest military decoration (Tower and Sword with Palm) by a seemingly grateful President Thomaz on 31 May 1973. While the regime purposefully sought a position for this potential political bombshell, the General quietly wrote a book. In January he was named Vice-Chief of Staff under a friend, a younger general, Costa Gomes. On

February 18, Spínola's 'awaited' book was published in Lisbon. It was titled *Portugal and the future*. If the year 1968 was called 'the year of the chair' (when Premier Salazar suffered a headblow and stroke after a deck chair collapsed under him), then 1974 will be called 'the year of the book'. Book sales reportedly reached 50,000 copies in a few days; in a country where sales of 3-4,000 mean a best seller. *Portugal and the future* is the most sensational and sought after book in the twentieth-century history of Portugal or of Portuguese Africa.

What this famed General proposes in the book may be no more important than the way he justifies these proposals. Reports in the American press have not done full justice to the book's contents. First, the General's analysis of the question of Portuguese Africa. His main point is that Portugal's national survival is at stake, not merely possession of colonies or territories. Perhaps the most controversial judgment, like a *cri d'coeur*, long bottled up, is found in the following passage:

> The very national survival will be in danger, if we persist in the concept that it is world opinion that is wrong, and that all our problems result only from the greed or lack of vision of others.[6]

Spínola says that Portugal has reached a crucial crossroads where she has a choice of several extreme solutions: (1) status quo and the war will last forever and drain Portugal; (2) 'betrayal of the past' or abandon Africa. The General then proposes a 'third way' in building Portugal's future in a 'Lusitanian Commonwealth' where the overseas states and provinces are in an equal relationship with Portugal. The General proposes the creation of a Federation of equal states, a 'political pluralism' where different types of political systems can, flourish under Portuguese culture with autonomy for each part. His solutions to the problem of how to create such a Federation or Commonwealth involve a structure where Brazil will be a part of the new community or Portuguese-speaking states, and where all the African states get more than progressive autonomy as promised by Caetano but actual self-determination by means of plebiscite or popular referendum which will ask the people, after some unspecified length of preparation, if they want to remain in the Commonwealth or secede. Implicit in Spínola's proposed institutionalisation of this plan is the idea that basically the African masses in overseas are mainly pro-Portuguese, and will vote 'yes' in a plebiscite. If this happens, Spínola postulates the West will give greater support to Portugal's creation of a peaceful Commonwealth in which the wars will cease or become quite manageable. Also implicit in his book is the advocacy of local African autonomy; laws not voted on freely by Africans, he suggests, will not be fully acceptable.

Spínola's somewhat vague but idealistic proposals envisage, then, a 'plurinational state', some 25 million strong, with 'member-nations' joining by free votes. There are distinct similarities between his scheme and General de Gaulle's 1958 Franco-African 'Community' which was a prelude to French decolonization in Africa. What is not clear is the extent to which Spínola's proposals encompass the division of powers and how power will be divided locally when Portuguese settler groups are involved. The proposals in the book are more startling still when one studies the proposed changes in government in the metropole. Spínola calls for a massive de-centralisation of home Portuguese administration and government from top to bottom; by this he would free Portugal itself of Lisbon's centralised control that has been so characteristic of the New State since 1926. According to Spínola's plan the central government in Lisbon would remain, but would retain control in Portugal and in Africa only of certain fields; foreign affairs, defence and finances. In this respect, the General joins a century of Portuguese reformers who have sought to lessen Lisbon's monopoly of power and privilege.

Perhaps the most sensational idea of Spínola is that Portugal cannot win the African wars by military means and that if they persist in military means they will lose the current good will of the majority of the African masses. This suggests that Spínola is contradicting the Government's promise of military victory, and that since 1971, when interviewed by international journalists; he has changed his mind on the feasibility of military victory.

Under previous circumstances, these last statements alone might have sent a less privileged public figure to jail in a matter of hours. Spínola concludes his book by proposing a new government structure which distinctly downgrades the Executive, abolishes the Overseas Ministry, reduces bureaucratic power and puts forth an independent judiciary and the Armed forces as the political watchdogs to see that the Lusitanian Commonwealth works well.

The timetable of crisis was telescoped by the publication, and public reaction to this book. In early March, the dispersed establishment flew in from Africa and marshalled right-wing support against the ideas of Spínola. On 5 March, an episode without constitutional precedent in the New State occurred in the National Assembly in Lisbon. Premier Caetano went before that hand-picked body and called for a formal 'vote of confidence' for a Government which by law is not responsible to the legislature; he got a laudatory vote and statement which defended his African policy and claimed there were ample means for continuing the war in Africa; it stated that negotiating with nationalists in Guinea would lead to collapse in Angola and Mozambique. Caetano then made a speech in which he gave an orthodox instant replay of his policy since 1968 and finally; attacked (without naming the General or his book) Spínola's proposals.

Interestingly, Caetano's rationale appears forced and somewhat less formidable than his usual performance as a spokesman for the establishment. Caetano said that his plan for progressive autonomy for African states was quite satisfactory; the new proposals were impossible and erroneous since (1) the mass of Africans are not prepared to make a real choice, due to their illiteracy; (2) the votes result – if truly free – might be *negative*, if the nationalists participated (3) and Portugal has the means to continue the war and continue progressive economic development. In other words, Portugal is doing better than ever; beware of impatient, 'words, facile ideas and gaudy fantasies' of false prophets.

The crisis came to a head when, on 14 March, the Government fired both Spínola and the Chief of Staff, Costa Gomes, with no reason mentioned, and military units were placed on alert. On the morning of 15 March, 200 men of the Fifth Infantry Regiment stationed at a town (Caldas da Rainha), north of Lisbon, mutinied against the command of the regiment, locked some officers in the barracks and took off in trucks toward Lisbon, supposedly intending to topple the regime. They were stopped; no shots were fired and later the police arrested them.

Within a week some 35 officers, including one Lt. Colonel, and 180 enlisted men, were under arrest; Spínola remained free but inactive, and the Government had also sacked senior officers in the Military Academy and Navy Command.

What of the future? What will follow this crisis, the most extraordinary internal crisis connected with the African situation since April 1961, when some senior officers failed to tire Salazar, and were fired in turn by him?

Observers who view Spínola – even if he were free to act as a kind of liberal man-on-horseback – should be cautious. Is he a potential De Gaulle who can inspire the armed forces to support his views, and his eventual rise to supreme power? Some may hope that he is, but his background, and the historical and cultural context to which he relates might mark him more as a dynamic throwback than as a man of the future. His proposals and pleas for democratic processes are refreshing, his justifications, fairly free of cant. But Spínola states that Portugal must somehow retain Portuguese Africa at least with economic ties or not survive as a free nation. He thus implies a disembodied, external threat, perhaps the historic Spanish menace, an old idea in Portugal. Moreover, his policies appear to be a curious mixture of radicalism and conservatism, more like a modern version of Portuguese Integralism than liberalism or democracy; like Presidentialists, he respects plebiscites; he like many monarchists of the pre-New State era calls for popular sovereignty as against elitism, like his ideological kindred nineteenth century heroes 'of Africa', is for decentralization of administration and a political role for the Military. He despises bureaucrats and, especially, lawyers. Indeed, Spínola appears to be a new old 'Hero of Africa', of the stamp of the generation of 1895, which conquered Portuguese Africa and set a new colonial policy. He is, perhaps, a new Mousinho with a monocle.

I have no penchant for presumptuous prophecy, but I can see the possibility of three scenarios based on a new prominence of the Portuguese Army in internal politics, continuing wars, and rising opposition to the war at home.

An Algerian scenario: (within 5 years)

Political crisis/coup in Lisbon/leadership changes to moderate executive willing to put in Spínola as Premier or President;

Elements of Portuguese army and settlers in Angola, and especially Mozambique 'pronounce' and refuse to allow a plebiscite of masses; create UDI in those states;

Lisbon gives Guinea a form of independence through a 'client' regime of moderate nationalists

OAS - Algerian scenario

Political crisis in Lisbon/army attempts coup right-wing suppressed briefly

Army elements from Africa return and put down moderates, re-instate status quo;

Client States set up in all 3 territories;

Cape Verde kept by Portugal;

Guinea given over to the 'client' African leaders;

Angola given over to 'client' white leaders, composed of settlers-Army-administrators;

Mozambique (south of Zambique) given over to 'client' state of settlers, Army in co-operation with South Africa; Rhodesia north of Zambesi let go to FRELIMO state;

Facade of a 'commonwealth' is kept for public consumption

Status quo for 3-5 years

Wars get out of hand, Caetano quits or is ousted by Right; replaced by rightwing hard-liner, Military regime;

Guinea given 'independence' by means of facade of client state run by Africans;

Status quo (development as fast as possible with 'mobile industries' in Angola and Mozambique)

There are too many variables: action of African nationalist parties, the progress of the wars, the home economy, the health and determination of the leadership, and the internal opposition in the Army to the war, to make easy predictions.

But the 'year of the book' crisis has brought some lessons. The timetable of change for Portuguese Africa has been speeded up by Spínola's effort, his book and the popular response to it in the major cities. Secondly, the unity of the armed forces command may be the key element of change in the long run. If disunity increase, even the police state apparatus may be unable to contain the opposition forces; if the Army officers who oppose the war, can get allies in other sectors as in business, the Church, and middle class, then there may well be civil strife in Portugal which would inevitably weaken Portuguese efforts to resist African nationalism overseas. Portuguese African armies would not then be immune to such conflicts. Growing disunity at home over the war policy is more significant than the sporadic bombings and sabotage by young Portuguese revolutionaries, whose acts serve largely to provoke further intransigence. Elements of the 'pro-Europe' business community, led in party by the *Expresso* weekly newspaper, strongly encouraged Spínola in his recent efforts to oppose Caetano and to bring a changed policy toward Africa.

Even in Europe's longest surviving dictatorship, the armed forces represent a double-edged sword. The Army overthrew the parliamentary Republic 48 years ago and it is not inconceivable after the March 1974 crisis that it could play a key role in overthrowing the Caetano regime. After 13 years of war in Africa, the Army has experienced unprecedented expansion in numbers, additions of equipment, trauma, and casualties, which number perhaps 12,000 dead and 50,000 wounded.

Despite Government attempts to satisfy military needs, and to reward aspirations, certain policies may have resulted in alienation which affects an officer group wider (broader) than the junior ranks. Potential Army grievances could include: the policy of creating numerous and competitive para-military, non-Army controlled forces such as police, the secret police (DGS), the Republican National Guard, and various militia groups; subordination of the military to ultimate civilian control which has preceded a pace under Caetano's leadership; transfers of officers, censorship, and recent military arrests, and firing of Spínola and his colleagues. In Short, elements of the Armed Forces command may increasingly perceive that they are being used in ways that will adversely influence national opinion about the future position of the military in society. An Army blamed for 'defeat' in Africa is a potentially dangerous Army at home. If, Army discontent - and this is the service in which it appears to be most serious – gets out of hand, and militarism and praetorianism revive within Portugal, the causes will not lie solely in Africa with Portugal's costly wars and the 'infectious' example of the increasingly important role of African armies in African politics. Militarism in Portuguese politics has venerable roots.

Since 1808 Portuguese politics is replete with the military intervening in politics. Such traditions that became a national disgrace during the first Republic, 1910-1926, even after a half century of the *Estado Novo*, may lay dormant but not dead. Military movements can overthrow dictatorships as well as democracies. This happened on occasion in Portugal in the nineteenth-century and again in 1910, when most of the Armed forces simply refused to defend the discredited Monarch.

As this writer noted four years ago,[7] Premier Salazar in 1962 stated that the Portuguese Army was 'the last bulwark which in the most serious crises defends the destiny and conscience of the Nation'. With the recent bold and daring action of Portugal's most acclaimed General, the Army evidently now nurses a divided conscience and a wounded honor. In the March 1974 crisis Portugal reached a new crossroads wherein a wider public awareness – stirred by a sensational book-perceived that the futures of both Portugal and Portuguese Africa are inextricably intertwined.

Notes:

*Department of History, University of New Hampshire, 27 March 1974

[1] I refer to books and articles by James Duffy, including *Portugal in Africa* (1962), which implied an early end to the wars, and the preface in Thomas Okuma's *Angola in ferment* (Boston, 1962), written by Rupert Emerson, and numerous journalists' reports of that period.

[2] Kahn, H. (1969), *Angola: some views of development*, vol. I, Hudson Institute, pp. 172-3.

[3] White Jr., L. (1974), 'Technology assessment', *American Historical Review*, 79, pp. 1-13.

[4] Degnan, M. (1973), 'Mozambique's three wars', *Africa Report*.

[5] Brinton, C. (1952), *The anatomy of revolution*, (revised edition), New York, NY, p. 278.

[6] Excerpt printed in *Expresso*, February 23, 1974 (Lisbon)

[7] In 'Thaw in Portugal', *Foreign Affairs*, July 1970.

9: The empire is dead, long live the EU

António de Figueiredo

Up until circa April 1975, it was possible for a Portuguese to travel and live thousands of miles away in the far-flung 'overseas provinces', some 24 times bigger than metropolitan Portugal, without ever going 'abroad'. Curiously enough, the advent of long distance flying from airport to airport even dispensed with the need to make a refuelling call at Capetown, on the way to Mozambique, and even then on Portuguese liners direct from Lisbon on an all-Portuguese route. Linguistic isolation, reinforced by an implacable system of censorship made all Portuguese and colonial 'natives' alike, captives of the jurisdiction of the autocratic regime of Salazar. I have long described its ideology as 'national-colonialism' to emphasize the colonialist dimension that differentiated the Salazarist doctrines and practises from those of the Nazis and other fascists to which it was originally related. I lived in Mozambique, to which I travelled to and from Portugal both in an ocean liner – incidentally, called the 'Colonial' – as well as by aeroplane during the six months leaves to which white settlers were entitled every four or five years. Over more than a decade, up to 1959 when I was honourably arrested and deported back to Portugal by the PIDE (the regime's state police) I acquired some empirical experience and insight into both white settler culture as well as to the plight of the African 'wards' under the Portuguese 'civilising mission'.

Having arrived as a would be settler in Beira, Mozambique, at the age of 18, not so much by choice but by decision of influential white settler relatives who wanted to help, an orphan since five weeks of age, to start a new life. I was soon struck by two facts: one the rampant exploitation of Africans, who were simply described as indigenas (natives), which seemed to imply a status even below the pobre (poor) of the majority back home in Portugal, including my impoverished widowed mother, who had also died young, leaving my two teenage sisters and myself even poorer.

The other fact was of lesser importance but equally surprising to me, namely the closeness of British-Portuguese relations in the area. My arrival had coincided with the Portuguese nationalision of the British owned Beira Railways and port facilities, which provided the nearest outlet to the sea for the vast mineral rich hinterland comprising Southern and Northern Rhodesia and Nyasaland, under a financial agreement on account of the accumulated British debts to Portugal during the recently ended Second World War.

Salazar who had only veered from his equally profitable collaborationist neutrality with the Nazis, by allowing facilities for US air forces in the strategic mid-Atlantic Azores in 1943, when the Allies were on the way to victory, had bounced back and would soon qualify for inclusion in NATO and, as such, a defender of the 'free world'. In reality Portugal's far spreading 'archipelago' of oppression and serfdom, from Mozambique – surrounded by five British possessions and South Africa – to Goa, in India, Macau, near Hong Kong, and East Timor, near Australia, or British interests in Angola and elsewhere, added an imperial dimension to the centuries old Anglo-Portuguese Alliance which had long become just a matter of convenience for England-cum-Britain, while remaining of vital importance for Portugal.

The 'nationalization' was seen as further evidence of Salazar's nationalist dedication, but the fact is that while white settlers viewed it with mixed feelings due to their dislike of the regime, the Africans I tried to speak with were completely unaware of what was going on. Moved by the signs of their unarticulated distrust of any approach by whites, other than orders or commands, I started paying more attention to the plight of their subjected condition. I had been told that an uncle on my mother's side, much loved and respected for his intellect, who had preceded me as a would-be settler had actually committed suicide after only a few years of residence in Beira – the new experience of colonialism being one added factor for his depression. Africans seldom rose much above a subordinate hierarchy, even if they were exceptionally clever, as this could upset the established norm. This hierarchy was defined by their work role, rising from *pequenino* (child servant – from which the equivalent English word 'picaninny' derives); *moleque* (all-purpose domestic servant); *mainato* (laundry-boy), and *cozinheiro* (cook). This full complement of servants in itself showed the standards of domestic service to which they grew accustomed, and only diminished when it became uneconomical as house accommodation and wages increased. The most blacks could aspire too were menial jobs in workshops or *continuos* (office messenger boys).

I joined the clandestine Movement of Democratic Unity, that had emerged during the Presidential campaign of 1949, when the democratic candidate, General Norton de Matos, had to resign before the poll. Even most of my Communist friends did not seem too concerned with local issues which, any way, required some inclination for, or knowledge of, sociology. The real experts were to be found in the administrative cadres or Catholic missionaries, with their own hierarchy of administrators and chefes de posto. Only they had access to the rural countryside, scarcely inhabited, and hardly ever transversed by other than hunters or traders, also mostly whites, as the mass of Africans themselves lived within a walking distance world. The Marxist theories on imperialism and industrial capitalism were obviously much above the vicissitudes of colonialism without capital and, in short, they did not know what to think of the local situation other than simplistically believe that it would be resolved in the world wide revolution that at that time seemed to be irreversible. I had to look elsewhere for others with a keener interest on the plight of Africans and sense of moral urgency in exposing a colonialist situation that was as degrading for the exploited 'natives' as it was for the Portuguese who exploited and oppressed them.

Having read some of the Pastoral Letters by the Bishop of Beira, D. Sebastião Soares de Resende who, since his arrival in 1943, vehemently denounced forced labour and forced crops and the appalling exploitation of African poverty, I, a newly arrived agnostic boy of 18, decided to ask him for an audience. Kind and curious enough to receive me, the meeting gave me the impression that, except for his religious faith, he was perhaps even lonelier than I was. At one point in our conversation, when I voiced my disappointment with white settler communists, he charitably pointed out that may be because, 'like so many Catholics', being human, 'they did not live up to their beliefs'. I became a regular reader of his Pastoral Letters, only recently published in a book, *Profeta em Moçambique*,[1] and, as I improved my knowledge of English, even translated the passages concerning conscripted labour and forced crops which reduced Africans to a condition of servitude that had expanded through the years as both the number of white settlers and the economy increased. I kept my rudimentary translations hoping I would meet humanitarian foreign visitors who could improve on them and 'tell the world'. The Bishop Soares de Resende's writings were, and still are, the most authoritative first hand documentary sources on the subject.

The abuse of African labour had attracted the attention of international observers from time to time, Henry Nevinson's *A Modern Slavery* (1906), being one of the earliest. His concluding appeal '…even if their cries are not heard by God, they will be heard in the hearts of the just and the compassionate', was heard by Professor Edward Ross in 1925, when, as a sociologist at the University of Wisconsin, with ample experience of the evolution from slavery in his own country, he submitted a report to the Temporary Slavery Commission of the League of Nations, detailing his field observations in both Angola and Mozambique. He referred to the systematic 'embezzlement of wages' and concluded labour conditions amounted to a 'state of serfdom'. In 1956, I myself, after reading Basil Davidson's pioneering books, *Report on Southern Africa* and *The African Awakening*, assisted a young visiting Professor, Marvin Harris of Columbia University, in writing his first-hand report *Portugal's African Wards*, on labour and education in Mozambique.[2] He stayed for almost a year up to May 1957 and, as requested, omitted the names of those who provided him with information.

I myself, through the years up to 1959, was well placed to collect evidence that the labour system outlined in the Statute of the Natives of Angola, Mozambique and Guinea-Bissau and other laws, was fully operative. I collected information from old settlers of the circle of friends of one Eduardo Saldanha, who had written extensively on the subject, apart from what had been set in print but not allowed to circulate. I made frequent visits to the port docks and railways of both Beira and Lourenço Marques (Maputo), or public works, factories and plantations, in and of towns, where conscripted labourers (*shibalos*) concentrated. 'Natives' were really treated as children, the prevailing penal system being corporal punishment, mostly confined to the palmatoria – a flat wooden bat applied to the palms of the hands, heavier than those used in Portuguese primary schools until the 1940s. I noted that it was, as a general rule, applied by uniformed policemen (*cipaios*), to involve black complicity in the pain it caused and dilute anti-white resentment. The palmatoria was indeed an apt symbol for a colonial system of exploitation based more on autoritarian paternalism than on excessive violence that might be morally unacceptable and obviously counterproductive. White settler colonialism in general, did not aim at making the standards of 'native' life worse, but was based upon the belief that the 'natives' had more to gain than to lose by being colonial servants. Instead of seeing themselves as a community of occupiers, they saw themselves as 'civilising' agents and, as such, white settlers had their own code of paternalist behaviour.

There was a tacit, instinctive, realization that since the settler community was overwhelmingly outnumbered, settlers had to set an example of more 'civilized' standards and hopefully avoid anti-white resentment. 'Natives' were, after all, a complement to settler life, as domestic servants, cooks and nannies to their children, and as such there was a vested interest in their health and improved welfare.

The regime had developed an impenetrable and insidious system of informal apartheid as effective as that which was institutionalized in South Africa, but even more effective since censorship and linguistic isolation prevented scrutiny or evidence to back up tentative international protests or appeals for intervention by the International Labour Organization or the UN.

This applied equally to the Portuguese who were deprived of the right of communication between themselves. The whole system was based upon dictatorial dogmas such as those implied in Art.141 of the Penal Code, which prescribed:

> Any Portuguese who attempts, by violent or fraudulent means, or with foreign help, to separate the Motherland [from the overseas provinces], or hand to a foreign country all or part of the Portuguese territory, or by any of those means offends and endangers the independence of the country... shall be liable to a sentence of from 20 to 25 years in prison.

This would make any discussion of colonial sovereignty impossible. Other clauses dispersed in legal codes or decree-laws reinforced the protection of the colonial administration. One example was a clause in the Labour Code of the Natives of Portuguese Colonies, published in 1928, little more than two years after the emergence of the Estado Novo Salazar would dominate for nearly 40 years:

> All Portuguese, as well as all individuals of other nationalities residing in

> Portuguese territory, who intentionally in public speeches, manifestos, books, booklets, newspapers or other periodicals to be sold or distributed free of payment to the public, propagate false information aiming at showing the existence of slavery or the traffic of slaves within the Portuguese colonies, will be punished with fines from 20,000 escudos, or up to two years imprisonment, and may still be liable to expulsion from Portuguese territory.

This code would be superseded by the Statute of the Natives of Angola, Mozambique, Guinea-Bissau, but since legislation on such as matters was vague, and its application uncertain, no one could be sure whether the authorities would chose to follow its letter or its spirit. I, for instance, upon being arrested in 1959 – ostensibly for writing a pamphlet protesting against not only the electoral fraud, but also the arrest of the democratic candidate General Delgado – was a victim of the insidiously discretionary methods of the regime. During the inquisitorial investigation, the PIDE had seized all my books and papers on slavery and colonialism, together with manuscripts with my thoughts that the censorship would not allow to be published had I wanted to do so. I could not, therefore, be accused within the terms of the repressive laws. However, Marvin Barris' critical pamphlet, *Portugal's African wards*, then being discussed in New York, was included in the evidence, and I was tacitly accused of being 'its moral author'. Amongst my papers, there were essays describing Salazar's Portugal as 'a caravel gone aground', and Portugal and its empire heading for a collapse. The regime would implode from in inside, or fall like a 'rotten fruit'. After three months of an inquisitorial process during which I remained incommunicado, except for long interrogation sessions, I ended up in a hospital room with uniformed guards outside the door, due to the intervention of psychiatrists who diagnosed a reactive neurosis that could leave me permanently damaged. One night I was taken from hospital and put on a plane direct to Lisbon, separated from my young wife and six year-old daughter, having lost my home and career, plunged into destitution. I was only told: that I had been arrested and was being expelled – not so much for what I had done, but because of 'what I could do'. I pleaded to be allowed to leave for Brazil with my family, but expulsion was meant to be deportation so that I could be under Portuguese jurisdiction – in the circumstances a euphemism for PIDE control. All I had left was my youth – and at 29 I arrived in London, intending to join General Delgado and Henrique Galvão in Brazil, but having developed my inadequate knowledge of English I decided it would be better if I stayed in London as the representative of the movement in the United Kingdom. When the ocean liner, *Santa Maria*, was captured, I translated the Galvão Report and offered it to *The Observer*, and a copy of the original to the *Estado de São Paulo*. Despite its pertinence as background information to the daring seizure of the *Santa Maria* – which was promptly renamed *Santa Liberdade* – few other British or US newspapers went beyond the coverage of the most sensational features of the event that reached the headlines of the world's media only for its meaning as a pioneering act of protest. But we were no political adventurers, we were but one of the many Portuguese and African nationalist groups organizing for the liberation struggle to come.

The mounting international and domestic pressures eventually strengthened the hand of the reformists within the regime, notably Minister Adriano Moreira, a friend of the Bishop of Beira, Soares de Resende, who achieved the abolition of the Statute of the Natives of Angola, Mozambique and Guinea-Bissau, which institutionalized the difference between the minority of qualified *assimilados* and the mass of 'natives' reduced to the administrative vagaries of the system of conscripted labour that had become one of the mainstays of the colonial economy. But it was too late, and the timing of the abolition of the Statute was surrounded by tragic-comic, but significant circumstances.

Comical because the regime was in no position to give the reform the publicity it deserved for fear that abolition might be taken as confirmation for the abuses that had been internationally suspected or denounced. Comical also because it had been overshadowed by the sensational world news concerning the captured Santa Maria, reported to be heading towards Luanda. But also tragic because its timing coincided with the attack on Luanda prison on 4 February 1961, followed soon after by the much more violent attacks by the predominantly ethnic Bakongo nationalists on the coffee plantations in Northern Angola where conscripted labourers from Southern Angolan ethnic groups had been used for decades within the 'native policy' of the regime. These events, in which thousands of white settlers and tens of thousands of black insurgents were slaughtered, marked the beginning of the colonial wars. From London, I followed the evolution of events where the perspective of distance and constant contact gave me a better overall view than would been the case had I stayed back in Eurocentric Portugal or its overseas provinces, which were like 'islands of separateness'. Soon after those events, I pleaded for a process of decolonization similar to those that Britain and France had managed to accomplish. Salazar, who, for all his dedicated nationalism and supposed wisdom, had never even taken the trouble, or the risk, of ever visiting the 'overseas provinces', was really governing an empire of his own imagination. At the time the regime had developed a special relationship with apartheid South Africa, where many like-minded white supremacists expected that the 'Portuguese in Mozambique and Angola' might also come to adopt their system. I wrote that in their self-defence, white settlers could still drag the unhappy continent into further misery and loss of life, but by a process of a process of peaceful change the white communities could fulfil a useful role in the immediate future of emancipated Africa. It is now known that under President Kennedy and through the US Ambassador, Admiral Anderson, in Lisbon, Washington offered to underwrite the economic assistance required for the gradual disentanglement from the colonial economy. Salazar declind the offer, proclaiming that Portugal 'was proudly alone', seeing the danger of a take-over from US imperialism due to the newly discovered Angolan oil-reserves.

Incredibly, as I found out through 'dissidents' within the regime, Salazar's main and only hope was that the crisis in the Congo would be unstoppable and, while diverting attention from Portuguese colonialism, would change the West's perspective on the 'Portuguese cause'. The strategic calculation of the Cold War over the Azores base, as well as French and British vested interests in avoiding potential communist agitation in their African 'spheres', conferred the regime a degree of diplomatic protection. In the meantime, if any process of decolonization developed, it was confined to the increasing contacts between exiled groups of activists gathered in Algiers or meeting elsewhere. The common realization was that Portugal could not decolonise, because it could not 'neo-colonise'. In that first book I foresaw that when 'the twin black and white awake and shake off their cocoons' there would be no time to reflect that the black peoples, turned into rebels, and the whites, turned into reactionaries, were alike – the victims of the overall drama of the end of colonialism that had already reached Angola. To add to the drama, the only faction of the clandestine and exiled resistance to the regime, both amongst black nationalists and Portuguese democrats, that was better organized and supported were the Communists. For me, as General Delgado's former chosen representative in the conspiratorial action in Mozambique, as well as representative of his National Independence Movement in London, our cause was summed up in a simple formula: If, without dictatorship, censorship, forced labour and the British and NATO alliances, there could be an empire – with the empire there could be no freedom or democracy.

After the assassination of General Delgado in Spain in 1965 I carried on with my career as a writer, journalist and broadcaster, committed to a common struggle for a common cause. I write, therefore, both with the benefit of being an informed witness as well as a participant in the subject of 'decolonization'. My interrogators in PIDE had been particularly irritated by my description of Portugal has 'a caravel gone aground', but the fact was that the regime – despite the liberalising efforts of Salazar's successor Prime Minister Caetano – was to remain up to the libertarian military pronunciamento of 25 April 1974, as a fixed target of a concerted war in three extensive and far flung fronts of guerrilla action, as well as attacks from Portugal's own National Liberation Front – broadcasting from Algiers, which after independence had become the meeting point of the Guinea-Bissau, Angola and Mozambique nationalist movements.

It did not amount to a process of decolonization in the conventional British, Dutch, French and Belgium precedents, but more of a sudden jump from dictatorship to common liberation and disintegration broadly within the principle enunciated by Agostinho Neto, leader of MPLA and first President of Angola during a lecture given in Dar-es-Salaam on 2 February 1974, less than three months before the coup: 'The system that oppresses and exploits the peasants in Portugal is also the system that oppresses and exploits the Angolan, with different motives, different methods but always the same purpose – exploitation! And between the Portuguese, the Angolans and Mozambicans – and the Guineans, it is possible to establish relationships, which will prevent the exploitation of man by man. The racial factor will play only a minor role and will last only a little longer, once the relationship between master and slave is brought to an end'. This and other statements of reconciliatory intentions on the part of the leaders of the liberation movements must have been in the mind of Norrie MacQueen when he concluded his book with the remark: 'Whatever their fate, the projects of the post-independence of lusophone Africa were probably the most principled and decent ever proposed for the continent. They have not been superseded in this regard, and seem unlikely to be'.[3]

However, empires do not end and nor do nations emerge according to plan; they are conditioned by the influence of many external factors that are out of the control of those directly involved. In the Portuguese case there is an obvious differentiation between the chronologically spaced end of the last remnants of the Portuguese empire in Asia and the much faster, almost simultaneous withdrawal from the last five colonies in Africa.

Looking first and briefly at the end of the empire in Asia, it really started as far back as 1961 when India – after more than a decade of appeals for negotiation – summarily expelled the Portuguese administration from Goa in a lightening military operation with little violence or bloodshed. The cases of Macao and East Timor provide a dramatic contrast, which seems to show that the success or otherwise of decolonization depends as much – if not more – on the decolonized than on the colonisers. In the case of Macao, the Chinese established the principle that it was up to them, and not to the 'temporary administrative powers', to determine the dates, terms and conditions for the transfer of powers. By contrast, the Indonesian regime, a remote pro-Western ally in the Cold War, still maintained the most amicable relations with the Portuguese regime up until 1972, with the Portuguese Ambassador publishing a rather cordial book on the history of the 'Portuguese in Indonesia'. In the wake of the libertarian coup in Portugal, as is well known, the Jakarta regime unleashed the most brutal war of annexation on East Timor, causing an unnecessary devastation and the deaths of tens if not hundreds of thousands. With the emotions of mourning and panic touching the entire population, and an oppression dramatically contrasting with the comparatively benign Portuguese colonial administration, the summary Indonesian takeover must rank as one of the most disgraceful episodes in the history of decolonization. After yet another outburst of violence upon the overwhelmingly adverse results of the UN sponsored referendum on independence in 1999, the Australians were asked to intervene to re-establish law and order and, at the at the time of writing, East Timor still remains a major humanitarian concern for the UN and an unhappy *post-scriptum* to the end of empire. By contrast, after more than two decades of transition and preparation by both China and Portugal, Macao must rank as one of the most successful achievements in the annals of decolonization.

Let me therefore repeat, bearing in mind also the case of Cape Verde which proved to be prepared for self-government, despite its share of the same oppressive rigours of obscurantist colonial rule, that the success or otherwise of independence, while conditioned by circumstances, can depend as much, if not more, on the former colonized, than on the former colonisers, before jumping, as it were, straight from colonialism to the separated evolution in democratic Portugal and the newly independent PALOPs until the creation of the Community of Portuguese Speaking Countries (CPLP), and the common attempt to salvage from the disintegration of old empire, whatever positive historical and cultural links might be worth forging on a basis of mutual respect.

The challenge of the CPLP: Community of Portuguese Speaking Countries

The pace of change in political thinking has accelerated so much in the past 25 years since the Portuguese completed their radical withdrawal from Africa upon leaving Angola formally at midnight on 11 November 1975, that the first and last words – discoveries and decolonization – more often used to describe the beginning and the end of the five-centuries old empire, have become 'incorrect' and controversial. During the successive commemorations of the arrivals of Columbus to America and Alvares Cabral to Brazil it was said there had been no discoveries at all since lands and peoples were already there for millennia. The Brazilians even adopted the synonym achamento (finding), in their commemorative literature.

I have become weary of such semantic controversies since the Portuguese used to be accused of arrogance for using descriptions such as Portuguese India, Portuguese Guinea, Portuguese East or West Africa when, on reflection, they turned out to be humble recognitions of the necessity of differentiation from much bigger neighbours, such as British India, French Guinea, or British and German East and West Africa, particularly in postal and telegraphic messages. With perhaps more reason, the use of the term decolonization has been put into question by most African nationalists when applied to the sudden and hectic Portuguese withdrawal. In fact, unlike the case of the former French colonies which, with the exception of Guinea, moved into autonomous status within the Francophone community, or the former British colonies which became independent states within the Commonwealth, with provisions for a transition from white settler to full African rule where applicable, the Portuguese breakaway from the empire was so decisive that it was marked by the uprooting and exodus of the mass of white settlers and the severance of all the previous official and social-conomic links – with the exception of the Portuguese ownership of the Cabora Bassa Dam, one of the biggest in Southern Africa, which was built in the 1960's when most Africans countries were attaining independence.

Paradoxically therefore, having been the most oppressed under a regime that some Marxists described as 'ultra-colonialism' the five PALOP countries jumped straight into a more genuine state independence and choice of international relationships than was, and remains, the case with most of the other African countries. In fact, under the first Marxist revolutionary governments, led by Agostinho Neto and Samora Machel, at least Angola and Mozambique – if not also Guinea-Bissau – sought closer links with the Soviet Union and other Comecon bloc countries that had supported their armed wars of liberation. In the case of Angola, the Cubans – overcoming Soviet reservations over another involvement in Africa –

after their frustrating experience in the Congo in the early 1960s, came to assume such a prominent role in Angola, due to the threat from white dominated South Africa that, until the Americans forced their removal, it appeared they would succeed the Portuguese in Angola (albeit within a different ideological aim).

Personally, I welcomed the success of the lightening and non-violent military pronunciamento on April 1974 with jubilation tempered by mixed feelings of sadness and concern over the eventual consequences for the colonies-cum-overseas provinces. Sadness because, after all, as a former member of General Delgado's candidacy in 1958 and fellow fighter in exile up to his assassination in 1965. I knew that the aims of the Armed Forces Movement behind the Carnation Revolution were essentially the same as those we had been fighting for. In fact, during his years of exile in Brazil and Algiers, Delgado had often exhorted the armed forces to direct their courage to the overthrow of the Salazar regime rather than towards the African peoples fighting their just wars of liberation. One of my first contacts with one of the (until then) unknown leaders of the Armed Forces Movement, the then Major Victor Alves, had been somewhat disappointing. Upon being asked, at a public meeting in Britain, why the April 1975 revolution had succeeded when all previous ones had failed, the Major had replied triumphantly that it was due to the fact that 'the military, unlike the civilians, know how to keep secrets'. I could not help but rise up to remind him and the audience that his answer was misleading- 'in fact we civilians,' I stated, 'had needed to conspire not with, but against the armed forces which had been after all the very mainstay of the regime'. The flippant distortion or sheer ignorance implied in the Major's statement did not augur well. I decided, unlike many of my exiled friends, to suspend any involvement in party politics, and opted for a new career as a correspondent for *The Guardian* and other papers, while pursuing my long standing work as a commentator for the BBC Portuguese Service that had made me well known as an opponent of the former regime.

It was in this new role as a visiting press correspondent that I came to meet many of the Armed Forces Movement leaders to whom my voice had become familiar when the BBC was heard regularly in Portugal and the African territories as the most reliable source of news in the years before the coup. In fact at a memorable press conference given by General Costa Gomes, then the would – be successor of President Spínola, and other leaders of the Armed Forces Movement, I had to move from the ranks of the international press to act as an interpreter because none of the army officers present spoke English with the required fluency if at all. This lack of preparation was at least a sure sign that the coup had been a purely spontaneous national affair. In the course of time, as many of my close friends assumed positions of power – notably António de Almeida Santos – who had been a fellow member of the board sponsoring General Delgado's candidacy in Mozambique, and had become the head the improvised Ministry of Interterritorial Affairs, even before the crucial decision that led to turning the 'overseas provinces' into independent states, I was to acquire a better insight into the irreversible evolution that was then called the 'revolutionary process'. To the 1974

General Assembly, I managed to combine my native knowledge of the situation with the cosmopolitan experience I had gained during my eventful 16-year exile in London. In addition to what has been written, both in Portugal or abroad, on this agitated period, I would only add that the explanation for some of the major developments that took place has to take into account a less known factor – namely the strong oral sub-culture the Portuguese developed as a tacit strategy of national survival. One must bear in mind that if in the Iberian Peninsula the Spanish were looked upon not so much as neighbours than as latent enemies, and that in the oceans and the colonies there were other powerful imperialist rivals – including the not so reliable England-cum-Britain – to understand that, both within the regime as in the ranks of the clandestine opposition, there were those who believed that upon leaving the empire, one of the super-powers engaged in a Cold War for world hegemony, would simply take over, even if only to anticipate the other in expansionist rivalry. Cunha Leal, a respected former Republican minister and lifelong opponent of the regime, was as explicit in his books on colonial issues as Salazar himself in his confidences within the regime. In this respect the emergence and development of black 'nativist' nationalist movements eventually destroyed initial claims and arguments that they were only manipulated agents of either Soviet or American imperialism. This had a decisively disturbing moral impact in a country where the first native fighter – *Viriato* – whose heroic deeds precede the emergence of Portuguese nationality, let alone monarchy. Moreover, the hundreds of thousands of Portuguese peasants that were conscripted to fight black peasants turned into nationalist rebels, were increasingly demoralized by the legitimacy of the struggle for independence. On a fact-finding tour of Angola and Mozambique, where the then transitional governor, Dr Soares de Melo – also a lifelong opponent of the former regime was a friend of mine – I was told by middle ranking officers that the ordinary soldiers had long been questioning these moral issues and even evading orders. The strong oral sub-culture extended to the higher ranks of the military, governance and diplomacy. The coup was achieved through a mixture of daring of a few young officers, notably Salgueiro Maia, who almost single-handedly arrested Caetano and most of his cabinet, and perhaps a few officers outnumbered by those former supporters of the regime who surrendered peacefully. The Armed Forces were, afterall, the institution that, by definition, is devoted to professional nationalism. Having been the mainstay of the regime when Salazar's national-colonialism seemed to be viable, they changed their loyalty when the alternative of joining the then EEC offered a way out of empire. The much-publicized campaigns against the Vietnam War, as well as the ominous precedent of the American withdrawal from Saigon, provided both the model and the face-saving cover for the strategic withdrawal from Africa. With a far flung empire which, with Brazil, had been 125 times larger than Portugal, and afterwards, with Angola and Mozambique, still larger than Western Europe, Portuguese governance and diplomacy abided by a guideline expressed by an anonymous nineteenth century diplomat: 'since Portugal is too small and poor a country with a history only rich in experiences of survival, it obviously knows more about the outside world, than the outside knew or cared about it.' Even the disdain over the centuries old alliance-cum-protectorate from England-cum-Britain was often cynically dismissed as a protection racket for which a toll had to be paid – but the toll was after all, an ill-gotten gain from the empire.

Kenneth Maxwell describes these traditions of governance in the following eloquent passage of his book, which is the clearest analysis of the subject to date:

> There was a pathology to Portugal's intransigence. Antonio de Figueiredo has called it the 'metaphysics' of empire, though it can also be explained by the psychology of a small power as it responds to unwelcome outside pressure. Portugal is a classic case of a country that survived the enveloping power of its dominant neighbours. Sharing the Iberian Peninsula with a larger and more powerful Spain and the oceans with the British, it is no accident that the Portuguese diplomatic service became absolute masters at delay, obfuscation, and manipulation, and finding ways of protecting Portuguese national interests in situations were overt power alone would have overwhelmed the Portuguese. Thus, while Salazar's ability to manipulate the international situation to Portugal's favor was considerable it was a so a skill that emerged out of Portuguese history. In the end, however, this skill was harnessed to the defense of intransigence and indefensible positions. The result was that Portugal was backed into a situation in which there remained no options whatsoever.[4]

I could not put it better myself. But my description of Portugal's 'metaphysical colonialism' was not only an allusion to the spiritualist and religious claims of Portuguese expansion, blessed by the Catholic Church, but an ironic title for a chapter devoted to the vicissitudes of Portuguese rule. Portugal could be said to belong to that group of small nations that feeling themselves threatened by extinction, (in the Portuguese case absorption by Spain), turn into oppressors and exploiters of other peoples. It is true that, when one looks at Spain and the endless struggle of the Catalans, and the Basques, to escape the centralist rule of Madrid, the Portuguese determination and zeal to retain its independence looks valid; when one sees, in the light of events in the former Congo or more recently the potential risks in Zimbabwe, the radicalism of the Portuguese withdrawal and exodus of the white settlers seems wiser than it did 25 years ago.

However, the millions of Africans in the empire paid the tremendous cost of the achievement – an empire that was a construct of Salazar's own nationalistic imagination since the ultimate paradox is that he never even went to Africa.

The empire is dead, long live the EU

Portugal's latest 'discovery' is that integration into the EU is proving to be a far better proposition than the latter day colonialism – even in the richer colonies of the former overseas empire. In the EU context, Portugal's post-colonial record of stability and impressive economic growth since the qualifying stages for admission in 1986, up to the smooth transition into the EMU by the turn of the century, might be comparable to those of Spain, Greece or Ireland, which likewise have shared in the 'cohesion funds' from Brussels, increased investments and tourism and other factors coincidental or related to the current dizzying technological and consumerist revolution.

But for Portugal, the return to its European condition after centuries of colonialist introversion in the colonies-cum-'overseas provinces' of the empire, and the short-lived but traumatic dislocation caused by the radical withdrawal from Angola and Mozambique, has had a much deeper impact and significance. Having joined the then EEC, side by side with Spain, which has historically been regarded as a potential threat to Portugal's independence, seemed to prove that the empire had, after all, fulfilled its role as a provider of the means to preserve Portuguese statehood. This also implicitly meant that the six-centuries old alliance with England-cum-Britain, already superseded by the joint membership in NATO, had become redundant, with Portugal, unlike Britain, having found a new comfortable role as a beneficiary within the EU so soon after losing the empire. Moreover, membership of the EU for a small country with inherited bilateral relationships outside Europe, such as with the US over the Azores, or Indonesia and Australia over East Timor, offers other diplomatic and consular advantages. At a diplomatic level, at least at the present stage of integration, being able to act on a bilateral basis when convenient, or to count on EU support when necessary, is a considerable asset. Reliance on the EU is also consistent with the belief that European unity is a way to contribute to the balance of peace and international co-operation, on the principle that, if power corrupts, super-power supremacy might corrupt absolutely – whatever nation holds it. Moreover, in relation to the newly independent PALOPs (African Countries of Portuguese Official Language – as they described themselves), the new EU membership status added strength to Portuguese diplomacy, as is evidenced by the fact that soon after admission in 1986 Portugal was able to participate as a full member at the first EU-Africa summit in Harare.

At a consular and individual citizenship levels, membership of the EU added immeasurable value, strength and benefits to Portuguese nationality, particularly for the millions of the diaspora outside Europe and Brazil (where Portuguese nationals enjoy privileged status on a reciprocal basis), in countries as far apart as the USA, Australia, Canada and South Africa – as well as other African countries, including notably the five PALOPs.

The overall impact of Portugal's new status as a member of the EU in accelerating the development that was already beginning to be felt since the lessening of the budgetary burden with the colonial wars and the support given to the *retornados* (returned settlers) from Angola and Mozambique from public reserve funds, was aptly summed up by the Brazilian journalist Eduardo Salgado in the popular weekly, Veja, during 1999, in a report ironically entitled 'A Portuguese miracle made in Brussels':

> For as long as we can remember, we Brazilians have derided Portugal, our little relation across the Atlantic. We recall that in the 1960s, half of

> Portugal's homes had no electricity, and we still think of it as a backward place where each citizen's sole desire is to emigrate. We must think again: For Portugal is undergoing a miracle, and Portuguese immigrants to Brazil are now queuing up to return home. In the past decade, its per capita income has trebled and its economic growth has outstripped most of Europe. So many streets, bridges and tunnels are built each year that road maps are out of date as soon as they are printed. All this has been due to one simple fact: membership of the EU (and latterly the EMU). It turned a marginal country into part of a major trading bloc whose other members, taking advantage of its cheap labour costs, have been eager to invest there. But even more important than the material benefits of entry has been the change in outlook: the hidebound conservatism of yesterday has been replaced by a spirit of innovation and tolerance. Long taboo issues – gay rights, legalising drugs – are now openly discussed.[5]

The picture described by the Brazilian journalist reflects the fact that Portugal, which in colonial times had less than that half of the average per capita income of Western Europe and only 54 per cent in 1986, attained 74 per cent of the EU average income in 1999. This achievement is also reflected directly in a better balance of migration, with more immigrants returning to Portugal, while a new generation avails itself of the right of free circulation within the EU to seek employment with the added incentive of language and cultural learning.

However, this success story is not exceptional in the European context; other terms of comparison that are more directly pertinent to Portugal's transition from centuries of overseas imperialism to less than two decades of full integration in the EU and the EMU are even more impressive and politically significant.

According to the SADCC's at the time of its foundation in 1984 – thus still excluding 'apartheid' South Africa – while Mozambique's development was comparable to that of Tanzania, at the time of independence, the development of Angola, where economic and infrastructural development of Angola, where industry already accounted for 20 per cent of GDP, compared favourably with that of the most developed countries of Southern Africa, excluding South Africa, i.e. seven former British colonies, including Zimbabwe. This was a surprising achievement for a small colonialist country which, determined to hold on to its 'overseas provinces' and even increase their white population, made a considerable administrative investment in both Angola and Mozambique, including the constrction of the Cabora Bassa Dam, one of the biggest in Africa, and designed to have South Africa as one of its main customers.

At the time, Portugal's GDP was still only US$23bn – or just over the combined GDP of the nine founding members of the SADCC – with an area much bigger, incidentally, than that of Western Europe and a population of 60 million – about six and a half times that of Portugal.

But when it come to comparisons with South Africa, Southern Africa's regional super power, and the home to an estimated half a million Portuguese, or 10 per cent of its white population, the picture was much different. By 1980 Portugal's

GDP was only US$28bn compared with South Africa's US$78bn. Given the geographical dominant proximity of South Africa in relation to Mozambique, the nearest outlet to the sea for the landlocked Transvaal, the richest of South Africa's provinces, and to Angola, the fact that its economy dwarfed that of small Portugal, the oldest but also by far the poorest 'colonial powers', was naturally the cause of much embarrassment. At the time it used to be said, amongst white separatist settlers as well as the more educated blacks, that Johannesburg alone had more cars than the whole of Portugal. This might not have been too surprising, considering that Johannesburg was the capital of the gold-rich Rand (now Gauteng), often described as the industrial heart of Southern Africa, and the need for motor cars in a much bigger country with undeveloped and racially segregated public transport was much greater. Nevertheless, it was an embarrassing reference to Portugal's anachronistic inadequacy for its role as a coloniser, let alone as a promoter of modern development.

This situation, however, was to change dramatically in just two decades following the withdrawal in 1975, and particularly since Portugal, emerging from its illusory status as the oldest old style-colonial power, returned to its European condition to become a member of the EU.

The following table, based on World Bank, OEDC and South African data, which compares the growth of Portugal's GDP to that of South Africa between 1980 and 1999, and reflects the contrast between the upsurge trend of the

Table 9.1:
GDP, Portugal and South Africa (US$m)

	1980	1998	1999*
Portugal	28 729	106 650	121 900
South Africa	78 744	116 730	118 000

*estimated

Table 9.2:
Average annual GDP growth, Portugal and South Africa (%)

	1980-90	1990-98	1999*
Portugal	3.1	2.3	3.1
South Africa	1.2	1.6	0.9

*estimated

Portuguese economy and South Africa's gradually declining growth rate:

The contrasting economic trends reflected in this table should not make anyone gloat, least of all the Portuguese who have an immigrant and descendant community in South Africa amounting to nearly 10 per cent of its white minority and, like everyone else, wish all the best to the new South African democracy. Moreover, if the contrast is so favourable to Portugal, the fact is that, first and foremost, it also confirms that whereas Portugal, upon withdrawal from colonialism, made such a comparatively quick recovery with the help fellow EU member countries, post-apartheid South Africa has had to rely on itself, despite the consequences of adverse terms of trade, the outflow of capital and other factors that are reflected in the sharp devaluation of the Rand. It is perhaps also a sad reflection of the old economic social order whereby the whiter you are the mightier are the chances that you will succeed.

But its pertinence as a point of comparison in the period in which both countries needed to readjust and recover from traumas of major events – the 'end of empire' for Portugal, and the 'end of apartheid' for South Africa – is that Portugal is now much better qualified to cooperate with both the Portuguese-speaking countries – its fellow CPLP members – as well as with other countries in the SADC, including South Africa.

Since the withdrawal in 1975, having absorbed the impact of the collapse of the regime, the end of empire and the reintegration of over half a million settlers and African-born citizens, Portugal has bounced back as an increasingly prosperous member of the EU.

By dramatic contrast, most of the former colonies, from East Timor to Guinea-Bissau, Mozambique and Angola, have turned their independence into nation-building in the most adverse conditions and circumstances. On personal visits, as well as through my close professional contacts with Angolans, Mozambicans, Guineans and Cape Verdians in the BBC Portuguese for Africa Service, where I am now the oldest serving contributor, I acquired some insight into their own oral sub-culture. I will spare you details, since their various political dramas and, in the case of Angola, war and corruption, have been well publicized. In short, they are too busy in the task of nation building to care to participate or read studies on decolonization. The situation, albeit in even more adverse conditions, can be summed up by recalling the comment of an Italian who had fought side by side with Garibaldi for Italian unification: 'Italy we already have; what we need now is Italians'.

This applies just as well to the African situation – Angola, Mozambique, Guinea-Bissau and now East Timor have emerged as states. Nation building has only started.

For 'decolonization' one should read a 'splitting of ways'. No one should be misled into thinking that in comparison with the outcome for the former colonies, and particularly East Timor, Portuguese colonial administration has been somewhat redeemed.

Successive Portuguese governments have offered co-operation, assistance and intercession within the EU on behalf of the emerging PALOP nations – as matter of duty as much as reciprocal advantage. In the splitting of ways and dramatically contrasting trajectories, it was not until 1996 that the CPLP, originally suggested by Brazil as far back as the 1960s as a way out of the Portugal colonial impasse, was created. In addition to the criticisms that have been voiced concerning the reciprocal lack of interest – for their own different reasons – of most of the various member countries, I still think it is a worthwhile challenge and particularly in what concerns education and the development of a shared or related culture. Comprising at present seven countries of vastly varied dimensions the CPLP, given the demography of Brazil, has already a majority of black and mixed Afro-European peoples – an indication of how slavery is, after all, one of the main features of the Portugal-Angola-Brazil relationship. It is also the group where the common language, Portuguese, is one of the most devalued of international languages due to the high rates of illiteracy and lower standards of living. What better challenge could there be for a joint effort for progress?

I have reached an age when one is weary of predictions and exhortations. In the context of the transition from empire, 'the past is another country' – or, more properly, other countries. Africans do not question their natural right to independence, and as for the Portuguese – freed from the empire they have become an open, modernized society, with no need for secrecy, censorship, oppression or subterfuge.

The old idealisms are gone, and as if to prove that European integration also implies uniformization, the latest survey of public opinion showed that over 70 per cent of the Portuguese have no interest in politics. The passing of generations will inevitably bring an amnesia of the errors and injustices of the past.

As for myself, I am pleased that I am now regarded as a pioneer long overtaken by events – after all, we can only be pioneers of causes that were worthy and lasting.

As a Portuguese, I say: the empire is dead, long live the EU! But as a fellow anti-colonialist fighter I join Africans in saying: the empire is dead, long live freedom!

Notes:

* António de Figueiredo, 10 September 2000

[1] Resende, D. Sebastião Soares de (1994), *Profeta em Moçambique*, Lisbon: Difel.

[2] These books were published in the African Today Series of the American Committee on Africa, New York, in 1958.

[3] MacQueen, N. (1997), *The decolonization of Portuguese Africa: metropolitan revolution and the dissolution of empire*, London: Longman.

[4] Maxwell, K. (1995), *The making of Portuguese democracy*, Cambridge: Cambridge University Press.

[5] Salgado, E. (1999), 'A Portuguese miracle made in Brussels', Veja.

Bibliography

Abecassis, R. (1998), 'CPLP vive num mar de equívocos', *O Independente*, 9 April, p. 18.

Abreu, W. P. de (1983), *Do 25 de Abril ao 25 de Novembro: memória do tempo perdido*, Braga: Intervenção.

Aguiar, L. (1977), *Livro negro da descolonização*, Braga: Intervenção.

Albino, C. (1994), 'Mudança radical em 24 horas', *Diário de Notícias*, 13 July, p. 10.

Ameal, J. (1968), *História de Portugal*, 6th edition, Oporto: Tavares Martins.

António, V. (ed.) (1981), *Atlas eleitoral: resultados eleitorais 1975-1980*, 2nd edition, Lisbon: Editorial Progresso Social e Democracia.

Antunes, J. F. (1981), *O segredo do 25 de Novembro*, 3rd edition, Mem Martins: Europa-América.

Antunes, J. F. (1990), *O factor africano (1890-1990)*, Venda Nova, Bertrand.

AP World Politics (2002), 'East Timor says dispute over maritime boundary tests friendship with Australia', ww.globalpolicy.org/security/issues/etimindx.htm, accessed 26 July.

Avillez, M. J. (1997), 'Faço hoje o que dizia há 20 anos', *Expresso Revista*, 28 June, pp. 46-56.

Avillez, M. J. (1996a), *Soares: democracia*, Lisbon: Público.

Avillez, M. J. (1996b), *Soares: ditadura e revolução*, Lisbon: Público.

Bacalhau, M. (1994), *Atitudes, opiniões e comportamentos políticos dos portugueses 1973-1993*, Lisbon: Heptágono.

Baganha, M. (1998a), 'Portuguese emigration after World War II', in Pinto, A. C. (ed.), *Modern Portugal*, Palo Alto, CA: SPOSS, pp. 189-205.

Baganha, M. (1998b), 'Immigrant involvement in the informal economy: the Portuguese case', *Journal of Ethnic and Migration Studies*, 24 (2), pp. 367-85.

Baldwin-Edwards, M. (1999), 'Where free markets reign: aliens in the twilight zone', in Baldwin-Edwards, M. and Arango, J. (eds.), *Immigrants and the informal economy in southern Europe*, London: Cass, pp. 1-15.

Barata, T. (1998), *Timor contemporâneo*, Lisbon: Equilíbrio.

Barreto, A. and Mónica, M. F. (eds.) (1999), *Dicionário de história de Portugal*, Vols. VII-VIII, Oporto: Figueirinhas.

Barreto, A. M. (1986), *L'état et la société civile au Portugal: révolution et réforme agraire en Alentejo, 1974-1976*, Lisbon: Gradiva.

Barrows, P. W. (1990), *The historical roots of Cape Verdean dependency, 1460-1990*, unpublished Ph.D. dissertation: University of Minnesota, pp. 199-217.

Bernardes, L. (1994), 'Cimeira lusófona até ao final do ano', *Diário de Notícias*, 26 July 1994, p. 5.

Birmingham, D. (1995), *The decolonization of Africa*, Athens: Ohio University Press.

Bragança, A. de (1987), 'Independence without decolonization: Mozambique 1974-1975', in Gifford, P. and Louis, W. R. (eds.), *Decolonization and African independence: the transfers of power 1960-1980*, New Haven MA: Yale University Press.

Branco, V. (1999), 'L'Immigration au Portugal: une nouvelle immigration dans un ancien pays d'emigration', unpublished MA thesis, Paris: IEPPCSS.

Brookshaw, D. (1992), 'Islands apart: tradition and transition', *Index on Censorship*, 6, pp. 13-4.

Cabral, M. V. (1996), 'CPLP, potencial e contradições', *Diário de Notícias*, 22 July.

Caetano, M. (1973), *Razões da presença de Portugal no Ultramar*, Lisbon: n.p.

Caetano, M. (1974), *Depoimento*, Rio de Janeiro: Distribuidora Record.

Caetano, M. (1976), *O 25 de Abril e o Ultramar: três entrevistas e alguns documentos*, Lisbon: Verbo.

Cahen, M. (2001a), 'L'Afrique de langue officielle portugaise: le premier quart de siècle', *Pays lusophones d'Afrique: sources d'information pour le développement. Angola, Cap-Vert, Guinée-Bissau, Mozambique, São Tomé e Príncipe*, Paris: Ibiscus, CEAN.

Cahen, M. (2001b), 'Afrique lusophone: approche socio-linguistique', *Pays lusophones d'Afrique. Sources d'information pour le développement. Angola, Cap-Vert, Guinée-Bissau, Mozambique, São Tomé e Príncipe*, Paris: Ibiscus, CEAN.

Cahen, M. (1999), 'Îles do Cap Vert: d'un micro-monde au système-monde?', *Lusotopie*, pp. 525-30.

Cahen, M. (1998), 'La francophonie contre la France', *Politique Africaine*, 70 (June), pp. 137-40.

Cahen, M. (1997), 'Des caravelles pour le futur? Discours politique et idéologie dans l'"institutionnalisation" de la Communauté des pays de langue portugaise', *Lusotopie*, pp. 391-433.

Cahen, M. (1994), 'Angola, Moçambique, que futuro para os crioulos?', *InformÁfrica Confidencial*, 63 (July), pp. 18-19.

Cardoso, F. H. (1996), *Discurso do Senhor Presidente da República Federativa do Brasil, por ocasião da sessão solene de abertura da Reunião de Cúpula da Comunidade dos Países de Língua Portuguesa*, Lisbon, 17 July.

Carey, P. and Bentley, G. C. (eds.) (1995), *East Timor at the crossroads: the forging of a nation*, London: Cassell.

Carrascalão, M. A. (2002), *Timor: os anos de resistência*, Lisbon: Mensagem.

Carvalho, R. de (ed.) (1978), *'Dossier' Carlucci/CIA*, Lisbon: Avante!

Castelo, C. (1998), *'O modo português de estar no mundo': o luso-tropicalismo e a ideologia colonial portuguesa (1933-1961)*, Oporto: Afrontamento.

Castilho, J. M. T. (2000), *A ideia de Europa no Marcelismo (1968-74)*, Lisbon: Afrontamento.

Céu Esteves, M do (ed.), *Portugal: país de imigração*, Lisbon: IEPD.

Chabal, P. (1996), 'The transition to multi-party politics in lusophone Africa: problems and prospects', *Lusotopie*, pp. 57-70.

Chan, S. and Jabri, V. (eds.) (1993), *Mediation in southern Africa*, London: Macmillan.

Chissano, J. (1996), *Discurso do Presidente da República de Moçambique. Cimeira Constitutiva da CPLP*, Lisbon, 17 July.

Coissoró, N. (1979), 'O caso de Goa', in *A descolonização portuguesa*, vol. 2, Grupo de Pesquisa sobre a Descolonização Portuguesa, Lisbon: Instituto Democracia e Liberdade, vol. 2, pp. 137-55.

Comissão para o Estudo das Campanhas de África (1961-1974) do Estado-Maior do Exército (1988), *Resenha histórico-militar das campanhas de África, 1° volume: enquadramento geral*, Lisbon: CECA-EME.

Corkill, D. (1999), *The development of the Portuguese economy: a case of Europeanisation*, Routledge: London.

Corkill, D. (1996), 'Multiple identities, immigration and racism in Spain and Portugal', in Jenkins, B. and Sofos, S. (eds.), *Nation and identity in contemporary Europe*, London: Routledge, pp. 155-71.

Corkill, D. (ed.) (1993), *The Portuguese economy since 1947*, Edinburgh: Edinburgh University Press.

Corkill, D. and Eaton, M. (1998), 'Multicultural insertions in a small economy: Portugal's immigrant communities', *South European Society and Politics*, 3 (3), pp. 149-68.

Correia, P. P. (1991), *Descolonização de Angola: a jóia da coroa do império português*, Lisbon: Inquérito.

Costa, B. (2002), 'Imigração', *Focus*, 141, pp. 26-30.

CPLP (1996a), *Comunicado final da sessão de trabalho da Conferência de Chefes de Estado e de Governo. Constitutiva da Comunidade dos Países de Língua Portuguesa*, Lisbon, 17 July.

CPLP (1996b), *Declaração Constitutiva da Comunidade dos Países de Língua Portuguesa*, Lisbon, 17 July.

CPLP (1996c), *Estatutos da Comunidade dos Países de Língua Portuguesa*, Lisbon, 17 July.

Cravinho, J. G. (1998), 'Cooperação e contribuintes', *Expresso*, 1 May, pp. 22-4.

Cruz, M. (1996), 'Lusofonia constitui âncora da identidade nacional', *Diário de Notícias*, 8 December, p. 8.

Cunha, C. A. (1992), *The Portuguese Communist Party's strategy for power, 1921-1986*, New York NY: Garland.

Cunha, L. M. de J. (1991), 'A nação e o império: a (re)invenção do lugar de Portugal no mundo', *Cadernos do Noroeste*, 4 (6-7).

Davinson, B. (1989), *The fortunate island: a study in African transformation*, Trenton NJ: Africa World Press.

Delgado, I. and Figueiredo, A. de (eds.) (1991), *Memórias de Humberto Delgado*, Lisbon: Dom Quixote.

Dias, A. S. (1995), 'Em Português nos desconhecemos', *Público-Magazine*, 7 May, pp. 40-54.

Dias, J. (1996), 'As actuais importações portuguesas com origem nos PALOPs e a importância da anterior ligação colonial', *Lusotopie*, pp. 93-103

Dias, P. C. (1998), 'Dependência, independência?', *Expresso*, 18 April, p. 22.

Domingues, J. M. (1998), 'Identité, cooperation et influence: l'enterprise politique de la CPLP', *Diplôme d'Études Approfondies*, Université de Paris 1 (Sorbonne), in www.terra vista.pt/PortoSanto/1646, accessed 22 June 1999.

Drain, M. and Domenech, B. (1982), *Occupations de terres et expropriations dans les campagnes portugaises: présentation de documents relatifs à la période 1974-1977*, Paris: Éditions du CNRS.

Dupraz, P. (1999), 'Pour une bibliographie des immigrations africaines au Portugal', *Lusotopie*, pp. 516-24.

Eaton, M. (1999), 'Immigration in the 1990s: a study of the Portuguese labour market', *European Urban and Regional Studies*, 6 (4), pp. 364-70.

Eaton, M. (1998), 'Foreign residents and illegal immigrants in Portugal', *International Journal of Intercultural Relations*, 22 (1), pp. 49-66.

Edmonds, R. L. (1993), 'Macau: past, present and future', *Asian Affairs*, 3 (24).

Eurostat (1997), *Eurostat yearbook 1997: a statistical eye on Europe, 1986-1996*, Luxembourg: Eurostat.

Eyzaguirre, P. B. (1989), 'The independence of São Tomé and Príncipe and agrarian reform', *Journal of Modern African Studies*, 27 (4), pp. 671-8.

Far Eastern Economic Review (2000), 'Ghosts in paradise', 31 August.

Far Eastern Economic Review (1999), 'Scorched earth', 16 September.

Fernandes, M. S. (2002), 'A iniciativa gorada de Franco Nogueira para o estabelecimento de relações diplomáticas entre Portugal e a China continental em 1964', *Revista Administração de Macau*, 56 (XV), 2, pp. 559-602.

Fernandes, M. S. (2000), *Sinopsis de Macau nas relações Luso-Chinesas*, Lisbon: Fundação Oriente.

Ferreira, J. M. (ed.) (1998), *Portugal em transe*, Vol. 8 of Mattoso, J. (ed.), *História de Portugal*, Lisbon: Círculo de Leitores.

Ferreira, M. E. (1997), 'Les contour économiques de la CPLP', *Lusotopie*, pp. 11-34.

Ferreira, M. E. (1994), 'Relações entre Portugal e Africa de língua portuguesa: comércio, investimento e dívida (1973-1994), *Análise Social*, XXIX (129), pp. 1071-121.

Filho, J. (1996), 'Inmigrantes caboverdianos en Portugal', *Arbor*, 154 (607), pp. 151-70.

Fola Soremekun, F. (1983), *Angola: the road to Independence*, Ile-ife: University of Ife Press.

Fonseca, M. (1997), 'The geography of recent immigration to Portugal', unpublished paper presented to conference on *Non-Military Aspects of Security in Southern Europe: Migration, Employment and the Labour Market*, Santorini, Greece.

Freyre, G. (1961), *Portuguese integration in the tropics*, Lisbon: n.p.

Freyre, G. (1952), *Casa-grande e senzala: formação da família brasileira sob o regime de economia patriarcal*, Rio de Janeiro: José Olympio.

Fundação Joaquim Nabuco (1996), 'Os trópicos na era da globalização', *Reunião Especial comemorativa dos 30 anos do Seminário de Tropicologia*, Fundação Joaquim Nabuco, Setúbal, in http://fundaj.gov.br/docs/tropico/semi/trop30-2.html, accessed 22 June 2000.

Gallagher, T. (1983), *Portugal: a twentieth century interpretation*, Manchester: Manchester University Press.

Gama, J. (1983), *Por uma nova comunidade dos países de língua portuguesa*, 15 November.

Gleijeses, P. (2002), *Conflicting missions: Havana, Washington, and Africa, 1959-1976*, University of North Carolina Press, 2002.

Gomes, V. (1980), *Tempo de resistência (I Parte)*, Lisbon: Ler.

Gonçalves, A. (1996), 'A paradigm of autonomy: the Hong Kong and Macau SARs', *Contemporary Southeast Asia*, 18 (1), pp. 36-60.

Gonçalves, A. (1993), 'Les implications juridico-constitutionelles du transfert de la souveraineté de Macao à la République Populaire de Chine', *Revue Internationale de Droit Comparée*, 4, pp. 36-60.

GPDP—Grupo de Pesquisa sobre a Descolonização Portuguesa (1982), *A descolonização portuguesa: aproximação a um estudo*, Vol. 2, Lisbon: Instituto Democracia e Liberdade.

GPDP—Grupo de Pesquisa sobre a Descolonização Portuguesa (1979), *A descolonização portuguesa: aproximação a um estudo*, Vol. 1, Lisbon: Instituto Democracia e Liberdade.

Graham, L. S. (1973), 'Portugal: the bureaucracy of empire', *LADAC Occasional Papers*, 2 (9), Austin: University of Texas.

Guerra, J. P. (1996), *Descolonização portuguesa: o regresso das caravelas*, Lisbon: Dom Quixote.

Guibentif, P. (1996), 'Le Portugal face à l'immigration', *Revue Européenne des Migrations Internationales*, 12 (1), pp. 121–38.

Guimarães, F. A. (1998), *The origins of the Angolan civil war: foreign intervention and domestic political conflict*, Basingstoke: Macmillan.

Gunn, G. C. (1999), *Timor-Lorosae: 500 years*, Macao: Livros do Oriente.

Gusmão, X. (1994), *Timor Leste: um povo, uma pátria*, Lisbon: Colibri.

Hamilton, K. A. (1992), 'Lusophone Africa, Portugal, and the United States: possibilities for more effective cooperation', *CSIS/FLAD Significant Issues*, XIV (11).

Harvey, R. (1978), *Portugal: birth of a democracy*, London: Macmillan.

Heimer, F. W. (1979), *The decolonization conflict in Angola 1974-76: an essay in political sociology*, Geneva: Institut Universitaire de Hautes Études Internationales.

Henriques, I. C. (1999), 'Portugal e as realidades africanas: práticas e preconceitos', *Janus 99-2000: anuário de relações exteriores*, Lisbon: Público-UAL.

Heriksen, T. H. (1978), *Mozambique: a history*, London: Rex Collings.

Hintjents, H. M. and Newitt, M. D. D. (eds.) (1992), *The political economy of small tropical islands: the importance of being small*, Exeter: University of Exeter Press.

Hodges, T. and Newitt, M. D. D. (1988), *São Tomé and Príncipe: from plantation colony to microstate*, Boulder CO: Westview.

Horta, J. R. (1994), *Amanhã em Dili: textos de Xanana Gusmão*, Lisbon: Dom Quixote.

Instituto Nacional de Estatística (2002), *http://www.ine.pt/*, Lisbon: INE.

Instituto Nacional de Estatística (1999), *Estatísticas demográficas*, Lisbon: INE, p.153.

Jaime, D. and Barber, H. (eds.) (1999), *Angola: depoimentos para a história recente*, vol. 1, Luanda: Edição dos Autores.

Jardim, J. (1976), *Moçambique: terra queimada*, Lisbon: Intervenção.

Johnston, R. (ed.) (1994), *The dictionary of human geography*, Oxford: Blackwell.

Jolliffe, J. (1978), *East Timor: nationalism and colonialism*, St. Lucia: University of Queensland Press

Jornal de Letras (1994), *Especial CPLP*, 23 November, pp. 5–9.

Kayman, M. (1987), *Revolution and counter-revolution in Portugal*, London: Merlin.

Keaton, G. W. (1969), 'The international status of Macao before 1887', in *The development of extra-territoriality in China*, vol. 2, New York NY: H. Herting.

King, R., Fielding, A. and Black, R. (1997), 'The international migration turnaround in southern Europe', in King, R. and Black, R. (eds.), *Southern Europe and the new migrations*, Brighton: Sussex Academic Press, pp. 1-25.

Kramer, R. D. (ed.) (1995), *Macao: city of commerce and trade*, Hong Kong: API Press.

Léonard, Y. (1999), 'As ligações a África e ao Brasil', in Bethencourt, F. and Chaudhuri, K. (eds.), *História da expansão portuguesa*, Vol. 5, Lisbon: Círculo de Leitores.

Lewis, J. and Williams, A.M. (1985), 'Portugal's *retornados*: reintegration or rejection?', *Iberian Studies*, XIV (1-2), pp. 11-23.

Lima, T. (2000), 'Soares deu os parabéns a Guterres', *Público*, 29 June, p. 11.

Livro Branco (1984), *Livro Branco da 5ª Divisão, 1974-75*, Lisbon: Ler.

Lopes, J.V. (1996), *Cabo Verde nos bastidores da independância*, Praia: Instituto Camões.

Lourenço, E. (1999), *A nau de Ícaro seguido de imagem e miragem da lusofonia*, Lisbon: Gradiva.

Lourenço, E. (1992), *O labirinto da saudade*, Lisbon: Dom Quixote.

Macedo, J. B. de (1989), 'O luso-tropicalismo de Gilberto Freyre: metodologia, prática e resultados', *Boletim da Academia Internacional da Cultura Portuguesa* (16).

Machado, F. (1997), 'Contornos e especificidades da imigração em Portugal', *Sociologia: Problemas e Práticas*, 24, pp. 9-44.

Machado, F. (1994), 'Luso-africanos em Portugal: nas margens da etnicidade', *Sociologia: Problemas e Práticas*, 16, pp. 111-34.

MacQueen, N. (1998), *A descolonização da África portuguesa: a revolução metropolitana na dissolução do império*, Mem Martins: Inquérito.

MacQueen, N. (1997), *The decolonization of Portuguese Africa: metropolitan revolution and the dissolution of empire*, London: Longman.

MacQueen, N. (1985a), 'Macao: end of a special case', *The World Today* (Aug-Sept), pp. 167-9.

MacQueen, N. (1985b), 'Portugal and Africa: the politics of re-engagement', *Journal of Modern African Studies*, 23 (I).

Madrinha, F. (1997), 'Uma visita indesejada', *Expresso*, 25 October, p. 2.

Magalhães, A. B. de (1999), *Timor-Leste na encruzilhada da transição Indonésia: notas democráticas*, Lisbon: Gradiva.

Magalhães, A. E. M. de (1998), 'O princípio de separação de poderes na Lei Básica da futura Região Administrativa Especial de Macau', *Revista Administração*, 41 (XI), pp. 709-33.

Malheiros, J. (1998), 'Immigration, clandestine work and labour market strategies: the construction sector in the metropolitan region of Lisbon', *Southern European Society and Politics*, 3 (3), pp. 169-85.

Manuel, P. C. (1995), *Uncertain outcome: the politics of the Portuguese transition to democracy*,

Lanham, MA: University Press of America.

Marcum, J. (1978), *The Angolan revolution*, vol. 2: (1962-1976), Cambridge MA: MIT Press.

Marshall, M. and Ferreira, H. G. (1986), *Portugal's revolution: ten years on*, Cambridge: Cambridge University Press.

Martins, A. C. (1981), *Esperanças de Abril*, Lisbon: Perspectivas e Realidades.

Mattoso, J. (1998), *História de Portugal*, vol. 8, Lisbon: Estampa.

Maxwell, K. (1995), *The making of Portuguese democracy*, Cambridge: Cambridge University Press.

Maxwell, K. (1982), 'Portugal and Africa: the last empire', in Gifford, P. and Louis, W. R. (eds.), *The transfer of power in Africa: decolonization 1940-1960*, New Haven MA: Yale University Press.

Meireles, L. and Guardiola, N. (1994), 'O (des)encontro lusófono', *Expresso*, 25 June, p. 22.

Meneses, F. R. de (2000), *União Sagrada e sidonismo: Portugal em guerra, 1916-18*, Lisbon: Cosmos.

Ministério dos Negócios Estrangeiros (1996), *A Comunidade dos Países de Língua Portuguesa (CPLP)*', Lisbon: Ministério dos Negócios Estrangeiros—Direcção-Geral de Política Externa, 9 May.

Ministério dos Negocios Estrangeiros (1995), *Portugal: dez anos de política de cooperação*, Lisbon: Ministério dos Negócios Estrangeiros.

Monteiro, A. M. (1996), *Discurso do Presidente da República de Cabo Verde, no acto solene de institucionalização da Comunidade dos Países de Língua Portuguesa*, Lisbon, 17 July.

Monteiro, H. (2000), 'A lógica da humilhação', *Expresso*, 29 April, p. 13.

Monteiro, N. G. and Pinto, A. C. (2000), 'Mitos culturais e identidade nacional portuguesa', in Pinto, A. C. (ed.), *Portugal contemporáneo*, Madrid: Sequitur, pp. 232-45.

Morais, C. A. de (1980), *A queda da Índia portuguesa: crónica da invasão e do cativeiro*, Braga: Intervenção.

Moreira, A. (1984/85), 'Introdução à cooperação no espaço lusotropical', *Boletim da Academia Internacional da Cultura Portuguesa* (13).

Moura, V. G. (2000), 'Um chavão que serve para uns discursos', *Expresso*, 25 March, p. 25.

Nascimento, A. (1994), 'A Liga dos Interesses Indígenas de S. Tomé e Príncipe', paper presented at the *Congresso Luso-Afro-Brasileiro de Ciências Sociais*, Lisbon.

Neto, M. da C. (1997), 'Ideologias, contradições e mistificações da colonização de Angola no século XX', *Lusotopie*.

Newitt, M. (1995), *A history of Mozambique*, London: Hurst and Co.

NHPC (1990), *Encyclopaedia of Public International Law*, vol. 12, Amsterdam: NHPC, pp. 223-5.

Nicol, B. (1978), *Timor: the stillborn nation*, Melbourne: Visa

Nóbrega, J. M. (2000), 'João de Deus Pinheiro', *Diário de Notícias-DNA*, 27 May, pp. 20-7.

Nogueira, F. (1984), *Salazar, vol. V: a resistência (1958-1964)*, Oporto: Livraria Civilização.

Nunes, M. L. (1982), *A Portuguese colonial in America: Belmira Nunes Lopes. The autobiography of a Cape Verdian-American*, Pittsburgh PA: Latin American Literary Review Press.

Nunes, R. (2000), 'Portuguese immigrants in Brazil: an overview', *Portuguese Studies Review*, 8 (2), pp. 27-44.

Oliveira, C. (1996), *Portugal: dos quatro cantos do mundo à descolonização, 1974-76*, Lisbon: Cosmos.

Oliveira, C. (1993), 'Do isolamento à abertura: a descolonização e a política externa portuguesa', *Boletim da Academia Internacional da Cultura Portuguesa* (20).

Oliveira, J. A. (1997), 'Um projecto de geopolítica económica', *Público*, 1 March, p. 12.

OneWorld.net (2002), 'East Timor to seek 'least developed' status', http://www.feer.com, accessed 10 July.

Oppenheimer, J. (1997), 'Réalités et mythes de la coopération Portuguaise', *Lusotopie*.

Pacheco, C. (2000), 'Lusofonia e regimes autoritários em África', *Público*, 3 February, p. 10.

Pacheco, C. (1996), 'A África e a miopia portuguesa', *Público*, 11 May, p. 15.

Pélissier, R. (1979), *Le naufrage des caravelles: études sur la fin de l'Empire portugais, 1961-1975*, Orgéval: Pélissier.

Pinheiro, J. de D. (1988), 'Grandes eixos da política externa no Portugal de hoje', *Nação e Defesa* (January-March)..

Pinto, A. C. (1999a), 'A guerra colonial e o fim do império Português', in Bethencourt, F. and Chaudhury, K. (eds.), *História da expansão portuguesa*, Vol. 5, Lisbon: Círculo de Leitores.

Pinto, A. C. (1999b), 'Da África à Europa', in Bethencourt, F. and Chaudhuri, K. (eds.), *História da expansão portuguesa*, Vol. 5, Lisbon: Círculo de Leitores.

Pinto, A. C. (1998a), 'Dealing with the legacy of authoritarianism: political purge in Portugal's transition to democracy (1974-76)', in Larsen, S. U. et al. (eds.), *Modern Europe after fascism, 1945-1980's*, New York NY: Columbia University Press Social Science Monographs.

Pinto, A. C. (1998b), 'Twentieth-century Portugal: an introduction', in Pinto, A. C. (ed.), *Modern Portugal*, Palo Alto CA: SPOSS

Pires, M. L. (1991), *Descolonização de Timor: missão impossível?*, Lisbon: Dom Quixote.

Pires, R. P., Maranhão, M. J., Quintela, J. P., Moniz, F. and Pisco, M. (1984), *Os retornados: um estudo sociográfico*, Lisbon: Instituto de Estudos para o Desenvolvimento.

Porch, D. (1977), *The Portuguese armed forces and the revolution*, London: Croom Helm.

Rayner, L. (1987), *Macau: the Round Table*, 76 (302), pp. 199-206.

Reis, A. (1994), 'O poder central', in Reis, A. (ed.), *Portugal: 20 anos de democracia*, Lisbon: Círculo de Leitores.

República Portuguesa (2000a), *Programa do X Governo Constitucional*, http://bill.publico.pt/servico/proggov/governo10/prog/index.html, accessed 23 May 2000.

República Portuguesa (2000b), *Programa do XI Governo Constitucional*, http://bill.publico.pt/servico/proggov/governo11/prog/index.html, accessed 23 May 2000.

Ribeiro, A. de M. and Saldanha, A. V. de (1995), *Textos de direito internacional público*, Lisbon: ISCSP.

Robinson, R. A. H. (1979), *Contemporary Portugal: a history*, London: Allen and Unwin

Rocha-Trindade, M. (ed.) (1995), *Sociologia das migrações*, Lisbon: Universidade Aberta.

Rodrigues, L. R. (2002), *Salazar-Kennedy: a crise de uma aliança*, Lisbon: Notícias.

Rule, E. (1996), 'Portuguese nationality law in outline', *Immigration Nationality Law and Practice*, 10 (1), pp. 12-5.

Sá Pereira (ed.) (1976), *Jornal 'O Retornado' denuncia ao mundo o pavoroso caso de Timor*, Lisbon: Literal-Selecta

Saldanha, A. V. (1996), *Estudos sobre as relações luso-chinesas*, Lisbon: ISCSP.

Sampaio, J. (1996), *Discurso do Presidente da República Portuguesa*, Lisbon, 17 July.

Sánchez Cervelló, J. (1993), *A revolução portuguesa e a sua influência na transição espanhola (1961-1976)*, Lisbon: Assírio e Alvim.

Santos, A. A. (1993), 'Uma política para África, já', *Público*, 1 August, p. 20.

Santos, B. de S. (1998), 'No verão com exposcópio', *Visão*, 13 August, p. 29.

Santos, J. E. dos (1996), *Discurso pronunciado por S.E. o Presidente da República de Angola, na cerimónia constitutiva da Comunidade dos Países de Língua Portuguesa*, Lisbon, 17 July.

Schmitter, P. C. (1999), *Portugal: do autoritarismo à democracia*, Lisbon: Instituto de Ciências Sociais

Schneidman, W. W. (1987), *American foreign policy and the fall of the Portuguese empire, 1961-1976*, unpublished Ph.D. thesis, University of California.

Seibert, G. (1999), *Comrades, clients and cousins: colonialism, socialism and democratization in São Tomé and Príncipe*, Leiden: Research school of Asian, African and Amerindian studies.

Silva, A. E. D. (1997), *A independencia da Guiné Bissau e a descolonização portuguesa*, Oporto: Afrontamento.

Silva, B. da (ed.), *'Dossier' Goa: Vassalo e Silva—a recusa do sacrifício inútil*, Lisbon: Liber.

Silva, C. (1988), *Intervenção no Instituto de Defesa Nacional*, Lisbon: Presidência do

Conselho de Ministros, 27 May.

Silva, D. (2002), 'Portugal to revive ties with Africa', *Business Day*, www.bday.co.za/bday/content/ direct/1,3523,1119611-6078-0,00.html.

Silva, J. R. (1999), 'Les relations économiques luso-brésiliennes au temps de la mondialisation', *Lusotopie*, pp. 55-90.

Silva, R. da (1997), 'Rafael Branco: apesar de tudo optimista', *Jornal de Letras (CPLP-Primeiro Aniversário)*, 16 July, pp. 5-7.

Soares, J. M. de A. (1997), 'África, o alvo triangular', *Expresso-Economia*, 18 October, p. 22.

Soares, M. (1994), 'Uma iniciativa histórica', *Jornal de Letras*, 23 November, p. 5.

Soares, M. (1982), *Democratização e descolonização: 10 meses de Governo Provisório*, Lisbon: Dom Quixote.

Soares, M. (1976), *Portugal: que revolução? Diálogo com Dominique Puchin*, Lisbon: Perspectivas e Realidades.

Sousa, T. (1996), 'A EU é o nosso maior parceiro', *Público*, 7 December, p. 14.

Spikes, D. (1993), *Angola and the politics of intervention*, Jefferson: MacFarland.

Spínola, A. de (1978), *País sem rumo: contributos para a história de uma revolução*, Lisbon: Scire.

Spínola, A. de (1976), *Ao serviço de Portugal*, Lisbon: Ática.

Tavares, M. S. (1999), 'África e Portugal', *Público*, 5 February, p. 13.

Tavares, M. S. (1995), 'A hora de pagar a conta', *Público*, 24 November, p. 19.

Teixeira, C. et al. (1995), 'As trocas desiguais do Império', *Público*, 25 April, pp. 2-4.

Teixeira, N. S. (1998), ' Between Africa and Europe: Portuguese foreign policy, 1890-1986', in Pinto, A. C. (ed.), *Modern Portugal*, Palo Alto CA: SPOSS.

Teixeira, N. S. (1996), *O poder e a guerra, 1914-1918*, Lisbon: Estampa.

Telo, A. J. (1998), 'O fim do ciclo africano do império', in *Portugal na transição do milénio*, Lisbon: Fim de Século.

Telo, A. J. (1997), 'Treze teses sobre a disfunção nacional: Portugal no sistema internacional', *Análise Social*, XXXII (142), pp. 649-83.

Telo, A. J. (1995), 'Portugal e a NATO: dos Pirinéus a Angola', *Análise Social*, XXX (134), pp. 947-73.

The Economist (1999), 'East Timor's uncertain birth', 23 October.

Time (2000), 155 (11), 20 March.

Trindade, M. de A. (1993), *Memórias de um bispo*, 2nd edition, Coimbra: Gráfica de Coimbra.

Valença, F. (1977), *As forças armadas e as crises nacionais: a abrilada de 1961*, Lisbon: Europa-América.

Vasconcelos, J. C. (1998), 'As relações com os PALOP', *Visão*, 9 July, p. 32.

Veiga, U. (1999), 'Immigrants in the Spanish labour market', in Martin Baldwin-Edwards and Joaquin Arango (eds.), *Immigrants and the informal economy in southern Europe*, London: Cass, pp. 105-28.

Venâncio, J. C. (1996), *Colonialismo, antropologia e lusofonias*, Lisbon: Vega.

Venâncio, M. (1993), 'Mediation by the Roman Catholic Church in Mozambique, 1988-1991', in Chan, S. and Jabri, V. (eds.), *Mediation in southern Africa*, London: Macmillan.

Venâncio, M. and Chan, S. (1996), *Portuguese diplomacy in southern Africa (1974-1994)*, Braamfontein: South African Institute of International Affairs.

Venâncio, M. and McMillan, C. (1993), 'Portuguese mediation of the Angolan conflict in 1990-1991', in Chan, S. and Jabri, V. (eds.), *Mediation in southern Africa*, London: Macmillan.

Vieira, J. B. (1996), *Intervenção de S.E. o senhor Presidente da República da Guiné-Bissau, por ocasião da Institucionalização da CPLP*, Lisbon, 17 July.

Wheeler, D. L. (1980), 'Portuguese withdrawal from Africa: the Angolan case', in Seiler, J. (ed.), *Southern Africa after the Portuguese coup*, Boulder CO: Westview.

www.ingramcontent.com/pod-product-compliance
Ingram Content Group UK Ltd.
Pitfield, Milton Keynes, MK11 3LW, UK
UKHW051849210426
5322IPUK00025B/633